Defining lies as statements that are intended to deceive, this book considers the various contexts in which people tell lies, how they are detected and sometimes exposed, and the consequences for the liars themselves, their dupes, and the wider society. The author provides examples from a number of cultures, with distinctive religions and ethical traditions, and delineates domains where lying is the norm, domains that are ambiguous, and the one domain (science) that requires truthtelling. He refers to experimental studies on children that show how, at an early age, they acquire the capacity to lie, and draws attention to the lack of studies showing how they learn when it is appropriate to do so and when it is not. He reviews how lying has been evaluated by moralists, examines why we don't regard novels as lies, and relates the human capacity to lie to deceit among other animal species.

In this judicious, and often witty, account, Professor Barnes concludes that although there are, in all societies, good pragmatic reasons for not lying all the time, there are also strong reasons for lying some of the time.

A pack of lies

Themes in the Social Sciences

Editors: John Dunn, Jack Goody, Geoffrey Hawthorn

A pack of lies
Towards a sociology
of lying

J. A. BARNES
Australian National University

CAMBRIDGE
UNIVERSITY PRESS

Published by the Press Syndicate of the University of Cambridge
The Pitt Buildings, Trumpington Street, Cambridge CB2 1RP
40 West 20th Street, New York, NY 10011–4211, USA
10 Stamford Road, Oakleigh, Melbourne 3166, Australia

First published 1994

Printed in Great Britain at the University Press, Cambridge

A catalogue record for this book is available from the British Library

Library of Congress cataloguing in publication data
Barnes, J. A. (John Arundel), 1918–
A pack of lies : towards a sociology of lying / J. A. Barnes.
p.   cm. – (Themes in the social sciences)
Includes bibliographical references and index.
ISBN 0 521 45376 3. – ISBN 0 521 45978 8 (pbk.)
1. Deception.   2. Truthfulness and falsehood.
3. Deception – Social aspects.
4. Truthfulness and falsehood – Social aspects.
I. Title.   II. Series.
BF637.D42B37   1994
177′.3–dc20   93–23455   CIP

ISBN 0 521 45376 3 hardback
ISBN 0 521 45978 8 paperback

CE

My first thought was, he lied in every word,
That hoary cripple, with malicious eye
Askance to watch the working of his lie
On mine, and mouth scarce able to afford
Suppression of the glee, that pursed and scored
Its edge, at one more victim gained thereby.

BROWNING
'Childe Roland to the dark tower came'

Contents

Contents

Preface

I cannot hope to list all those who have helped me in writing this book. To do so would entail producing an almost complete muster of my relatives, friends and colleagues, all of whom have had something to say on this topic. I maintained for so long that I was writing a book about lying without being able to demonstrate tangible signs of progress that I soon acquired the reputation, not of becoming an expert on lying, but of being already a liar, at least in respect of my academic pretensions. This long delay, however, gave me the opportunity to benefit from the innumerable suggestions made to me about what questions I should tackle, what sources I should seek to tap, and what conclusions I might be able to draw. When at last I began to write I was already halfway towards my goal. I must thank the graduate students who participated in my course on lying at Flinders University in 1990 for stimulating me to begin writing; I am most grateful to Riaz Hassan for giving me the opportunity to discuss this topic with them and to Jillian Litster for trying out some of the ideas that emerged. I must however also express my debt to Jerzy Zubrzycki for having, many years earlier, dobbed me in as an expert on a topic about which I then knew nothing, thus starting me on the trail leading to this book.

Of the very many people who have made suggestions and answered queries there are some who must be mentioned by name: Judith Barbour, Rory Barnes, Michael Black, the late Bob Brissenden, John Sutherland and Ian Watt helped me to avoid many pitfalls in the, to me, unfamiliar territory of English literature; Judith Dunn, Nicholas Mackintosh and Candida Peterson kindly answered my questions in developmental psychology; Rick Bigwood, the late Sir Richard Eggleston, Marcia Neave and John Spencer guided me to legal sources; Raquel Ackerman, Barbara Bank, Elizabeth Colson, Malcolm Crick, John Dunn, Nicholas Evans, Mariane Ferme, Paula Brown Glick, Esther Goody, Alma Gottlieb, Deborah Kaspin, Al Klovdahl, Lamont Lindstrom, Mary Luszcz, Margaret Middleton, Ann

Moyal, Grant Noble, Nicholas Peterson, Charles Piot, Robin Pope, Skip Rappaport, Margaret Rose, Loyal Rue, Bambi Schieffelin, Timothy Shopen and Charles Richard Snyder drew my attention to papers and books in linguistics, philosophy, sociology and anthropology and answered numerous queries; Paul Ekman and Jack Goody helped with obtaining access to sources, as did Anton Ploeg. He and Stephen Mugford commented on draft chapters, and Wes Whitten kept me in touch with the world outside the social sciences; Anthony Barnett, Marjorie Bull, Fay Goddard, Jo Habib, Frances Michaelis and Peter Underwood kept their eyes open for relevant material. The tea room in the Coombs Building of the Australian National University has long been a fertile ground for gleaning stimulating ideas and erudite information; among the many fellow tea-drinkers to whom I am indebted I must mention in particular Lisbeth Haakonssen, Ken Inglis, Harry Rigby and Barry Smith. Likewise I am very grateful to Frank Jones and my colleagues in the Sociology program for them congenial and stimulating working environment which I have enjoyed for many years. Geoffrey Hawthorn has been most encouraging and helpful in getting the book into print. Jessica Kuper has been a great help in overcoming the unavoidable difficulties of communication between Australia and Britain.

Finally I must thank Frances Barnes for her wise comments on draft chapters and her enduring support and forbearance over the years while I have been preoccupied with lies.

Acknowledgments

I am indebted to Raquel Ackerman and Charles Richard Snyder for permission to quote from their unpublished manuscripts, and to Philip Kerr for permission to use his translation of Ingannevole's *Enchiridion mendacii*.

Quotations from 'Cultural patterning in speech behavior in Burundi' by Ethel M. Albert are reprinted from *Directions in sociolinguistics* edited by John Joseph Gumperz and Dell Hymes by permission of Blackwell Publishers, copyright 1972 Holt, Rinehart & Winston Inc.

Quotations from *The biology of moral systems* by Richard D. Alexander are reprinted by permission of Aldine de Gruyter, copyright 1987 Richard D. Alexander.

Quotations from *Between past and present* by Hannah Arendt (copyright 1954, 1956, 1957, 1958, 1960 and 1961 by Hannah Arendt) are used by permission of Viking Penguin, a division of Penguin Books USA Inc.

Excerpts from 'Lying in politics: reflections on the Pentagon Papers' from *Crises of the republic*, copyright 1971 by Hannah Arendt, reprinted by permission of Harcourt Brace and Company.

Quotations from *The prevalence of deceit* by F. G. Bailey are reprinted by permission of Cornell University Press.

Quotations from *Lying* by Sissela Bok are reprinted by permission of Random House Inc., copyright 1978 by Sissela Bok.

The passage from *Mambu: a Melanesian millennium* by Kenelm Burridge is quoted by permission of the publishers, Methuen London.

Quotations from *How monkeys see the world* by Dorothy L. Cheney and Robert M. Seyfarth are reprinted by permission of The University of Chicago Press, copyright 1990 by the University of Chicago.

The verses by T. M. Conway are reprinted by permission of The Observer Ltd, copyright the *New Statesman*.

Quotations from 'Age changes in deceiving and detecting deceit' by Bella M. DePaulo and Audrey Jordan are reprinted from *Development of nonverbal behavior in children* edited by Robert S. Feldman by permission of Springer-Verlag.

Quotations from 'Telling lies' by Bella M. DePaulo and Robert Rosenthal are reprinted from *Journal of Personality and Social Psychology* by permission of the American Psychological Association.

Quotations from *Portrait of a Greek mountain village* by Juliet du Boulay are reprinted by permission of the author.

Quotations from *Lies and truth* by Marcel Eck are reprinted by permission of Macmillan Publishing Company, copyright 1970 the Macmillan Company.

Quotations from *Telling lies* by Paul Ekman are reprinted by permission of the author.

The quotation from *Jokes and their relation to the unconscious* by Sigmund Freud and published by Routledge & Kegan Paul is reprinted by permission of Routledge.

Quotations from 'Lying, honor and contradiction' by Michael Gilsenan are reprinted by permission of the author.

Quotations from *Knowledge and power in a South Pacific society* by Lamont Lindstrom are reprinted by permission of Smithsonian Institution Press.

Quotations from *The double-cross system* by Sir John Cecil Masterman are reprinted by permission of Yale University Press, copyright 1972 Yale University.

The quotation from *Lies as allies* by Viscount Maugham is reprinted by permission of Oxford University Press.

Quotations from *The will to power* and *Basic writings of Nietzsche* by Friedrich Wilhelm Nietzsche, edited by Walter Kaufmann, and published by Random House are reprinted by permission of Random House Inc.

Quotations from *Ecology, meaning, and religion* by Roy A. Rappaport are reprinted by permission of North Atlantic Books (Berkeley, Calif.), copyright 1979 by Roy A. Rappaport.

Quotations from *The sociology of Georg Simmel*, translated and edited by Kurt H. Wolff, copyright 1950, renewed 1978 by The Free Press, a division of Macmillan, Inc., are reprinted by permission of the publisher.

Quotations from *Social evolution* by Robert L. Trivers, published by Benjamin/Cummings, are reprinted by permission of Addison-Wesley Publishing Company.

Quotations from 'The evolution of reciprocal altruism' by Robert L. Trivers are reprinted from the *Quarterly review of biology* by permission of the University of Chicago Press, copyright 1971 Stony Brook Foundation Inc.

Quotations from 'A phenomenological approach to human deception' by Lucy Fontaine Werth and Jenny Flaherty are reprinted from *Deception*, edited by Robert W. Mitchell and Nicholas S. Thompson by permission of the State University of New York Press, copyright 1986 State University of New York.

1

What is a lie?

Lies are everywhere. We hear continually about lying in public and private life. Very few people would claim never to have told a lie, and even fewer would say they have never been duped by a liar. Writing in a magazine in January 1889 Oscar Wilde (1989:216) complained that, with the possible exception of the speeches of barristers, lying as an art had decayed. A hundred years later, most people would say that there is now more lying than there used to be; a British journalist (Lott 1990) has labelled the 1980s as 'the decade of lies'. In 1991, an American journalist (Bradlee 1991) commented that 'It seems to me that lying has reached epidemic proportions in recent years and that we've all become immunized to it.'

Whether lies are in fact told more often nowadays than previously is anyone's guess, but at least there is a greater awareness of the prevalence of lying, partly because public lying is now often exposed more promptly. As Rasberry (1981:2–3) says:

History has recorded numerous situations where political leaders have lied, but most of these lies were not revealed for years. Because of media improvements in the last 25 years, citizens today see and hear deception as it occurs.

We see lying as a regrettable human failing and assume that unless we make great efforts to train children to be honest, they will follow a natural tendency and tell lies. In a survey conducted in ten west European countries in 1981, respondents were asked to rank the qualities they wished to pass on to their children; in nine countries out of ten, most respondents ranked honesty first (Harding and Phillips 1986:19–21). But efforts by parents bring only limited success; most adults tell lies from time to time. Indeed, Oliver Wendell Holmes seems to have believed that as

1

children grow up they lose an initial propensity to be honest. According to Alexander (1987:197), he is reputed to have said 'Pretty much all the truth-telling in the world is done by children.' Rejecting this view, developmental psychologists assume that lying by children is something that can be taken for granted. For instance, children's agreements to the statements 'I tell the truth every single time' and 'I never lie' were accepted as evidence, in an American study, of their propensity to falsify their responses (Castaneda et al. 1956:319).

Journalists and students of the mass media have shown the prevalence of lying in selected domains of social life (e.g. Glasgow University Media Group 1976, 1980) but it is anthropologists who have effectively shown that in some cultures lying is ubiquitous. Gilsenan (1976:191) described how, in the community he studied in the Lebanon, lying was 'a fundamental element not only of specific situations and individual actions, but of the cultural universe as a whole'. Likewise Ernestine Friedl (1962:78–81) reports that in rural Greece parents deliberately lie to their young children as a way of teaching them that other people's actions and words should not necessarily be taken 'at face value'. She mentions an occasion when, at the end of a social evening, one of the participants remarked jovially 'Let's tell a few more lies and then go home.' Yet this usage suggests that no-one was being deceived. Most writers make deceit or deception, terms I shall be using synonymously, part of their definition of lying, but Friedl mentions that the Greek word *psemata*, which she translates as 'lies', is used 'with less emotional intensity, and with a milder pejorative connotation than Americans use the English word'. Perhaps some *psemata* are better described as untrue stories that only a stranger would think were true. This Greek usage parallels the use of the expression 'telling lies' by some Black speech communities in the United States as a synonym for 'talking shit', i.e. 'making a point by indirection and wit' with the expectation that there will be a similar response (Abrahams 1974:258).

Lying has been a human activity for a long time and is not merely a recent and lamentable innovation. There is no shortage of lies in the tales told by Homer and Hesiod in ancient Greece, nor, as Ruskin (1905:351–352) pointed out, was lying always regarded as reprehensible. As Scheibe (1979:83) notes:

Prometheus gained fame not only for stealing the fire of civilization for mankind but also for his skill at confabulation.

Admiration for successful liars has not been confined to ancient Greeks. The anonymous author of *The Lying Intelligencer*, introducing his satirical newsheet, with its motto *Splendide mendax*, to his London audience, wrote:

Let not my readers imagine, that I propose writing a panegyric upon the art of lying. It were absurd to recommend to mankind, what is already in such universal esteem. In courts it assumes the name of good breeding; in religion it is called pious fraud, it is mystery in trade, and invention in poetry. In our political contests, it is stiled opposition, liberty, and patriotism. (Anon 1763:3)

Even John Locke (1894:146–147), while disapproving of the deceit he saw engendered by oratory, observed that

It is evident how much men love to deceive and be deceived, since rhetoric, that powerful instrument of error and deceit, has its established professors, is publicly taught, and has always been had in great reputation; ... men find pleasure to be deceived.

The pleasures of deceit are captured in the words of Robert Browning's (1981:839) *Mr Sludge, 'The medium'*

> ... there's a real love of a lie,
> Liars find ready-made for lies they make,
> As hand for glove, or tongue for sugar-plum.

Locke wrote in 1690 and Browning in about 1860; the subsequent supplementation of individual rhetorical skills by professional advertising agencies and government departments of disinformation confirms the truth of their comments.

Some writers, notably the philosopher Thomas Hobbes (1839:36; 1840:25) and the psychoanalyst Sandor Ferenczi (1955:72), have even singled out the ability to lie as one of the criteria that distinguish human beings from other animals, though, as we shall discuss later, many animals practise other modes of deceit, including, in some cases, using their voices deceitfully (see Rappaport 1979:224; Thorpe 1972:33). Arendt (1968:250; cf. 1972:5) goes one step further, and proclaims that

our ability to lie – but not necessarily our ability to tell the truth – belongs among the few obvious, demonstrable data that confirm human freedom.

Lacan (1988:244) presents a somewhat similar view when he states that 'the characterising feature of intersubjectivity' is 'that the subject can lie to us'. The same sentiment was expressed more elegantly in the sixteenth century by Bartholomaeus Ingannevole when he wrote that

never to lie admits of no imagining which is all that God did give man to distinguish him from the beasts of the field. (Kerr 1990:100)

It is perhaps the perception of lying as evidence for freedom and imagination that explains the attraction of compilations of lies, both scholarly and demotic (e.g. Jones 1984). Kerr (1990:99–101) includes in his anthology the only surviving fragment of what he describes as the first book of lies, dating from the sixteenth century. Lying may be reprehensible and we are offended if we become dupes, yet from a safe distance we can admire and enjoy the wit and audacity of successful liars. A recent *Liars' handbook* (Dale 1992) is classified by booksellers as a humorous work, as indeed its editor intended it to be. Accusations of lying, despite the risk of suits for slander or libel, are made much more readily than many other aspersions against good character. Max Black (1983:117–118) provides a good example of an almost frivolous use of this accusation when he cites a statement made by Mary McCarthy about the writings of fellow writer Lillian Hellman:' I once said in an interview that every word she writes is a lie, including "and" and "the" '. Black cannot decide whether or not the statement is an instance of humbug.

It is only in contrast to lies and falsehoods that we are able to construct the concept of truth. As Barwise and Perry (1983:18) note:

If people said only what they knew to be the case, then we would never notice truth as a property of some utterances and not others. It is because people sometimes violate the conventions of language, inadvertently or otherwise, that we come to recognize truth as a uniformity across certain utterance situations.

With the contingency of the relation between sign and referent in mind, Eco (1976:7, 58–59) proposes that 'the definition of a "theory of the lie" should be taken as a pretty comprehensive program for a general semiotics.'

Given the interdependence of the concepts of the truth and the lie, the central attention paid by Habermas and other members of the Frankfurt school to the concept of truth seems out of proportion to the lack of critical attention he and his followers have given to deception, even though that is the element in his conceptual kit antithetical to truth. We might even say that the language games discussed by Habermas (1970; see also McCarthy 1973) are akin to chess, where everything is, or ought to be, above board, whereas in studying lying we are looking at a language game closer to poker, where there is no board to be above. But even if there is no board, there are still rules, both stated and unstated, to the game of poker which have to be learnt (Hayano 1980, 1982). The language-game of lying 'needs to be learned like any other one' (Wittgenstein 1953:90e). Unfortunately, as we shall see, there is a shortage of evidence on how the game of lying is learnt (cf. Searle 1975:326).

Yet despite its ubiquity, antiquity, theoretical interest and, if Hobbes is right, its human specificity, most social scientists and philosophers have given lying comparatively little attention, at least by comparison with the amount of scrutiny they have given to telling the truth (cf. Bok 1978:5; Steiner 1975:220–222). By far the greater part of what philosophers have written treats lying as a form of deviance, and not sometimes as an instance of conforming to special norms and expectations. For purposes of the present study, we can ignore the formidable philosophical literature on the self-referencing pair of sentences in St Paul's 'Epistle to Titus' (ch. 1, vv. 12, 13) which have been studied variously as the Cretan or Epimenides or Liar Paradox (or paradoxes) (Anderson 1970; Barwise and Etchemendy 1987; Farb 1973:129–131; Mates 1981:6, 15–19). This paradox is of great interest in the development of set theory but has little direct sociological relevance. Helen Daniel (1988:3), in her literary critique, *Liars*, links the classical Liar Paradox to certain statements uttered by characters in some recent Australian novels, including Peter Carey's *Illywhacker*, but in my view the link is weak. When for example Herbert Badgery, on the first page of *Illywhacker*, says 'I am a terrible liar and I have always been a liar' (Carey 1985:11), the reader soon realizes that Badgery is in truth a consummate liar, and not a mere antipodean Cretan.

Instead of turning to the critical theorists, logicians and moral philosophers for help, the sociologist interested in lying might be tempted to think that game theorists, with their analyses of the Prisoner's Dilemma and the game of Chicken (Kuhn 1963:335; Schelling 1960), might provide useful philosophical underpinning. Unfortunately the theory of games can provide only limited help. Axelrod (1984) reports experimental evidence for the advantages of following a policy of tit for tat, of being initially honest and subsequently responding in like manner to honest and deceitful moves by one's opponent. But Williams (1988:5–6) gives reasons why Axelrod's results bear 'only indirectly on the question of human cooperation in society'. As Hollis (1989:168, 176–178) points out, 'game theory deals only with games where rational choices are instrumentally rational' (cf. Wolfe 1989:42–43). In the real world, games are embedded in social life and players choose to act honestly or dishonestly for reasons that are expressive or instrumental or both. The players are citizens, and the public interest is therefore also their own interest, however narrowly or widely 'the public' may be perceived. The typical players of games theory are more at home in the world of what Fortes (1957:160) called 'billiard-ball sociology' rather than in the muddled and complex real social world.

Despite its pervasiveness, card-carrying sociologists have done disappointingly little work on lying. Apart from the pioneering work of Simmel at the beginning of this century, little sociological analysis has been carried out (cf. Steiner 1975:221). Even the monumental scholarly survey of lying edited by Lipmann and Plaut (1927), with its twenty-four chapters, contains hardly any sociological discussion, despite the claim in the subtitle that the book includes an account of lies from a sociological viewpoint. Larson (1932) comes nearer the mark, but his source book is aimed primarily at the practical task of detecting the lies told by criminals rather than at locating lying in a wider context. Durandin (1972) comes closer still, with a broader-based discussion of the reasons why individuals tell lies, supported by the results of a questionnaire survey. There are just a few good field studies of lying, though most of these have been carried out by ethnographers working as outsiders away from their native cultures. I regret the scarcity of empirical findings but am glad to be spared the chore of rehearsing the definitions and analyses of lying that might otherwise be found in standard sociological textbooks; they are not there.

The relative neglect of lying has been noted by a trio of psychiatrists who recently complained (Ford et al. 1988:554) that lying had 'only seldom been the object of psychiatric or psychological investigation'. They may be right about their own discipline of psychiatry, but their judgment on psychology needs qualification. Developmental psychologists have written at length about children's ability to tell lies and to detect them, though even they have said surprisingly little about how and when children use these skills outside the laboratory.

Though the Liar Paradox has little to do with the sociology of lying, there are other associations of the word 'lie' that do have a bearing (cf. Lutman 1988). The English verb 'to lie' carries a complex semantic load through its double meaning, to speak deceptively and to be lying down, a conjuncture that Ricks (1975:123) describes as 'simply the most important pun in the language'. The pun, enriched by sexual connotations, was of great attraction for Shakespeare, and is exemplified in the final couplet of his sonnet 138:

> Therefore I lye with her, and she with me,
> And in our faults by lyes we flattered be

(cf. Ricks 1975:130–131; Ewbank 1983:137–138). On the same theme, but in more light-hearted vein, is the description of psychoanalysis as 'lying on the couch' (Forrester 1989). According to Wolf (1988):

Patients inevitably deceive psychiatrists and clinicians, consciously or unconsciously, and it is not uncommon for them to lie consciously.

Surprisingly, Freud (1958) wrote little about lying as such, yet broad notions of lying and deception, particularly self-deception, are central to psycho-analytic theory and praxis. Forrester speaks of psychoanalysis as 'the science of lying' and says that 'A central preoccupation of Freudian psychoanalysis is deception' (Forrester 1989:156; 1990:119; cf. Eagle 1988; Ferenczi 1955:77–80; Forrester 1980:136–137; Goldberg 1973:99–104).

Lying occurs ubiquitously. Although Douglas (1976:68) says 'Certainly

6

people do not lie much of the time', he maintains that 'falsehood knows no class lines', and that 'almost all research reports (probably all) are laundered'. However, his sociologist colleagues 'have not lied. They have merely evaded the issues' (Douglas 1976:xiii). Yet his own evidence shows that most people, or at least most Americans, lie some of the time. Likewise the existence of so-called pathological liars, who do indeed lie most of the time, is well established (Ford et al. 1988). The propensity to lie varies widely within communities and across communities, and within and across specified domains of social life. Developmental psychologists have studied extensively how this propensity, and the ability to detect lying, varies with age and gender (DePaulo et al. 1985). Thus for example over a hundred years ago Hall (1891:212) reported the results of a study of Boston adolescents disclosing that:

Boys keep up joint or complotted lies which girls rarely do, who 'tell on' others because they are 'sure to be found out', or 'someone else will tell' ...

The efforts of psychologists have focussed mainly on children. Adults have been less often studied from this viewpoint, even though interest in the topic goes back at least as far as Chaucer (1975:164) who maintained:

> For half so boldely kan ther no man
> Swere and lyen, as a womman kan.

Centuries later, David Hume (1987:564) repeated this sweeping generalization with his claim that women have 'an appetite for falshood' (cf. Battersby 1981:308).

The ubiquity of lying prompts the question: why should we ever tell the truth? But while this normative inquiry may be appropriate for moral philosophy, social science is more properly concerned with answering slightly different questions: not why *should* but why *do* we so often tell the truth, and *when* do we not do so? For we find empirically that, in societies and cultures of great diversity, with their distinctive codes of religion and ethics, the truth is told more often than not. The ubiquitous, though far from universal, preference for the truth suggests that, quite apart from any moral or religious merit that in various ways may be ascribed to telling the truth, there are also strong pragmatic reasons why, in many social contexts though not in all, it is in everyone's interest not to lie. Indeed, Sir Thomas Browne, writing in 1646 in his *Pseudodoxia epidemica*, went even further. He maintained that:

so large is the Empire of Truth, that it hath place within the walls of Hell, and the Devils themselves are daily forced to practise it; ... in Moral verities, although they deceive us, they lie not unto each other; as well understanding that all community is continued by Truth, and that of Hell cannot consist without it. (Browne 1964:76)

I doubt if Sir Thomas had any hard evidence to support this assertion (cf. Bok 1978:18–19; Johnson 1963:362), but it certainly tallies with our socio-logical understanding of the necessary conditions for sustained social life. We might though want to qualify Sir Thomas's assertion that the devils do not lie to one another; if they are anything like humans, they are more likely to tell lies not only continually to their victims but also, from time to time, to one another.

There are many books, both popular and scholarly, on how to detect lies and deter liars (e.g. Ekman 1985, 1989), and there are many articles in psychological journals on how the ability to tell lies and to detect them is correlated with age, gender, social class, ethnic affiliation and so on. Notably absent are accounts of how children learn to distinguish white lies from black lies in their own distinctive cultural milieu, and by whom they are taught this vital information. Learning to lie properly is an important feature of the process of human socialization, for we have innumerable good accounts of adults, in a wide variety of social and cultural contexts, exercising their social skills in telling the right lies at the right time, and to the right people. By 'right' I mean successful in achieving deception. Ochs (1986) has outlined a framework for the analysis of 'language socialization' that would suit admirably a comparative inquiry into the way in which children learn to use lying in diverse cultures, but it seems that unfortu-nately no such inquiry has been undertaken.

Karl Scheibe (1980:15) defends lying 'on practical psychological grounds'. Curiously, this favourable comment by a psychologist is exceptional, for although many of them have discussed how the pro-pensity to lie can be curbed by parental action, psychologists have given much less attention to possible benefits from telling the right lies (cf. Tudor-Hart 1926). The orientation of most psychologists contrasts with the writings of psychiatrists, some of whom discuss the beneficial con-sequences of certain lies. For example, Joseph Smith (1968:62), an American psychiatrist, speaks of a child's first lie as 'a decisive further step into separateness and autonomy'. Ford and his psychiatric col-leagues state that:

Lying becomes an important, perhaps essential mechanism by which the child can test the limits of his or her own ego boundaries in order to define and establish autonomy. (Ford et al. 1988:555)

Kavka (1985:401) asserts that lying is a means for maintaining 'narcissistic equilibrium', while the poet Joseph Brodsky (1979:32) maintains that 'the real history of consciousness starts with one's first lie.'

The thesis that lying forms an essential component in the development of consciousness and autonomy is carried a step further, into adult life, by the novelist David Malouf (1976:170). He ends his novel *Johnno*, about a persistent and imaginative liar, by saying:

Maybe, in the end, even the lies we tell define us. And better, some of them, than our most earnest attempts at the truth.

Favourable or sympathetic evaluations of lying by psychiatrists and novelists are hard to match in the writings of developmental psychologists. We shall look at their findings in chapter 8.

Most psychologists prefer to work in laboratories rather than in the field. Studies of the process by which children learn when to speak the truth and when not to do so are therefore scarce (cf. Bok 1978:298). We all have to acquire these skills before we can live as fully encultured members of our communities. At home and on school playgrounds, as well as later in the workplace and the conjugal bed, we learn when it would be unwise, treacherous or rude to tell the whole truth and nothing but the truth. Regrettably, but understandably, psychologists have been reluctant to venture into these muddy research fields, even though the study of how and when people lie in real life was an area of research proposed for psychologists by DePaulo and Rosenthal (1979:1720–1721) in their 1979 programme for studies of deception. Surprisingly, anthropologists, who traditionally have been eager to forsake the university campus for the attractions of the field, have also neglected to study the process of socialization into lying, even though it is they who have given us the best accounts of lying by adults. Psychologists, sociologists and anthropologists alike seem to have neglected an important area of study.

Curiously, little is said about lying in the formidable body of literature on moral stages inspired by Lawrence Kohlberg. Truthtelling is recognized as a norm (Colby and Kohlberg 1987a:42, 51–52; Kohlberg and Turiel 1971:433; Kohlberg et al. 1983:96) but the decision whether to lie or tell the truth receives comparatively little explicit attention in this analytical scheme (Colby and Kohlberg 1987b:281, 518, 568–569, 584; Kohlberg and Turiel 1971:422–424; cf. Blasi 1980). According to Kohlberg (1964:385–387) the only moral virtue is justice, whereas honesty is merely a character trait (cf. Rich 1986:215–216). Peters (1971:262) criticizes Kohlberg for his cavalier treatment of honesty, and maintains that he 'is really prescribing one type of morality among several possibilities' (cf. Snarey 1985).

In his analysis of conversational norms, Grice (1989:27) argues that people talking to one another assume that their interlocutors, like themselves, are being cooperative, and that one of the maxims they follow (part of Grice's category of Quality) is 'Do not say what you believe to be false'. Paley (1825:123) referred to this assumption as a tacit promise, while earlier Grotius (1925:613–614) saw it as 'that mutual obligation which men had willed to introduce at the time when they determined to make use of speech and similar signs'. Lies usually succeed because dupes mistakenly assume that liars mean what they say. Dupes will not make this assumption unless their experience has been that, most of the time, most people do indeed mean what they say. In any sustained system of interaction, lying being one example, the majority of actors must pay their way; only a minority can be free riders. Hence a search for an optimal level of lying, if optimality were to be measured by maximum success, might be rephrased as a quest for an optimal number of free riders.

The topic of lying is large, while the field of deception, of which lying is one mode, is larger still. I shall aim to avoid getting lost in the labyrinths of deception by focussing firmly, though not exclusively, on lying. Some consideration of the wider topic must be provided to set lying in its proper context. I shall pay little attention to the presence of deceptively concealed bias in the mass media, a topic examined by Cirino (1971) and many others. Some aspects of lying I shall mention only in passing, partly because of lack of data, partly because of the limitations of my expertise, and partly because they appear to have only slight importance for a study intended to highlight the social significance of lying. Thus I shall have little to say about the manipulation of quantitative data to achieve deception. I recognize the truth in the words attributed, probably erroneously, by Mark Twain (1960:149) to Disraeli:

There are three kinds of lies: lies, damned lies and statistics.

For present purposes, however, I shall concentrate on damned lies.

DEFINITIONS: LYING AND DECEPTION

If we are to talk about lies, we need a clear idea of what a lie is. Unfortunately, but for powerful reasons, clear ideas are scarce in the social sciences (Barnes 1990:13). 'Lying' is a slippery concept (Coleman and Kay 1981:42; Ludwig 1965:7). I cannot hope to do more than highlight some of the diversities of lying as we move from one domain of social life to another, and from one cultural setting to another. This exercise should serve as an introduction to a field of inquiry that, in my view, has been strangely neglected. If it does nothing else, this book should expose those areas where inquiries are required if we are to gain an adequately grounded understanding of where and how and why people tell lies.

Some writers give a very broad meaning to the word 'lie' while others avoid the term, replacing it by euphemistic expressions such as 'elaborations of the truth', Churchill's 'terminological inexactitudes' and the game theorists' 'strategic misrepresentations' (Raiffa 1982:142). In my childhood we tried to avoid the unpleasant connotations of the word 'liar' by speaking of a '51 A R'. Ordinary lay conversation gives 'lie' many meanings (Coleman and Kay 1981; Sweetser 1987) as do children of different ages (Peterson et al. 1983). For present purposes I shall act like Humpty Dumpty, and make my own choice of meanings. I shall also try to keep my taxonomy as simple and sparse as possible. Following Bok (1978:13) a lie, for our purposes, is a statement intended to deceive a dupe about the state of the world, including the intentions and attitudes of the liar. Most of the deceptive statements usually labelled as lies meet this definition, though some lie-like statements made by young children do not, as discussed in chapter 8. Bok stresses that to meet her definition an 'intentionally deceptive message' must be *'stated'*. When discussing self-deception, I expand her definition somewhat to include statements that are merely thought, as part of an inner dialogue, rather than spoken or written. Lies, of course, are not static; making a lie has consequences, not only for the dupe but also for the liar, and after a while a statement that began as a lie may no longer fit easily under its initial rubric. We discuss this process of transformation in chapter 7, where we also examine the difficulty of applying the criterion of intention to persons who deceive themselves.

Our definition, unlike some proposed by other writers, ignores the success or failure of the attempted deceit. It also allows for a statement to be perceived incorrectly as a lie by those who hear or read it, when in fact its originator had no intention to deceive. By our definition, errors and misunderstandings do not necessarily constitute lies, provided they arise in good faith, even though in the speech of young children, and in some popular usages, they are sometimes labelled as lies. For example, Duncan and Weston-Smith (1979:1) introduce their symposium on *Lying truths* by asserting that 'what we now call the climate of opinion is made up of a series of lies ...' The symposium contains several chapters on popular misunderstandings, for example a discussion by a physicist on quantum theory (Davies 1979), which have nothing to do with lying as characterized by an intent to deceive. On the other hand there is a chapter by Thomas Szasz (1979:122) on 'The lying truths of psychiatry' in which he accuses psychiatrists of 'a host of ... mendacious propositions and deceitful practices'. In other words, Szasz says that psychiatrists are liars.

Chisholm and Feehan (1977) provide a detailed logical analysis of the meaning of 'intending to deceive'; for our purposes I take it to mean intending to cause a dupe to adopt an understanding of the state of the world and/or of the mind of the liar that the liar believes to be false. The commonest way of achieving this goal is for the liar to make a false statement which the dupe accepts as true, but this is not the only way for a

11

liar to proceed. As Saint Augustine (1952:56) pointed out, a dupe may be deceived by accepting as false a statement that is actually true.

At this point we have to make a distinction between the state of the world and the beliefs of the liar. Bok (1978:6–13), following Kant, draws a useful distinction between truth and truthfulness, on the one hand, and falsity and deception on the other. The distinction between truth and falsity hinges on issues of ontology and epistemology, on correspondence, or on some similar relation, between what is and what is said to be. Truthfulness and deception, on the other hand, belong to the moral domain of intention. If we intend to deceive, we are acting untruthfully; if our untruthful act consists of making a statement intended to mislead, we are lying. Habermas (1979:68) makes a similar distinction between truth and truthfulness as validity claims in his discussion of universal pragmatics. According to our definition, therefore, lies can consist of either true or false statements, or of statements that are partly true and partly false.

It is important to remember that the distinction made here between truthfulness and deceit refers to the intentions of the liar, and not to the actual state of the world. The liar may be mistaken about the state of the world, including the state of his or her own mind. Following Bok, our definition ignores the truth or falsity of the lying statement. For lying is not simply the opposite of telling the truth. We may speak sincerely and in good faith, thinking that we are telling the truth, and yet be in error. Ptolemy may have been deceptive in presenting his data but he was not lying when he said that the sun revolves round the earth. He believed his statement to be true, and he expected that his audience would accept his statement as true. Likewise the chemists of the early modern period were not lying when they posited the existence of phlogiston to explain the phenomenon of combustion, even though we now believe that they, like Ptolemy, were wrong. The source of the potentially socially destructive effect of lying, and therefore appropriately its sociological hallmark, is not error or falsehood but the conscious intention to deceive, as Montaigne (1926:34–35) pointed out some four centuries ago, and St Augustine before that:

For, a person is to be judged as lying or not lying according to the intention in his own mind, not according to the truth or falsity of the matter itself. (St Augustine 1952:55)

In particular, a plagiarizer may well speak and write statements that are both true and not intended to mislead; yet he or she is deceitful in purporting to be the true begetter of these statements (cf. Committee on Professional Ethics 1980:348).

We should not assume that truth and truthfulness are unproblematic and context-free notions. Current postmodern fashions merely highlight a longstanding area of controversy. As noted earlier, there is an enormous corpus of literature on the problematic character of the concept of truth; by comparison the idea of truthfulness has received much less scrutiny. Haviland (1977:185), generalizing on the basis of his ethnographic fieldwork in Mexico, reminds us that 'the notions of truth and falsity are in most social discourse themselves negotiable.' Although he speaks of truth and falsity, I think he is, in Bok's terms, referring here to truthfulness and deception.

Bok and many other writers on lying, often for good reasons, treat truth as if the concept is unproblematic. This intellectual stance, associated at least retrospectively with positivism, has since the early 1970s been attacked vigorously by many of those who adopt one or other version of postmodernism. Truth remains a contested concept and a fashionable topic for debate. To pursue comprehensively the variety of important issues raised by postmodern writers, and moreover to do so in a vocabulary that made sense to those readers unsympathetic to postmodernism, would be a formidable exegetical task even if it was limited strictly to those issues that bear directly on the topic of lying. I shall not attempt it (cf. Kermode 1991:10).

The distinction between truthfulness and deception turns on the intentions of the deceiver, and not on the success or failure of what is intended. The recipient of a message may be misled, even though it may have been truthfully transmitted. More importantly, the intended victim of a deceptive message may see through the deception, or may in some other way escape being misled. Lies remain lies, even when they fail to deceive.

As well as being categorized as successful or unsuccessful by reference to outcome, lies can be classified in terms of the intentions of the liar. From this standpoint, lies are often referred to as white, social or altruistic if the intentions of the liar are basically good, and as serious, cruel, blatant or grave if the liar intends to do harm. Protective lies may be constructed to shield the interests of some other person, who may or may not be the dupe, but they are often designed to protect the liar, without necessarily harming anyone. These are all useful folk categories but for an analysis aimed at elucidating the social context of lying, rather than its moral status (though in chapter 10 we look briefly at moral evaluations of lying), we may do better to adopt a different perspective. We can begin by making a broad distinction between benevolent and malicious lies, depending on whether the liar intends to enhance the interests of the dupe or to harm them. If A, visiting her sick friend B in hospital, says 'I'm sure you will soon be well enough to go home', her intention is to comfort B even though she believes that B is unlikely to get well. She hopes that B will believe her false statement, and is therefore lying. This lie might seem to satisfy Bok's (1978:58) definition of a white lie: 'a falsehood not meant to injure anyone, and of little moral import'. But this label is, for our purposes, not very satisfactory. As a folk term the label is applied rather more widely, as Bok points out, often being attached to any well-intentioned lie. The 'moral import' of different kinds of lie is the focus of Bok's book, but not of the present analysis. Furthermore recent experience has shown, somewhat surprisingly, that for some people 'white lies' are those lies told by Whites rather than by Blacks. Indeed, this is how the term is used in Sean Virgo's (1981:134) short story 'White lies'. I suggest we drop the label as an analytical term. If we need to refer specifically to lies in which the liar merely intends to enhance the dupe's interests by deceiving him or her, we might speak of 'simple benevolent lies'. Such lies are also benign, in that the liar has no intention to harm any third party.

We need the adjective 'simple' because there are other benevolent lies that do not fall under this rubric and which are not benign. The hypothetical lie discussed by Kant (1949), in which A lies to B about the whereabouts of C, whom B is seeking to murder, is benevolent, in that A intends to protect C, but it is not simple, for the dupe is B rather than C. Furthermore, although Kant refers to this type of lie as benevolent (*gutmüthige*), A's benevolence is limited to C and does not extend to the dupe B; the lie can therefore not be called benign. Kant's Anglophone translators refer to A's motives as 'altruistic' and this seems an acceptable label for this kind of lie, even though A, while putting C's interests ahead of B's, is not necessarily putting them ahead of his or her own. As Durandin (1972:44n) points out, lies told in order to benefit someone else can also benefit the liar. 'Altruistic' is certainly a better label than 'officious', the now obsolete term and its French equivalent *officieux* used in the eighteenth century by John Wesley (1986:284–285) and Rousseau (1946:65) and derived from Saint Thomas Aquinas' (1972:150) *mendacium officiosum*. Saint Augustine (1952:86), in his eight-fold classification of lies, gives as his third type the lie 'which is beneficial to one person while it harms another' but unfortunately does not offer a label for the type.

Clearly distinguishable from wholly or partly benevolent lies are malicious lies, those told with the intention of benefiting the liar at the expense of the dupe. Most, if not all, of the lies popularly described in bad terms – serious, grave, deadly and the like – fall into this category. Another common category consists of social lies, statements which, taken literally, are false but which are not intended to deceive. If, on leaving a manifestly ghastly party, I say 'What a pleasant evening this has been', I may expect to be judged polite but I do not expect to be believed. I cannot be said to have lied, at least not if I believe that my hosts adopt the same norms of politeness as I do. But what happens if they do not? If I know that my remark will be taken at face value, and yet persist in making it, then I am lying, and run the risk of being invited to another ghastly evening for my recklessness. If my sincere belief that they will not take my remark literally is false, they are deceived even though I have not lied. If they subsequently discover my true feelings about the party, they may then judge me a liar. In our terms, most so-called social lies are not lies at all, for no deception is intended. Unintended deception and unjustified accusations of lying arise when there is a discrepancy between the perceptions of the author of a statement, whether or not he or she is lying, and those of its recipient. As we shall see, this kind of discrepancy often occurs, not only in connection with social lies.

Many other kinds of lies have been distinguished by theologians and moralists: jocose, paternalistic, religious, trivial, medical and so on. For our purposes, however, the hairs we have split are quite sufficient.

The rough and ready partition of lies into benevolent and malicious is based on the liar's intentions. These labels do not necessarily indicate the actual effect of lies on the dupes. For example a social 'lie' such as 'What a lovely party', or a simple benevolent lie such as 'I'm sure you'll soon be well', may easily hurt a naive dupe who takes the remark literally, and later discovers the mistake. On the other hand malicious lies may fail to deceive an alert intended dupe, and may even backfire to harm the liar. In any analysis of lying we always have to take into account both perspectives, as Bok (1978:20–28) calls them, the perspectives of the liar and of the dupe. Would-be free riders may be unhorsed by sophisticated dupes, and would-be benign liars, misunderstanding the cultural and personal assumptions their dupes make about the coloration of lies, may inadvertently find themselves regarded as malicious deceivers.

Although Bok's definition matches the usages of many other writers, some do not conform. For Dr Samuel Johnson, somewhat surprisingly, the word *lie* applied also to 'a mistake or an errour in relation' (Boswell 1934:49; cf. Johnson 1963:361–366; Ricks 1975:126–127). The term has also been applied not only to statements uttered or written at particular times and in particular places, where the criterion of intent to deceive can be applied to identifiable persons, but also to whole conceptual schemes and systems of morality, where the criterion of intention has little relevance. The most notable example of this usage is to be found in the writings of Friedrich Nietzsche who referred to religion as 'the holy lie', invented by priests and philosophers so that, by deceiving the laity, they would be able to take over 'the direction of mankind' and gain 'power, authority, unconditional credibility' (Nietzsche 1968a:89–90; cf. Kaufmann 1950:265–266). Nietzsche's attack was aimed widely at all religions or at least at all religions embodying a belief in a god 'who punishes and rewards'. He mentions Hinduism and other world religions but his principal target is Christianity, 'the most fatal seductive lie that has yet existed' (Nietzsche 1911:214; 1968a:90, 117; cf. Gregory Bateson 1951:222–227).

More recently, Bailey (1991:xviii) makes what he calls 'basic lies' the cornerstones of his analysis of deceit. A basic lie is the product of people who collaborate 'in pretending that circumstances are other than they know them in fact to be'. A basic lie purports to be 'objective truth'; the fact that it is not becomes an open secret shared by the collaborators. Bailey illustrates the concept with ethnographic data from India, but does not limit its use to peasant societies. Hobbes' *Leviathan* and Plato's *Republic*, he says, can be read as basic lies (Bailey 1991:83, 91–92). They are 'charters for repressive regulation', and the collaborators are, it seems, the members of the elite who propagate the charters to legitimate their dominance. Indeed, at one point in his exposition, Bailey speaks of 'the basic hegemonic lie' and equates this with the 'dominant ideology'. Even 'lesser designs like functionalism or structuralism or postmodernism' are included under the basic lie rubric (Bailey 1991:122). This broad application is, I think, undesirable. The criterion of deceit has disappeared; also Bailey seems to have lost sight of his own earlier definition. I cannot see how postmodernists, for instance, can be said to collaborate 'in pretending that circumstances are other than they know them in fact to be'. The same objection applies to functionalists, structuralists and the protagonists of innumerable other 'lesser designs'. Bailey does not refer to Nietzsche, but like him uses the term 'lie' overenthusiastically, so that as an analytic tool it becomes unacceptably blunt.

Rappaport (1979:231) is another writer who paints the concept of lie in broad terms. He distinguishes ordinary lies from what he calls 'vedic lies'; these are 'states of affairs ... that do not conform to the specifications they purport, or are supposed, to meet'. Thus I suppose that a democratic republic, so-called, that was not democratic and/or republican would be an instance of a vedic lie. Somewhat less happily, Rappaport (1979:241) speaks of 'lies of oppression', statements made under coercion, when, he says, the person coerced is not a liar; it is the coercer who is the liar, and also the victim of the lie, for oppression is 'finally, self-defeating'. Our working definition is much closer to Bok's delimited usage than to Rappaport's. Likewise in the present study we shall ignore the use of 'lie' to refer to attempts to elaborate or modify appearances or personalities, as in the nudist comment 'You tell the first lie of the day when you put your clothes on' (*Connections* 1989).

Our focus is on the spoken or written lie, but we should note that even silence can be a means of deception. Silence is not necessarily a neutral state; indeed we even speak of 'pregnant silences'. As Disraeli (1927:277) says 'Silence is the mother of Truth'. An unexpected silence is like those areas on large-scale maps where surprisingly there appear to be no significant features. We know at once that we are looking at an area probably bristling with military installations, though we cannot tell exactly where and what they are (cf. Monmonier 1991:120–121). Likewise a silence conveys meaning. For example, in a children's book about lying, a woman is shown saying to her daughter 'Does anyone know what happened to the vase that was on the table?' The daughter is depicted as lying by thinking 'If I don't say anything, she'll never know that I broke it!' (Berry 1988). Though we might regard a deceptive silence as a minimal or null lie, it differs from a substantial lie in that while the latter is usually constructed so as to generate in the mind of the dupe a specific misleading belief, it is much harder to control or check just how a deceptive silence is inter-preted. A lie, as it were, sets our audience off more firmly along a specified false trail, whereas a silence may start a multitude of false hares. The same ambiguity is, of course, present when we attempt to determine the truth concealed by lies we have detected. As Montaigne (1926:36) says, 'the reverse of *truth* has a hundred thousand forms, and a field indefinite, without bound or limit'.

Lying is a mode of deception. Goffman (1975:83–123) has developed a detailed typology of what he calls 'fabrications':

the intentional effort of one or more individuals to manage activity so that a party of one or more others will be induced to have a false belief about what is going on.

Not all of his deceivers engage in lying; his very lively illustrations of the variety of deceptions encountered in ordinary life demonstrate the fer-tility of the human imagination but, alas, carry us well beyond the scope of the present study.

Chisholm and Feehan (1977), in their paper referred to earlier, analyse the distinction between lies and deception. They identify eight ways in which a person may deceive another person, and conclude that only two of their types can properly be called lying. Likewise Jack Douglas (1976:57), in his typology of the problems that must be tackled by anyone aiming at avoiding deceit, makes a distinction between what he terms 'lies', i.e. lies of commission, and 'evasions', which are, roughly speaking, lies of omission; the latter are, he says, 'not out-and-out lies' (Douglas 1976:59).

Thus Bok, and Montaigne before her, see deceptive intention as the distinguishing feature of lying, whereas Chisholm and Feehan distinguish one type of deception from another on the basis of outcomes, what happens to the beliefs held by the dupe. Definitions that hinge only on the intentions of liars or the beliefs of dupes may well be sufficient for discussions in moral philosophy but for a sociological analysis we cannot confine our attention to just these two social actors. Michael Gilsenan (1976:191–192) points out that:

Lying manifests itself to us socially as an attribution made by others to the actor of a specific intention, whether or not such an intention 'in fact' existed.

For example, Hingley (1978:86–87) reports that when showing Oxford colleges to Russian visitors and remarking 'This is a typical under-graduate's room', his visitors assume that he has begun to indulge in *vranyo*, a Russian custom of telling fanciful stories that polite listeners should pretend to believe but which are not true. In communications between individuals with differing cultural expectations, it is easy for one of them to assume that the other is being deceitful when no deceit is intended. This type of mutual misunderstanding is particularly likely to arise when untrue statements are made that, to the speaker, are harmless but which the hearer mistakenly assumes are true and hence is deceived.

A spoken lie may form only one part of an act of deception; the liar may use, consciously or unconsciously, what has come to be known as body language as a means of enhancing the chances of success for the deceit; on the other hand, unintended body movements may enhance the likelihood that a liar will be detected. Alternatively, deception may be attempted by body language alone, without a supporting spoken lie. A fascinating example of the distinction between deceiving by what is said and by the way it is said is provided by Oliver Sacks (1986:76–80), in his account of how aphasic hospital patients reacted to a television address by Ronald Reagan in 1984. They responded by roars of laughter. These patients suffered from global aphasia, and could not understand 'words as such'. But, says Sacks,

it was the grimaces, the histrionisms, the false gestures and, above all, the false tones and cadences of the voice, which rang false for these wordless but immensely sensitive patients. It was to these (for them) most glaring, even grotesque, incon-gruities and improprieties that my aphasic patients responded, undeceived and undeceivable by words.

We do not need to become aphasic to experience much the same phenom-enon, nor even to listen to The Great Communicator; watching almost any politician speak on television with the volume control turned right down is usually quite sufficient, as is well illustrated in, for example, a sequence in the film *The loneliness of the long distance runner* where two delinquent British boys respond in the same way as Sacks' American patients when viewing, on muted television, a politician's speech.

Although some kinds of deception, such as the production of fake antique furniture or of feigned passes in a football game, may not necessarily entail lying, lies may sometimes occur incidentally as part of some more elaborate deceptive ploy. Homer and the Old Testament provide numerous instances. A modern example is found in the Witness Security Program in the United States. This has given false identities to thousands of people who have become government-sponsored liars, not because they wish to harm their new neighbours and workmates, who are their dupes, but because they need to conceal the fact that their apparent identities have been fabricated. Their lies are merely a by-product of their larger deceit. Some of the witnesses may well have had plenty of experience of lying but this is not the case with members of their families, who experience considerable stress from the lies they are required to tell (Montanino 1984).

Summing up, we can say that people, as social actors, communicate with one another in a variety of ways, and not only with words. They cannot read each other's minds, and hence communication is always less than perfect; indeed, they may be misled about what is going on in their own minds. Given this imperfection, all messages may be or may become distorted, either deliberately or unintentionally. Different contexts, however, provide different possibilities for deceit. These we shall explore in the following chapters. In the next three chapters I present data about lying in various social domains, beginning with those where lying is frequent and expected and ending with those where it is regarded as reprehensible and probably infrequent. In chapter 5 we look at how cultural norms affect patterns of lying and in chapter 6 at how they are affected by the type of relation existing between liar and dupe. Chapter 7 is about self-deception, when liar and dupe are the same person. The techniques of lying and detecting lies, and how these techniques are acquired, are discussed in chapter 8. In chapter 9 we look at the notion of fiction, as an example of untrue statements that are not deceptive. In the last two chapters we see how a selection of writers have evaluated lying and attempt to assess its genesis and function in social life.

2

Where lies are expected

A DIVERSITY OF DOMAINS

Miss Shute, a character in the late nineteenth-century collection of short stories, *Some experiences of an Irish R.M.* (Somerville and Ross 1944:97), draws attention to the difference between deceit practised in the process of buying and selling a horse and deceit perpetrated during a game of cards. She asks:

No one will ever explain to me ... why horse-coping is more respectable than cheating at cards. I rather respect people who are able to cheat at cards; if every one did, it would make whist so much more cheerful; but there is no forgiveness for dealing yourself the right card, and there is no condemnation for dealing your neighbour a very wrong horse!

With a horse sale, and not only in Ireland, lies are expected; they are not thought to be reprehensible, whereas cheating at cards is. Miss Shute played whist, not poker, but even in poker misdealing the cards is condemned even though bluffing an opponent is applauded. Yet even horses do not provide a *carte blanche* for every lie. In Australian racing circles volunteering a racing tip that is not offered in good faith is regarded as reprehensible, whereas responding to a request for a tip with deceitful advice does not attract moral censure. Card games and horses illustrate the way in which attitudes towards lying vary across social domains. In this chapter and the two following we shall look in turn at a variety of domains to discern what kinds of lies are told and how they are regarded.

Different domains of social life exhibit different expectations of truthfulness. We do not expect invariably to be told the truth about a person's relationship with his or her spouse, parents or children. We may not necessarily expect to be decisively deceived, but we are not particularly surprised if we discover later that this is what has happened. We expect

20

not to be deceived by news items in the mass media, but are not surprised when we discover that some newspaper advertisements are deceptive.

Different expectations, not only about lying but about many other socially and culturally significant activities, are often signalled by markers which serve to distinguish one domain from another. Domain boundaries may be indicated by markers set either in physical space or in secular time, or by linguistic cues. For example, the architecture and trappings of the law court indicate to actors and onlookers alike, provided they are culturally aware, that within its walls distinctive expectations of lies and special sanctions against lying are in force. The same concrete indications of difference are seen with parliaments and churches. Electoral campaigns, with their special norms, are sharply delimited by time markers, and in ordinary conversation special phrases indicate a shift in assumptions about truthfulness and deceit. There are probably other kinds of markers in use; the uniform of Father Christmas is an obvious example of a sartorial marker. His red robe and white beard indicate that he is expected by parents to tell lies to their children. Clever children may soon discern that what he tells them are lies, but a conscientious Father Christmas should still make an effort to achieve deceit.

Not all lying, and not all avoidance of lying, can be explained in terms of the social context in which lies are told. Some lies are best understood by reference to the personalities of liars, notably so-called pathological liars, persons afflicted with *pseudologia fantastica*. Whereas pathological liars tell too many lies, there are indubitably other individuals who tell fewer lies than one would expect, bearing in mind their position in society. These latter persons, alas, constitute a neglected category, lacking any label in a taxonomy of liars. It would be unkind to label them 'pathologically honest', though indeed one of my friends who clearly belongs to this category did once earn for himself the description 'a notoriously honest cop'. Any extended discussion of these non-liars must await the findings of further research. For the present we can merely note the existence of the phenomenon of 'pathological truthtelling' (sometimes known as the George Washington syndrome); it is seen by some psychiatrists as a stage in the struggle to establish autonomy during adolescence (Goldberg 1973:105–108).

In his chapter on 'The pathological lie' Marcel Eck (1970:78ff.), a child psychologist, uses Dupré's (1905) term 'mythomania' to refer to 'a pathological tendency, which is more or less voluntary and conscious, to lying and the creation of imaginary fables'. Citing evidence from case studies, Eck (1970:81) makes the point that 'in mythomania the desire to attract attention takes precedence over the desire to deceive'. Thus we have the paradox that although the intention to deceive is the essential feature of lying, the individuals who tell the most lies, those we call pathological liars, are not primarily motivated by a wish to deceive others. Selling (1947:484) notes that 'the characteristic of pathologic lying is its apparent lack of purpose'. According to Scott Snyder (1986:1289) 'pathological lying often arises out of a need for the patient to produce narcissistic gratification' rather then from an intention to deceive. Aldrich (1989) speaks of 'the choice of lies as symptoms' by psychiatric patients. Eck (1970:79) maintains that children have 'a natural inclination to mythomania', with the implication that in children this is not an unhealthy condition. He notes that 'traditionally, girls have been considered more inclined to mythomania than boys, although the opposite is often the case'. As for adults, 'woman is the tightrope-walker of mythomania, while man is the jobbing workman'.

Nevertheless, from his own evidence, and from that reviewed more recently by Ford and others (1988), there is nothing to show that mythomania or other forms of pathological lying are correlated with any social characteristic except, perhaps, gender. Davidoff (1942) considers that a pathological lie 'is not determined by situational factors, unconscious motivations predominate, the lie appears to be compulsive and fantastic, and is destructive to the liar' (Ford et al. 1988:555). Thus we have another paradox in that whereas pathological liars are sometimes described in popular terms as 'born actors', in sociological terms they are very poor social actors. Our present study has as its focus the social context of lying; we shall therefore say little about pathological liars, despite the abundance of their context-independent lies.

We encounter lies in virtually all walks of life, along with an equally ubiquitous preference, either moral or pragmatic, for telling the truth. Even gods are portrayed as telling lies to trick or test humans, as exemplified in the Old Testament story of Jehovah instructing Abraham to sacrifice his son Isaac (Genesis 22:1; cf. Milton 1934:305).

Nevertheless, despite this ubiquity, Simmel's generalization remains true:

Sociological structures differ profoundly according to the measure of lying which operates in them. (Simmel 1950:312–313)

These differences arise, at least in part, because of the varying extent to which the activities of free riders upset the workings of different structures. Free riders cannot be kept in check without effort, and the effort required varies from one domain of social life to another; likewise the consequences of free riding are more or less serious depending on the context. For example, mutual trust is called for more strongly in marriage, rock climbing and relations between lawyer and client than it is in chance conversations in the street. Diplomacy might well be described as institutionalized insincerity; Sir John Masterman (1972:32) remarks that 'when dealing with diplomatic conversations and the rumours of embassies we are in the very realm of lies'. We should not forget Sir Henry Wotton's punning definition of an ambassador as 'an honest man sent to lie abroad for the good of his country' (Smith 1907:49; Walton 1951:92–93). In this respect the world of diplomacy is scarcely distinguishable from the world of espionage, of which it is so often the cloak of respectability.

An absence of mutual trust may lead to an abundance of lies, each party trying to deceive the other, but the presence of trust does not necessarily result in an absence of lies. In intimate face-to-face relations the shared expectation of mutual trust may lead to collaboration between, or more likely connivance by, liars and dupes in order to maintain the plausibility of a lie, as well as the plausibility of continuing trust. When this happens it is no longer obvious who is deceiving whom.

WARFARE

The domain of warfare is a good place to start looking for lies. Warfare lies right at one end of the trust–mistrust continuum, where mistrust dominates relations between friend and foe, but also colours relations between friend and friend, or what might naively be thought to be friend and friend. Phillip Knightley, historian of war correspondents, has aptly amended the quip about lies and statistics to read 'Lies, damned lies and military briefings' (1991). *A bright shining lie,* the title of Neil Sheehan's (1988) book on the war in Vietnam, refers not to lies told by Americans to Vietnamese or by Vietnamese to Americans but to lies told by United States military officials to their fellow Americans (cf. Ekman 1992:306–308; Wise 1973). Although in retrospect most Americans may now condemn this particular set of lies, the absence of any blanket disapproval of attempts by American liars to make dupes of other Americans was demonstrated dramatically in 1987. Lt.-Col. Oliver North, USMC, proudly defended his decisions to lie to members of the United States Congress, and to shred documents relating to what became known as the Irangate affair (North 1987; cf. Ekman 1992:299–302); overnight he became a hero in the eyes of many of his fellow citizens. Likewise James Angleton, one of the main participants in 'the invisible war between the KGB and the CIA' (Epstein 1989:18) maintained that in his working environment deception was 'a norm rather than an aberration'.

Yet deception as a norm cannot stand alone, except perhaps in some hypothetical Hobbesian world of non-cooperating and mutually antagonistic individuals. Even the most devious persons need sometimes to trust and be trusted. Norms of cooperation and deception can coexist, though not without tension, provided separate areas of applicability are recognized. This unavoidable latent tension is well demonstrated in the temporary fraternization by soldiers from opposed front-line trenches in France during Christmas 1914. These short-lived friendly episodes were perhaps possible only because of the military division of labour, whereby deceptive initiatives originated exclusively from officers, while the task of the rank-and-file soldiers was merely to obey orders. Except as part of an attempt at deception, it is difficult to imagine friendly games occurring between opposed guerilla forces, where the capacity to initiate is more widely distributed.

Cruickshank (1981:1) begins his book on military deception with an impressive list of examples, starting with the Trojan Horse. He also shows (Cruickshank 1977: chs. 5–8) that during the Second World War no conceivable imaginative deceptive ploy seems to have remained unused by the British. The deception practised during Operation Desert Storm in the recent Gulf War continued the tradition.

Discussing lies told to enemies, Bok (1978:145) maintains that 'the language of enmity and rivalry ... is private language not suited to moral inquiry'. Bok's retreat may be right for philosophers, but the general public has no hesitation about evaluating lying to enemies in moral terms. Overcoming one's enemies may or may not involve the use of deceit, but if 'one' is a nation-state rather than a private citizen, the use of deceit is tolerated and even applauded. It is this 'inversion of values' that leads Bartoszewski (1989:28) to draw parallels between spying and myth, for in myths the moral order is often turned upside down. In a conflict between nations, particularly if this includes war, many politicians and members of the armed forces are likely to engage in deceit, but it is spies who do so most comprehensively. Spies, to earn their keep, are expected to deceive and to lie whenever necessary. Here we encounter a sharp contrast between the perspective of the liar and that of the dupe. Those who spy on us are popularly regarded as morally despicable; they deserve harsh penalties when discovered. Those who spy for us are silent heroes whose achievements we regret we cannot honour openly.

This contrast becomes even sharper when hostility is openly recognized by a state of war. An Australian psychologist is reported as saying:

one of the best legacies the British have left in Australia is that there has always been in the educated British mind an abhorrence of lying and mendacity. (Beale 1988:25).

Fine sentiments indeed; but compare, for instance, comments made about deception at the beginning of the Second World War and immediately after its victorious end. In a pamphlet published in 1941 by Oxford

University Press, entitled *Lies as allies*, and written by Viscount Maugham, formerly Lord Chancellor of Great Britain, we read that:

Hitler believes in lying as a method of gaining his ends ... he doubtless will continue to follow it until he disappears from the scene, with the reputation of having been the Champion Liar of all modern history ...

Maugham contrasts this with the British position:

British statesmen and public men have never at any time used mendacity as an instrument of war, still less have they ever uttered such praises of lying as Hitler has done in *Mein Kampf* ... In Great Britain we believe in the ultimate power of Truth. (Maugham 1941:11–12)

Yet only four years after the publication of Maugham's pamphlet, in a report on counter-espionage written initially only for official use but subsequently published, J. C. Masterman, an academic who had spent the war working on counter-espionage, wrote:

... peace is unfortunately often a condition of latent war.
  Counter-espionage must be a continuous process, an activity which persists in time of peace as well as in time of war ... we are fully entitled to adopt counterespionage measures against any power which indulges in espionage, whether that power be for the time friend or foe ... To tackle enemy espionage (whoever the enemy may turn out to be) it is therefore of paramount importance to keep a firm hold on the enemy's own system of agents and informers. Knowledge of his methods, knowledge of his intentions, and knowledge of the personnel of his organisation are all vitally necessary. Surely all these objects are best attained by the maintenance of double agents! (Masterman 1972:34–35)

In time of war, each contestant assumes that its enemy will try to deceive it, and in turn claims the right to try to deceive the enemy; yet at the same time it endeavours to persuade its own citizens to accept as true its statements to them. One of the traditional tasks of government is to protect citizens against their enemies, to 'confound their politics' and 'frustrate their knavish tricks', to use the phraseology of the second verse of what was until recently the Australian national anthem (though in the anthem, these tasks are assigned to God). In fulfilling this task, the government has the support of the majority of its citizens, and thus its use of at least defensive deceit is legitimate in their eyes. When a country comes under enemy occupation, the obligation to lie selectively is extended from the government to all loyal citizens. In relations with the enemy, the citizen is expected to follow an inverted moral code, despite the perils of doing so.

  The duality manifest in the actions of government, offering truth to its citizens and lies to its enemies, provides a key to understanding why attempts at deception are sometimes successful and sometimes fail. As mentioned earlier, in a situation where most participants are honest, a few individuals can become free riders; the assumption of good faith generated by the actions of the majority ensures the success of the deceit practised by the minority. Likewise an individual who is honest most of the time is more likely to be successful with the occasional lie than is someone who tells lies all the time. But if a liar relies too heavily on the assumption of good faith and makes too small a contribution to its maintenance, he or she loses credibility and becomes unsuccessful in deceit. The free ride comes to an end. This can easily happen with governments, for the separation between the two tasks they undertake is easily eroded.

Since the late 1960s the strongest protests about excessive lying have been against lies told by governments to their own citizens. These protests have been particularly strong since the war in Vietnam, and in the United States were fuelled by the Watergate and Irangate scandals. Despite the vehemence of protests, assigning personal responsibility for morally controversial decisions to individual decision-makers becomes difficult and itself a controversial matter, for all modern wars are characterized by long chains of command. Military bureaucrats, like bureaucrats everywhere, are prone to conceal their actions behind a shield of confidentiality, a process that may well involve telling lies. For example, in discussing the inquiry into responsibility for the lack of preparedness of the American defences when Pearl Harbor was attacked in 1941, Toland (1982:323) makes the comment about the then Chief of Staff, General George Marshall, 'It is a tragedy that a man in his high position was forced to lie.'

Unfortunately the task of confusing the enemy is easily enlarged to become one of deceiving the citizens as well. In the distant days immediately following the First World War, the Cambridge philosopher Francis Cornford was able to define propaganda as 'that branch of the art of lying which consists in very nearly deceiving your friends without deceiving your enemies' (Guthrie 1953). He was writing well before the blossoming of black propaganda that occurred during the Second World War, and the emergence of the term 'disinformation' to cover deceit that is suffered as much by one's trusting supporters as by one's enemies.

Deception in wartime, when aimed at the enemy rather than at fellow citizens, is directed at making him act in some way harmful to his interests and helpful to one's own. Typically, the enemy is encouraged to misjudge the strength of one's forces (either positively or negatively), the use to which they will be put, the appropriate weapons he should use, and the timing of any operation. For instance, Whaley (1984:56) notes that up to 1935 German deception was aimed at concealing its preparations for war. In that year, policy changed; the government wished to postpone the outbreak of hostilities until it had overtaken its enemies. Accordingly, 'dissimulative deception' was replaced by 'simulative deception that concealed weakness'. 'Cover', a special form of deception, is aimed at inducing the enemy to do nothing, 'to decide that genuine hostile actions are harmless' (Cruickshank 1981:xi). Sexton (1986:351) claims that what the enemy thinks is only of secondary importance, at least in the short term. He says 'it is only what the enemy does that affects the outcome of battle'. But before battle can be joined, a great deal of thinking has to take place. The Second World War saw what Sexton describes as 'the systemization of military deception', though this comment applies more aptly to the United States than to its European allies and opponents, with their longer traditions of fighting foreign wars. Certainly the duration of the Second World War and its global extent allowed elaborate and comparatively slow-moving deceptive ploys to be worth undertaking; the success of many of these has been described at length by many journalists and historians (e.g. Brown 1975; Cruickshank 1981).

The production of successful disinformation calls for considerable ingenuity, whether the target is the actions of the enemy or the thoughts of one's own citizens. For example, deceptive dispatches from the field of battle must be almost as old as warfare itself; Napoleon became known for the unreliability of his bulletins (Bourrienne 1893:112–115). Since 1939 production of deceit has been professionalized, and it is not surprising that deceivers take pride in their work and adopt deception as their customary mode of addressing the public. Anthony Marro (1985:38–39) tells the story of the wedding cake recipe used when President Nixon's daughter was married. Many loyal Americans wished to try it, and the White House published a recipe, appropriately scaled down for domestic use. Cooks who followed the instructions experienced nothing but culinary disaster. Marro comments that if Nixon's staff were incapable of acting truthfully about a cake recipe, how could they expect to be believed about what was happening in Vietnam. These free riders were unhorsed by a cake, if they had not already been thrown off by the television coverage of the war. As Adrienne Rich (1980:186) remarks bitterly:

We assume that politicians are without honor ... The scandals of their politics: not that men in high places lie, only that they do so with such indifference, so endlessly, still expecting to be believed. We are accustomed to the contempt inherent in the political lie.

The cake incident well illustrates what Arendt (1972:4) describes as 'the commitment to nontruthfulness' of the Nixon administration at that time. In Nixon's case, Rich's evaluation was to be confirmed by his involvement in the Watergate affair (Rasberry 1981: Part II).

In 1971 the *New York Times* published what became known as the Pentagon Papers, a top-secret report on the Vietnam War. Hannah Arendt (1972) analysed the report at length; she claims that disinformation efforts during the war were aimed not at concealing secrets from the enemy but at concealing widely known facts from the American people, especially members of Congress. Arendt's choice of examples indicate that 'widely known' includes 'widely known to the enemy' (cf. Arendt 1968:236; 1972:14, 27).

Despite the erosion of belief in government honesty during the Vietnam War, the United States administration still tried to convey the impression to the public that it did not engage in disinformation. In 1966 Admiral Poindexter proposed a disinformation programme whereby the American media would generate the impression that Colonel Gadaffi faced serious internal opposition. President Reagan and his assistant Larry Speakes denied the existence of the proposal when it was revealed by journalist Bob Woodward. Their denials were made in predictable terms; that of an unnamed administration official is more interesting. He said 'You must distinguish between the audiences, you must distinguish between deception and disinformation' (Hoffman 1986). In other words, in his view deceiving Gadaffi was a legitimate task for the American government; disinforming its own people was not.

For the United States, Bok (1978:xviii, 141f.) identifies 1960 as a year when disbelief in the honesty of government increased significantly. It was then that Khrushchev and Eisenhower clashed over the alleged shooting down of a U-2 reconnaissance plane, and the whole world saw that Eisenhower had lied (cf. Rasberry 1981:61– 62). This event may well have served to open the eyes of many United States citizens to dishonesty in high places; elsewhere disbelief in the truth of government pronouncements has a longer history. For instance, I remember the adage current in the 1930s when the French Foreign Ministry was located on the Quai d'Orsay: 'It must be true; the Quai d'Orsay has already denied it.'

In some conflicts, the distinction between friend and foe is unproblematic. When the two sides in a conflict speak different languages, lies intended to mislead the enemy can be targeted in a way that will ensure that one's own side does not mistake them for the truth. For example, in 1944 black propaganda was broadcast by the British to the German army from stations such as Soldatensender Calais; because the programmes were in German, Anglophone troops in the area were unlikely to listen to them and even less likely to believe them.

In civil conflicts both sides may speak the same language, and the distinction between friend and foe may often be unclear. Black propaganda and other varieties of disinformation cannot be targeted so as to reach only the enemy. This can be seen in the history of disinformation in Northern Ireland from the early 1970s onwards, when, so it seems, the British government adopted a policy of black propaganda aimed at the Irish Republican Army. Unfortunately, the history of deceit is itself a suitable arena for further deceit, so that the prudent observer must take all claims as to what really happened with large doses of salt. Even so, the production of black propaganda in Northern Ireland seems clear, as well as its very limited success (see Foot 1989).

Deceit practised as an accepted tactic during hostilities does not necessarily cease with the achievement of victory. Both sides may claim victory, even when an outside observer would have no hesitation in identifying the loser. This age-old practice was continued at the conclusion of the recent war in the Gulf, though it is unclear who was trying to deceive whom and who, if anyone, was deceived.

William Paley (1825:124) draws a sharp distinction between the conduct of war, during which deceit is allowable, and the termination of war, when 'the most religious fidelity is expected'. An example of a breach of this distinction is provided by the Treaty of Waitangi of 1840 between the British and the Maori people of New Zealand (Kawharu 1989; McKenzie 1987). The treaty was negotiated with two texts, one in English and the other in Maori, with ostensibly identical meanings. This identity has been challenged by Maoris and others, who maintain that the Maori text does not imply that the chiefs who signed it were yielding sovereignty to the British, which is of course the implication of the English text. Sahlins (1983:533) maintains that the use of two discrepant texts was an act of deliberate deception by the British, and not an accident of translation.

Despite the ingenuity of wartime liars, not all their lies achieve unqualified success. Liars confuse their targets, and are likely to end up confusing their supporters as much as, or even more than, their enemies. They may start to admire their inventions and come to believe them. For instance, according to Whaley (1984:72), by 1941 Hitler had come to believe his own propaganda, and thought himself infallible. He therefore attacked the Soviet Union and declared war on the United States. We discuss in chapter 7 the process whereby liars come to believe their own lies. However, according to Arendt (1972:35), during the Vietnam War Pentagon propagandists *started* by believing their lies (cf. Royle 1987:203–211). Liars, then, may have a free hand in time of war but even so they encounter much the same set of hazards as do liars in other areas of social life where lying is less actively promoted and condoned.

POLITICS

The political arena is second only to warfare as a domain where lies are expected, do in fact occur, and are to a substantial extent tolerated. Isaac D'Israeli (1881:438) cites the definition of politics as 'the art of governing mankind by deceiving them'. In his anonymously published *Proposals for printing the Art of Political Lying* John Arbuthnot (1712:8; cf. Aitken 1892:51– 52, 293– 303; Beattie 1935:288–298; Pollard 1897:108) defines 'the nature of political lying' as 'The Art of convincing the People of Salutary Falshoods, for some good End'. In his short pamphlet he poses the basic dilemma of lying in the political domain, particularly in those societies where there is no impermeable division between 'the People' and the elite who generate the 'Salutary Falshoods'. Arbuthnot notes, on the one hand, that 'no Man spreads a Lye with so good a Grace as he that believes it'. On the other hand, he warns the Heads of Parties against 'Believing their own Lyes; which has prov'd of pernicious Consequence of late ...' (Arbuthnot 1712:18, 19; Pollard 1897:119, 120). Arbuthnot's sentiments are echoed in the twentieth century by Hannah Arendt (1968:227) who begins her discussion of 'Truth and politics' with the uncompromising statement that 'lies have always been regarded as necessary and justifiable tools not only of the politician's or the demagogue's but also of the statesman's trade' (cf. Kintz 1977:492).

Lies are to be found throughout the political process; Bailey (1988:3–5) provides an impressive collection of examples from events in the United States, China, the Soviet Union and Africa. Those who spend their lives in this context become skilled at lying; it is a requirement for occupational success. Bailey (1988:169) observes, echoing Machiavelli, 'that leaders who are conventionally virtuous are also likely to be ineffective'. As Ekman (1985:21) says, 'it usually will be far easier to spot behavioral clues to deceit in a suicidal patient or a lying spouse than in a diplomat or a double agent'. But though Ekman may be right when looking for 'behavioural clues' in suspected liars, he is surely wrong when liars utter their lies to audiences who are well aware of their status as diplomats, patients or whatever.

In listening to patients and spouses we usually start with a presumption of honesty; a diplomat or politician, however honest and sincere in appearance, is much more likely to be heard with suspicion. Hence the Russian joke:

Q. How can you tell when a politician is lying?
A. When he moves his lips.

Parliament is a forum where the smell of deceit is never entirely absent. In England, in the intellectually feverish years that followed the repeal of the Licensing Act in 1694, when pamphlets appeared in profusion, political lying was delineated in a memorable article in *The Examiner*, attributed variously to Jonathan Swift or John Arbuthnot (Swift 1940:10). The pamphleteer makes the observation that:

There is one essential point wherein a *Political Lyar* differs from others of the Faculty; that he ought to have but a short Memory, which is necessary according to the various Occasions he meets with every Hour, of differing from himself, and swearing to both Sides of a Contradiction, as he finds the Persons disposed, with whom he hath to deal.

Here we have notice of an important difference. In many other domains where deceit is attempted, an appearance of consistency is called for; liars should therefore have good memories, so that they avoid contradicting themselves and exposing their deceits. Already in the first century AD, there was a Roman proverb (Quintilian 1921:101) that a liar should have a good memory. Later Montaigne (1926:34) observed that 'he who has not a good memory should never take upon him the trade of lying'. These maxims do not apply to politicians; consistency in a politician is, we might say, too much to expect. Many of the statements made by politicians, in early eighteenth-century Britain as well as generally today, are of course truthful, and sometimes even true; each fresh pronouncement might turn out to be one of these, even if it is incompatible with earlier statements. We live in hope.

Within political life, electoral campaigns have their own special set of norms. In an election, each party accuses all others of trying to deceive the gullible electorate. The elector, suffering from a surfeit of propaganda from all sides, cannot distinguish between sincere promises and seductive lies. Politicians may acknowledge this. For example, the 1990 Australian federal election generated a good harvest of statements that were branded as lies. After the election John Howard, a prominent politician, appropriately appealed to his colleagues on both sides of politics to rely less, in their search for electoral support, on what he tactfully called 'semantic gymnastics'. Two remarks made by the Liberal Party leader in the 1993 Australian election illustrate the expectation that campaigns generate lies. Beginning the campaign, John Hewson expressed the hope that on this occasion there would be no lies; after the election he explained his party's defeat by saying 'I was too honest'.

In parliament itself expectations change, though indulgence in deceitful mythmaking during an election campaign is a habit not easily discarded the moment the campaign has ended. Statements about the future are often perceived by political opponents as intended to deceive, both during campaigns and afterwards in parliament. On the other hand, parliamentary statements about the past, and to a lesser extent statements about the present, are expected to be true. A British civil servant told a journalist, when interviewed about possible conflicts between his personal code of ethics and the briefs he was required to write for his minister, that:

telling untruths about the future doesn't matter because it's anyone's guess; telling lies about the present or the past is far more important. (Phillips 1991)

Parliamentarians, both ministers and backbench, are from time to time discovered to have made untrue statements about what has happened in the past and are then sometimes accused of lying. These accusations are made with such indignation as to indicate clearly that in this context, unlike on the hustings, lying is wrong. An illustration comes from a poetic comment on the 1963 Profumo affair. John Profumo, the British Secretary of State for War, was alleged, among other things, to have visited a young woman, Christine Keeler, in her London mews flat where she also received other male visitors, among them a Russian naval attaché. Challenged in the House of Commons about his association with Miss Keeler, Profumo first denied the allegations. Subsequently he admitted that the allegations were correct and resigned his parliamentary and government posts (Young 1963). A limerick circulating at the time ran

> What on earth have you done, said Christine,
> You have wrecked the whole party machine;
> To lie in the mews,
> That is just rude,
> But to lie in the House is obscene.

Respondents to a social survey were asked whether they regarded the security risk posed by the involvement of the Russian attaché, or Profumo's having a mistress, or his act of lying in parliament, as more important. Eighty per cent of them chose lying, then came the security risk, with the fact of having a mistress coming last (Irving et al. 1963:227).

A politician who is seen to have lied is less likely to be believed the next time he or she tells the truth. In recent times it is probably Ronald Reagan who has most clearly been identified with persistent, and even carefree, untruthfulness. In times of peace, politicians in high office usually restrict their lying to important occasions when they are particularly anxious to mislead the public. Yet Reagan's output of demonstrably false statements during his first term as President was sufficient to fill a book listing more than two hundred of them, together with their refutations (Green and MacColl 1983). But was Reagan lying? Did he intend to deceive? Perhaps sometimes, but hardly all the time. A saying current at the time is nearer the truth: George Washington couldn't tell a lie, Richard Nixon couldn't tell the truth, Ronald Reagan couldn't tell the difference. Given this attitude to the truth, are there grounds for complaint because his spokesman Larry Speakes invented statements that he attributed to the President? Broder (1988) thinks there are not and instead of Speakes blames 'the reporters and voters who have accepted manipulation and deception as a way of life.' Broder calls for politicians to 'Speak for yourselves' so that, among other things, they can be seen to be responsible for their own lies. In this case, whether or not Reagan intended to deceive, it is clear that Speakes did. Indeed, his successor as White House spokesman, Marlin Fitzwater, is reported as acknowledging that the publication of Speakes' book *Speaking out* (1989) would make it more difficult for administration officials to be believed (Cannon 1988).

The call for politicians to speak for themselves may, however, be a vain attempt to put the clock back to the time before political parties had become major clients of the advertising agencies. For, as Robert Adams (1977:44, 65) notes, 'political lying has entered, in our day, the era of mass production'. Departments of disinformation complement the activities of advertising agencies, and those run by governments in office stand out from the rest only because of the superior resources they command. Hence we reach the situation typified by President Nixon's advisers, who, in Adams' words,

lied, it would seem, not simply from greed ... not from malice or fear ... not even from a natural though corrupt love of the lie itself. ... They lied, it would seem, automatically, mechanically, out of teamwork, like the man who went to hell simply from reluctance to break up a good party.

Levitt and Levitt (1979:336) put the matter more simply. Referring to Nixon's lies about his own career, they say:

The citizenry could no longer trust Nixon's appraisal of their external reality since he had made such a mess of his own.

Luckily, in a democracy no-one can believe everything said by all politicians, for what one politician says is likely to be contradicted by another. Thus one argument in favour of democracy is that it prompts us to treat all statements by politicians with caution; in the words of an anarchist poster that appeared at the time of the 1983 Australian federal election, 'Don't vote for politicians: it only encourages them'. On the other hand coherent public life would, I think, be impossible if no-one ever trusted any politician. To maintain a complex social fabric we have to be prepared sometimes to give some politicians the benefit of the doubt; they have to avoid excessive, and hence counter-productive, lying.

According to the 'noble lie' doctrine discussed by Plato (see chapter 6), governments are empowered to tell lies that are in the national interest. Jody Powell, sometime White House press secretary, goes one step further; in his view: 'In certain circumstances government has not only the right but a positive obligation to lie' (Powell 1984:223). I think that most people would agree with this proposition; but there would be little consensus about specifying the 'certain circumstances'.

Governments typically protect themselves with a cloak of official secrecy, so that with luck many of their attempts to deceive their opponents and the general public succeed and never come to light. Rules about the release of official documents after a stated number of years allow historians and others to uncover past deceits, but usually only long after their perpetrators are safely out of the way. During the last few decades this form of protection for governments has in some countries been partially eroded by Freedom of Information Acts and similar legislation, which in turn has led to greater awareness of the risks in committing plans and decisions to paper. The shredder may be seen as the best defence against the photocopier, with the increased opportunities for leaks offered by the latter. The continuing revolution in information technology will presumably bring forth new struggles between deceivers and their dupes. But in the meantime the yearly release of previously classified material, written under pre-revolutionary conditions, reveals the deceits practised by governments in earlier years. Thus on 1 January 1992 Australian federal government papers from 1961 were released. At that time, married women could not hold permanent positions in the public service. A committee set up to inquire into this discriminatory practice had recommended that the restriction be removed, and this proposal was supported by the Public Service Board. The Prime Minister, R. G. Menzies, disliked the proposal and intended to reject it, but with an election in the offing did not want to reveal his opposition. His cabinet accepted his plan for telling parliament and the public that the matter was being considered by government but no decision had yet been reached (*Canberra Times* 1992). In other words, both parliament and the public were to be deceived. By 1992 Menzies was long since dead and the appointment of married women to permanent positions well established.

The domain of politics has two characteristics relevant to the prevalence of deceit: competition and leadership. Political competition, at least in a democracy, is more regulated and less violent than warfare but it provides many similar opportunities for achieving success by deceit. Likewise the necessity of providing leadership in the implementation of public policy opens the way for, or perhaps even requires, fooling at least some of the people some of the time. Bailey (1988:ix, x) asserts 'that leaders everywhere are like [academic] deans, inescapably polluted by what they do', and what they do is essentially 'malefaction'. Bailey then qualifies somewhat these sweeping claims but his point is well made. The combined requirements for success in conflict and leadership put a premium on the exercise of deceit, a premium whose existence is recognized, luckily by many but unfortunately not by all, of the intended dupes. This recognition provides at least a partial curb on the chances for successful deception. How great a curbing effect it has varies with the openness of the society concerned.

The domains of warfare and politics have many similarities, as innumerable political scientists have recognized. Among these similarities are resemblances in their patterns of lying. In both domains substantial amounts of lying occur, and are recognized as occurring, but whereas in warfare the generation of lies is officially and relatively overtly funded, in politics the production of lies is concealed and is, except in rare instances, denied rather than admitted. Both politicians and wartime propagandists run the danger of coming to believe their own lying inventions, but also confirm the truth of Arbuthnot's comment about the greater effectiveness of liars who do just this. Both groups devote a substantial amount of energy to misleading their supporters as well as their opponents. Compared with other domains we shall look at, these two stand out in the extent to which onlookers expect that lies will be told and their tolerance of, or at least resignation to, this state of affairs.

3

Ambiguous domains

COURTS AND POLICE

Warfare and politics occupy one end of the trust–mistrust spectrum; the other end might be assigned to academic references. At the mistrustful end we assume at least one side is being deceived, and that if a message happens to be true, it has been transmitted only in order to achieve deception more successfully at some later date. At the other end of the spectrum we assume that there is no intention to deceive, even if what has been written seems to be untrue. In between the two ends is a middle range where untrue messages are sometimes assumed to be lies and sometimes not. In her book *Lying* Bok lists several of these intermediate categories: statements made to protect others, or made to promote the public good, or told to the sick and dying. Some of the statements made to participants in experiments in social science are untrue and may be explained later when the experiment has been concluded. Bok discusses at length to what extent statements made in these various contexts are made with intent to deceive, and whether or not these lies are justified. Our interest however is less in the moral evaluation of these statements and more in the ways in which statements are classified as lies by others, including the persons to whom the statements are addressed.

Legal systems in most industrial societies, perhaps in all of them, are social domains where the blanket assumption of good faith found in the academic ivory tower does not prevail, and yet where the shameless deception required from spies attracts censure rather than praise. The domain is characterized by diverse expectations and evaluations of deceit attempted by persons in different jural roles, and by the strategic use of oral as well as written modes of communication. Commenting on the preference for speech over writing in court proceedings, Tallis (1988:174) notes that:

It is perhaps easier to lie in a written statement (which can be checked before submission for internal consistency and plausibility) prepared in the calm of the study than in a public inquisition.

'The calm of the study' may perhaps reign in the lawyer's chambers but is likely to be absent from the interrogation cell. The fabrication of evidence by the police comes to light from time to time in what are judged to be scandals. Yet the collection of evidence by the police, honest and dishonest officers alike, is predicated on two assumptions, one moral and the other methodological. We assume that suspected persons are likely to tell lies, but we also assume that deceitful questioning may uncover the truth a person is unwilling, or even unable, to reveal voluntarily. The same methodological assumption is made by social workers (Reamer 1982:228) and at least some ethnographers. The battle of wits between suspects and police goes on behind closed doors but the same assumptions of distrust can be seen floodlit in the courtroom arena. Here we assume that accused persons are likely to deceive in order to escape conviction. Trial procedures all over the world are designed to probe for indications that statements given as evidence are false, with the assumption, in general, that false statements are made with deceitful intent.

Courts are distinguished from other social domains by the frequent use of formal procedures aimed at emphasizing the requirement of honesty. It is in the courts that Mark Twain's maxim has most relevance:

Truth is the most valuable thing we have. Let us economize it. (Twain 1897:89)

The injunction to tell 'the truth, the whole truth and nothing but the truth' has been derided by Steiner (1975:220) as 'a fictive ideal of the courtroom or the seminar in logic'. Indeed, though the injunction presents its three parts as equally important, in practice lies of omission are widely regarded as less reprehensible than lies of commission; they also provide fewer possibly vulnerable statements for the opposition to latch on to.

Courts both expect deceit and deplore its occurrence. Thus for example, Ethel Albert (1972:88), an American linguist who during the 1950s worked in east Africa in what is now Burundi, says of local courts:

It is assumed that the self-interest and emotional involvements of disputants and witnesses will lead them to falsify evidence, to exaggerate accounts of damage or make excessive claims for compensation, and even to perjure themselves.

British and US courts are in this respect much the same as those in Burundi. There are however some significant differences. British courts, like their counterparts in America, seem to place great weight on demonstrated inaccuracies in the testimony of witnesses; as Dean and

Whyte (1958:37) point out, once a witness has been shown to have made a mistake, the whole of his or her testimony comes under suspicion. But on the other hand, if several lay witnesses offer identical stories, they are likely to be suspected of having been rehearsed in presenting a false account; a slight amount of divergence and vagueness adds verisimilitude. Identical stories presented by police witnesses, however, are perceived as testifying to their professionalism and accuracy of observation. According to the British *Police training manual* (English 1986:100), a police officer 'could be classed as a professional witness' and is expected to present facts 'correctly, impartially, and respectfully'. There is no room for any post-modern epistemological uncertainty in police training.

In general the judicial process entails, among other things, the discovery, construction or determination of the truth. It is therefore not surprising that lies told in court tend to be treated more seriously than those told outside the courtroom. Notably, these lies attract extra-judicial sanctions. A feature common to judicial processes in many tribal and pre-industrial societies is the use of supernatural agents to decide outcomes and in particular to punish witnesses who lie. Trials by ordeal or by adversarial oath-taking rely not on evidence brought before the court but on supernatural intervention to indicate verdicts. The Ten Commandments single out bearing false witness for special mention and in English law there has been a long association between lying and divine retribution. From the earliest times the administration of an oath, whereby a person swore to tell the truth, was adopted as a mechanism for enrolling God not only as an arbiter but also as a punisher, or, as Jeremy Bentham (1843:192) trenchantly put it, making 'God the sheriff and executioner – man the despot, God his slave' (cf. Criminal Law Revision Committee 1972:163). The oath, says Baker (1990:6, 87–88) 'was intended to obviate formal enquiry into the factual merits of the case'. As late as the eighteenth century an English judge held that understanding the nature of an oath administered in court meant that oath-takers realized that if they told lies they would burn in hell forever (Spencer and Flin 1990:45–46; cf. Wigmore 1976: s. 1816). But whereas English courts initially relied in many instances on divine intervention alone to determine the truth and, either instantly or in due course, to punish liars, by the sixteenth century this arrangement came to be viewed as unsatisfactory. The Star Chamber developed the concept of perjury, whereby a person who lied on oath became liable to secular as well as divine punishment. Disenchantment with the use of inescapable torment in hell as a deterrent under the old system of compurgation, or 'wager of law', was well expressed by Sir Edward Coke, in a comment on the landmark *Slade's Case* of 1602:

for experience now proves that men's consciences grow so large that the respect of their private advantage rather induces men to perjury, and principally those with declining estates. (Baker and Milsom 1986:441)

Yet despite the introduction of perjury as a crime with secular sanctions, evidence given on oath continued to be associated with the possibility of attracting divine wrath. Later, scepticism about the truth of unsworn evidence given by a defendant speaking from the dock came to be based on his or her freedom from cross-examination as well as on the absence of any invocation of the deity (cf. Spencer and Flin 1990:49–55).

Oath-taking by the defendant has a more complicated history. Anglo-Saxon defendants swore their innocence and medieval courts examined defendants forcibly on oath. The Star Chamber claimed and abused the same power, so that, after its abolition in 1641, there was a 'strong insistence ... that the administration of an oath to a defendant was contrary to the law of God and the law of nature' (Williams 1963:41). The defendant's right to remain silent, coupled with his or her inability to give evidence on oath, led however to what Williams (1963:45) describes as 'unmerited acquittals'. This was remedied by allowing defendants to make unsworn statements from the dock, a practice abolished in 1982 as a belated but desirable consequence of the change introduced in 1898 whereby the accused was allowed to give sworn evidence (cf. Criminal Law Revision Committee 1972:65–66).

Thus it is clear that attitudes towards oath-taking have shifted greatly over the centuries. Some of these shifts have been influenced by changes in arrangements for denying or allowing an accused person to be legally represented, a topic that would take us too far away from our present inquiry. Ignoring this complication, we can say in broad terms that evidence displaced divine intervention, instant or delayed, as the basis for deciding cases. English courts have consistently assumed that an accused person may well wish to tell lies to enhance his or her chances of acquittal. In early times swearing was seen as an effective deterrent against lying whereas the Star Chamber, by adding secular sanctions, placed its victims in double jeopardy. Later the common law came to recognize the accused's right not to be questioned, which Williams (1963:37–38) sees as analogous to the US privilege against self-incrimination. Towards the end of the nineteenth century public opinion moved against this right 'to shelter unheard in the dock' and introduced an option for the accused to give sworn evidence on which he or she could be cross-examined 'with a view rather to breaking down this shield than to providing the innocent defendant with better weapons' (Cornish 1978:58; Cornish and Clark 1989:618–619). The idea of double jeopardy had effectively disappeared. In its report on evidence the Criminal Law Revision Committee (1972:163–166) sets out the reasons why a majority of its members considered that the judicial oath should be replaced by 'an undertaking to tell the truth', one of which was that:

for a person who has a firm religious belief, it is unlikely that taking the oath will act as an additional incentive to tell the truth. For a person without any religious belief, by hypothesis the oath can make no difference.

Only a minority of members favoured the retention of the oath. The Committee nevertheless did not make any recommendation about abolishing oath-taking because 'the question is obviously an important one of general policy going beyond the criminal law'. Accordingly, when the Committee's recommendations were implemented in legislation, the system of oath-taking remained unaffected.

In some state jurisdictions in the United States and in some other European courts, the accused may be allowed to give evidence without taking an oath, so as not to attract punishment for perjury (Freedman 1975:31; Wigmore 1976: s. 1826). Other witnesses might be expected to respond to the secular and possibly supernatural threats of punishment by giving honest testimony; the motivation of the accused to lie would be too strong for either secular or divine intimidation. But if in industrialized communities belief in automatic intervention by God has declined, it still finds strong support in many rural areas. For instance Herzfeld (1990:310–315) reports the gravity accorded to divine punishment of perjurers by thieves and shepherd-monks in Crete during the 1980s.

Accused persons may be expected to lie; but how do we evaluate statements made by lawyers? Was Oscar Wilde right to exclude barristers from his lament over the decline in the art of lying? Tricky questions put in cross-examination are seen in retrospect as attempts to trip up a witness in the hope of exposing a concealed deceit. But 'tripping up' is only a euphemistic way of describing efforts to deceive the witness, at least momentarily. Raiffa (1982:142) remarks that most people

would choose not to label as 'lying' the exaggerations that are made in the adversarial confrontations of a courtroom. I call such exaggerations 'strategic misrepresentations'.

A fine line is sometimes drawn between what Scheppele (1988:132–133) calls 'intentional misrepresentation', which American courts will not allow, and the creation of a false impression by concealing information that was not required to be disclosed. This distinction is analogous to that between lying by commission and by omission, with greater reprobation being attached to the former mode of deceit.

While lawyers are reluctant to admit that in their pleading they may sometimes be lying, they are even more reluctant to agree that they have a duty to lie on behalf of their clients. Yet in 1821, Lord Brougham, during his pleading in defence of Queen Caroline, expressed the view that an advocate's duty to further the interests of his client was absolute, 'his first and only duty' (Freedman 1975:9). More recently an American jurist argued that a defending lawyer has a duty to be disingenuous, a duty which sometimes may require him or her to lie in the interests of the client (Curtis 1951:9; cf. Bok 1978:158). His contention was indignantly rejected by some of his legal colleagues (Drinker 1952); the majority view would seem to be the one adopted by Peters (1987:2) who draws a distinction between the courtroom and what takes place outside the court. In the courtroom there are strong injunctions against dishonesty, whereas in negotiations, lawyers, like other negotiators, 'are forbidden to lie, but are generally encouraged to deceive in other ways'.

We may note that the duty proposed by Curtis is limited to preserving and enhancing the truthful appearance of a client's evidence which the lawyer knows to be a lie; nevertheless it is a duty to lie and deceive. Furthermore the injunctions governing conduct in court conflict with one another, constituting what Freedman (1975:28) calls a trilemma: the lawyer 'is required to know everything, to keep it in confidence, and to reveal it to the court'. Freedman argues that, faced with these obligations, a lawyer may quite properly present testimony provided by the client which the lawyer knows to be a lie:

the rules appear to require that the criminal defense lawyer should urge the client to correct the perjury, but beyond that, the obligation of confidentiality precludes the lawyer from revealing the truth.

Yet at the same time as presenting this as his own resolution of the trilemma, Freedman elaborates on alternative resolutions proposed by other jurists or adopted by professional associations that emphasize the lawyer's duty to the court at the expense of his or her obligations to the client. Frankel (1975:1035) observes that under the existing adversary system of justice: 'The advocate's prime loyalty is to his client, not to truth as such'. For this reason, he suggests radical changes away from the adversary mode of arriving at a verdict.

These arguments have been put forward in the United States, where the system of legal advocacy differs significantly from that prevailing in Australia and Britain, notably in the financial stake the lawyer may have in securing the success of his or her client's case. However, Freedman (1975:29) notes that even in England, according to the Law Society, a lawyer must maintain the confidentiality of his or her relation to the client if told by the client, after the conclusion of a civil case, that a witness had been paid by the client to commit perjury. Woodbury (1984) has provided a fascinating analysis of the ways in which lawyers vary the grammatical form of the questions they put to witnesses according to the kind of response they are seeking to elicit. It would, I suppose, be stretching the concept of deceit unduly to say that asking the legendary question 'When did you stop beating your wife?' is an attempt to deceive but it is certainly an attempt to trap.

In the legal systems we have been considering, court hearings are designed to discover and/or constitute the truth; if there is to be successful deception it must take the form of fabricated evidence and bogus confessions. Questioning may be deceptive but, according to the rules, the answers that are elicited ought to stop short of actual lying. The search for truth is, however, not the dominant aim in all courts. In family courts a greater emphasis tends to be placed on reaching a settlement that will be accepted, however reluctantly, by all the parties to the dispute, even if the settlement is made legally presentable by the incorporation of fictions. Many peasant legal systems are likewise concerned with reaching acceptable compromise outcomes rather than arriving at some constituted truth, even when dealing with disputes that are not centred on the family. For example, Collier (1973:viii, 97), in her study of legal procedures in a rural Mexican community, reports that people 'were not concerned with crime and punishment. They cared about ending conflicts, to forestall supernatural vengeance'. The compromise solutions they reached 'may be based on outright lies, which everyone knows are lies but which offer the only possible route to agreement'.

It is not only in courts aiming at reconciliation that lies may abound. Competitive lying may flourish in courts when there is a scarcity of incontrovertible testimony. An example of aggressively contested lying in court is mentioned in chapter 5.

Police work is another activity where deception, including lying, is commonplace. As with the process of government and the conduct of psychological research, to be discussed in chapter 4, both deception and truthfulness are called for. In a democracy the police depend for the effective discharge of their duties on enjoying the confidence of the general public. At the same time police officers are expected to deceive individuals, not only to trap lawbreakers but also to test the truthfulness of the testimony offered by the innocent. Manning (1977:180–181) maintains that

police officers in the line of duty in a variety of situations, some involving possible criminal charges and others that deal with public-order maintenance, are virtually required to lie.

Indeed, Klockars (1984a:422) maintains that

It is generally conceded ... that in any situation in which police enjoy a legitimate right to use force they acquire a moral right to achieve the same ends by lying. (cf. Arendt 1968:229)

On the other hand

... in the police officer's view, to lie when one can achieve the same effect more efficiently and with less effort is not immoral but stupid. (Klockars 1984b:537)

Klockars gives several examples of the use of deceit by police. Although he does not raise this issue, his assumption seems to be that the police whose activities he studied were honest, practising deceit quite conscientiously in the performance of their role as law enforcers.

'Blue lies', as Klockars calls them, are told to control the dupe. Hence the individuals most likely to become the dupes of blue lies are those who do not respond submissively to the power and authority of the police or to non-deceptive attempts at persuasion. Klockars includes in the category of blue lies not only lies told to suspects to get them to 'come quietly' but also lies told to superiors in the police administration, or even to the court, so that the liar can continue to fulfil his or her duty, as he or she sees it. He reports an incident involving a shoe left behind by a rapist who had been interrupted *in flagrante*. Instead of storing the shoe in an evidence room, a police officer investigating the case kept it in a drawer of his desk. Later he matched the shoe with one found in a search of the rapist's lodgings. So that the abandoned shoe could be used as evidence in the trial, the officer forged an evidence receipt so that he could pretend that the shoe had been kept in proper custody ever since it had been retrieved from the scene of the crime.

Klockars discusses why a police officer with a well-deserved reputation for honesty would behave in this way. The officer knew that the shoe had not been tampered with, and was convinced that the rapist was guilty not only of this rape but of at least four others as well. Furthermore, the officer perceived the rules of evidence continuity applied by the court to be merely a technicality, 'a procedural rule the violation of which does not affect a perpetrator's factual guilt'. Forging the receipt had the effect of covering up the mistake he had made. It so happened that neither did he have to produce the shoe as evidence nor did the verdict of guilty hinge on that evidence. Thus his action conformed to police norms of morality.

Another deceitful ploy is what Klockars calls the 'police placebo'. As common examples, he cites

promises to keep a close watch on an area or dwelling after a person has been victimized or becomes fearful of being victimized by media reports of crime; assurances that burglaries with all the earmarks of a professional job were probably the work of 'just kids'; advising a seriously injured child or widow of an accident victim that the deceased is all right or receiving expert medical care; telling the family of a fatally injured accident victim that their loved one died instantly and painlessly when the officer knows the death was neither quick nor painless; and attribution of a decision not to effect an arrest to some generous or kindly motive rather than the futility of doing so in the face of inadequate evidence. (Klockars 1984b:535)

Klockars identifies four features that mark out placebos from other kinds of lying by the police. The perception of the situation by the dupe is wrong; the lie gives the dupe the impression that the police are efficient; the placebo is given partly or wholly for the benefit of the dupe; and the liar assumes that the dupe will not be better served by some non-deceptive response.

Police face the same dangers of excessive lying as do policy makers and, as we shall see in chapter 4, experimental psychologists. Police lies, says Klockars, are often 'intrinsically appealing, exciting and attractive'. Consequently 'as the police officer becomes comfortable with lies and their moral justification, he or she is apt to become casual with both' (Klockars 1984b:543). This hazard is not confined to the police. Indeed, Klockars suggests that in American society 'prison guards, keepers of mental institutions, and parents', as well as police have a legitimate right to use both force and lies. Given this legitimation of lying, we should not be surprised when police, like politicians, tell lies in situations where to tell the truth would be more in the public interest. Yet deceit by the police, as by other people, can succeed only if their dupes believe that most of the time the police are honest.

These examples of court hearings and police inquiries confirm one of the conclusions drawn from the discussion in chapter 2 of lying in warfare and politics: in those social institutions where lying and truthfulness are both called for, success in deceit encourages its practitioners to practise deceit more widely, leading in the end to a destruction of the assumption of honesty, and thus to diminished success. As Hannah Arendt (1972:7) puts it, 'There always comes the point beyond which lying becomes counterproductive.'

ADVERTISING

In a market economy, advertisements describe goods and services in favourable terms whose accuracy the customer cannot easily check. Even in those countries with legislation designed to protect consumers, some commercial advertisements are deceptive. Typically, deception in advertising is achieved by omission rather than commission and by making statements that, though true when taken strictly literally, carry implications that are false. For instance, some years ago an American brewery stated in an advertisement that the bottles used to contain its beer were 'washed with live steam'. The implication is that this procedure was distinctive of that brewery. This was false, for the procedure was also followed by all other American breweries (Garfinkel 1977). Likewise, a firm of tax accountants gave as one of the seventeen reasons why taxpayers should use its services the fact that one of its representatives would accompany any client who was called to the tax office for a tax return audit. Again, this undertaking was presented as part of a 'unique selling proposition' of the firm, concealing the fact that it was an obligation imposed by US law on all tax accountants.

'Misleading functionality' is another technique for deceiving consumers. Garfinkel instances an advertisement in which a firm of towel manufacturers claimed that its towels were heavier than those of any of its competitors. The implication is that heavier towels dry better; in fact these heavy towels dried no better than lighter ones.

Written advertisements are easier to monitor and control than are those that are only spoken. In street trading, it is comparatively easy for market stallholders to make fraudulent claims without risk of legal sanctions. For the most part the lies shouted out by sellers stress the presence of the same good attributes as appear, fraudulently or not, in written advertisements. However, it is only in oral claims that goods are stated to be stolen or smuggled. Sometimes these claims are correct, but not always. Klockars (1974:79) describes how a stallholder passed off some legitimate items as if they had been stolen, hoping thereby that his customers would think, wrongly, that they were getting a good bargain. A similar ploy was common among petty traders in Bombay in the 1970s, when watches manufactured in India were deceptively described to customers as having been smuggled into India by returning migrant workers. In both situations, a customer who discovers he or she has been cheated cannot appeal to the law for redress, for attempting to buy stolen or smuggled goods makes the customer an accessory to a crime.

Writing at the beginning of the twentieth century, Georg Simmel (1950:314) saw changes in advertising practice as part of an historical process whereby increasing social complexity brings about a decline in lying, a process which he thought was 'by no means completed'. He compared advertising in the wholesale and retail markets, and said that, compared with the retail trade, wholesalers 'can afford to proceed with complete sincerity when offering their goods'. What he called 'mendacious claims concerning certain merchandise' in retail trade he saw as historical relics, carried over from an earlier and simpler social state when lies were both permissible and expedient. He predicted that

Once the business of the small and middle-sized merchant reaches the same perfection, the exaggerations and outright falsehoods of advertising and praising, for which it is not usually blamed today, will meet with the same ethical condemnation which already is meted out wherever these falsehoods are no longer required by practice. (Simmel 1950:314)

Alas, we are still waiting for the retail trade to reach this state of perfection. Its 'mendacious claims', the product of collaboration between market researchers and creative advertising agencies, can hardly be regarded as 'historical relics'. Boorstin (1962:213–214) remarks perceptively, with reference to the United States, that

Few advertisers are liars ... Advertising befuddles our experience, not because advertisers are liars, but precisely because they are not ... The advertising profession was founded on 'Truth', but has survived by its power to give Truth a new meaning.

Simmel's predicted trend seems to be pointing in another direction. In a climate of so-called economic rationality, we are exhorted to assess the mendacity of claims according to the financial losses they cause rather than by the extent to which they depart from the truth. Craswell (1991:553) argues that deceptive advertisements should be subjected to cost–benefit analysis and compared to rewritten alternative advertisements 'designed to correct the misleading impression'. He introduces the idea that an advertisement be deemed 'legally deceptive if and only if its total injury [to consumers] exceeds the total injury that would have been produced by the alternative'. The future arena of honest transactions envisaged by Simmel is here replaced by a market-place in which ubiquitous deception is accepted.

There is a parallel between the growth of advertising agencies in this century and the formation of departments of disinformation within military establishments, made all the closer by the employment of advertising agencies by political parties for the presentation of their policies. Both kinds of institution are exposed to the risk of overkill as people become increasingly aware of the attempts to manipulate their attitudes and actions. Advertising material in newspapers and journals usually has a distinct format, signalling the existence of different expectations of truthfulness, though sometimes advertising material is given a deceptive appearance so that its status is concealed. Consumer organizations have developed as a defence against the marketing of deceptively described goods and services, but the expression 'the advertisements speak well of it' remains the modern equivalent of the ancient warning *caveat emptor* – 'let the buyer beware'.

BUREAUCRACIES

Physicians, lawyers, priests, personnel managers and many other professional and semi-professional persons possess substantial amounts of confidential information. If we try to penetrate this confidence without proper excuse, the answers we get may be deceptive and designed to throw us off the scent. Deception of a special kind occurs between spouses, partners and other family members when one member has an extra-familial role that entails access to information that cannot be shared with other members. A lawyer may lie to his or her spouse about having seen a common acquaintance if the deceit is necessary to protect the confidentiality of a professional interview. In the last half of the twentieth century many professional codes of ethics have been adopted, aimed at defining and promoting morally acceptable practices (cf. Barnes 1980:159–164). The codes may prohibit or discourage specified procedures pertinent to the concerned profession, but rarely if ever include a blanket prohibition on lying. For example, a textbook on professional ethics for social workers makes lying a lesser evil by saying that

rules against basic harms to the necessary preconditions of action (such as life, health, food, shelter, mental equilibrium) take precedence over rules against harms such as lying or deceiving (or violating agency guidelines). (Reamer 1982:101)

The same sentiments are expressed in a wider context of professional ethics by Goldman (1980:71) when he says:

People indeed must occasionally be lied to, deceived or coerced by political acts, but only when more fundamental rights are at stake.

Bok (1980:11) notes that when professionals function as members of collectivities they are more prone to engage in deceit than when operating as individuals. She uses the expression '*déformation professionelle*' to label what often happens 'when professionals debate deceptive practices among themselves'. A 'strict commitment to veracity', appropriate in ordinary affairs, is weakened to allow for the special conditions of professional practice, entailing, for instance, the protection of the interests of clients and the advancement of knowledge. This kind of deceit, says Bok, is disguised by euphemisms such as 'double book-keeping'.

Government bodies and large corporations, rather than universities and professional organizations, provide us with the closest approximations to the Weberian ideal type of bureaucracy; the gap between technical language and ordinary discourse is widest here and most potentially deceptive. There is what Jackall (1980:52–53) calls 'a distrust of intangible issues of value which threaten to disrupt the calculated achievement of goals'.

This distrust leads to a 'misguided alchemy of the moral into the pragmatic' and hence to the use of 'neutralizing vocabularies'. Jackall gives as examples 'price-stabilization' for price-rigging, 'handling the case' and 'making sure things don't get out of hand' for perjury, burglary and conspiracy in the Watergate affair, and 'a symptom complex' for byssinosis, a serious lung disease. Jackall argues that use of these euphemisms is part of a wider process whereby members of bureaucracies learn that to rise in the organization they must treat themselves 'in a quintessentially bureaucratic way – namely, as an object to be manipulated to achieve a certain result'. This in turn leads to 'the manipulation of others to achieve organizational ends' (Jackall 1980:57).

Recruits to bureaucracies bring with them their own ethical commitments; these may be at odds with the tasks assigned to the newcomers by their superiors. Phillips (1991) sets out evidence, mostly provided under the cloak of anonymity, for the moral conflict experienced by some members of the British civil service between their personal commitment to the truth and their obligation to produce deceptive statements for use by their political masters, or, as she puts it, to bend the facts to suit government policy. She makes the point that the extent of these conflicts may have increased during the Thatcher administration, for

with the arrival of television as the media became more informed and more questioning and as ministers became more nervous about public embarrassment, they got more and more involved in the details of policies and their presentation, which in turn put more pressure on their officials.

These pressures are felt more strongly by junior members of the bureaucracy than by those at the top. Juniors who complain may be transferred to some other branch of the civil service where there is less chance of a conflict between their official duties and their own conscience, but thereby are likely to lose chances of promotion. Those who get promoted are high-fliers 'who manage to combine ability with robust consciences'. This robustness is well illustrated by the comment made by a retired British senior bureaucrat: 'Economy with the truth is the essence of a reply to a parliamentary question.' Recently, Quakers in Britain initiated an inquiry into standards of integrity in the civil service, after one of their members resigned from his post as a junior official in the Cabinet Office, 'unable to stomach what he felt was a life of deception'.

Deception and manipulation in a bureaucracy may take the form of lying to subordinates about prospects for advancement and for reduction of workload. Hence we have the paradox that when bureaucratic scandals come to light, we so often discover that many of the main culprits are solid citizens, pillars of society. Indeed, it is precisely because prominent persons are involved that these instances of deception are given the status of scandals and receive publicity. While outraged by scandals, we should remember that deception, particularly lying to protect the confidentiality of information, is an accepted feature of bureaucratic activity. Like governments and members of the police, bureaucrats are expected to be both honest and deceptive.

HISTORY AND TRADITION

If we can be deceived about what is going on around us now, how much more readily can we be misled about what happened in the past? More than two thousand years ago Thucydides set out his criteria for historical writing and tried to distance himself from earlier writers, Herodotus among them, who had incorporated into their accounts what he regarded as mythical and supernatural elements (Vernant 1980:191). He criticized them not for being deceitful but rather for trying to enhance the charm of their accounts by the inclusion of fabulous material, and being thus diverted from the true task of the historian, understanding the events of the past. Oscar Wilde (1989:226) took a sterner view of Herodotus, dubbing him not 'the father of history' but 'the father of lies', thus appropriating Satan's title, derived from John 8:44.

In more recent times, several accounts of the past that conflict with generally accepted understandings have attracted the charge of deceit, notably the persistent attempts to deny the occurrence of the Holocaust under the Nazis. In Australia 1988 was celebrated either for two hundred years of peaceful settlement by Europeans or, in the eyes of many Aborigines, for two hundred years of illegal and contested occupation. In a talk given during the bicentennial year, the novelist Patrick White (1989:189–190) was moved to adopt a remark he attributed to Peter Brook: 'The moment a society wishes to give an official version of itself, it becomes a lie'. White therefore referred to 1988 as 'The year of the great Australian lie'. He then went on to describe as 'the weather lie' the distortion he alleged takes place in Australian weather forecasts, whereby bad weather prospects that might affect attendance at sporting events are systematically played down. The future as well as the past can be distorted deceptively.

In recent times the best known account of the continual deceptive revision of history is to be found in Orwell's novel *1984*. The novel leaves several aspects of the process of deceptive historical revision unclear (Klockars 1984a:418); maybe we shall have to wait for an editorial history of the *Great Soviet Encyclopaedia* before these questions can be answered (see Taubman 1980). But even if this analysis ever appears, could we trust it? Might it not be yet another example of making the past compatible with the present, written by experts in this procedure? Arendt (1968:238–239) grants every generation the right 'to rearrange the facts in accordance with its own perspective' but denies it 'the right to touch the factual matter itself'; unfortunately this distinction is inherently problematic (cf. Arendt 1968:249–250, 252).

For more than two millennia the writing of history in the West has been based on the study of documents that are contemporary, or nearly so, with the events they describe. In the East this tradition is at least as long. In all parts of the world where there has been a literate elite, popular perceptions of the past have been influenced by what has been written in the history books, though not fully determined by them. To a lesser extent, our perception of the past is influenced by works presented unproblematically as fiction, without any explicit claim for historical accuracy. Jane Austen's novels are obvious examples of this phenomenon, and if the picture she presents of English society at the beginning of the nineteenth century does not correspond to reality, we cannot complain that she has tried to deceive us; we may have been misled, but that is our fault, not hers. For deception to occur, there must be deliberate cooking of the books. In chapter 9 we discuss the connection between novels and deceit.

On the other hand, absence of books to cook does not remove the possibility of deception; people who lack a literate elite also have perceptions of the past, and a lack of correspondence between them and what actually happened may arise in very many different ways, including deliberate deception. In many pre-literate societies the rationale for existing social alignments takes the form of a genealogy, and attempts to alter these alignments are justified by appeal to incompatibilities with postulated genealogical linkages. Forgeries are written lies, and the conscious intention to deceive may be easier to ascribe to a forger than to a non-literate orator who proclaims his or her version of a contested pedigree; the latter is perhaps more likely to believe sincerely in the truth of what is proclaimed. The absence of writing drastically reduces the possibility of refuting official or accepted versions of the past by confrontation with enduring contemporary evidence. Borofsky (1987:144) comments that

by recording traditions in books, we, as outside anthropologists, are helping to make knowledge less fluid and diverse than it in fact is.

Likewise Bohannan (1952), in a classic paper on the manipulation of pedigrees in a pre-literate society, ends by predicting that when genealogies were written down they would become relatively immune to manipulation. The evidence from literate societies shows that fabrication occurs even in written genealogies. For instance, Elizabeth I purported to trace her pedigree back to Adam whereas the Emperor Maximilian only got as far back as Noah (Barnes 1967:118). In an encyclopaedia article Barron (1959:103) remarks wryly:

From the first the work of the genealogist in England had that taint of inaccuracy tempered with forgery from which it has not yet been cleansed.

The selective recollection of past events, and the manipulation of what are sometimes known as 'genealogical charters', are examples of the wider process of the social construction of the past. This process operates also on customary social practices, particularly in contexts where social groups distinguish themselves from one another by reference to so-called 'traditional customs' (Barnes 1990:120–129; Keesing and Tonkinson 1982). Constructing the past to serve present purposes may or may not be undertaken with intent to deceive. If the proponent of a contested view of the past does not believe in its truth, deceit must be present.

On the other hand, the transformation or translation of a series of events from an unfamiliar to a familiar idiom is not necessarily motivated by an intention to deceive, even if an outsider might think otherwise. Albert (1972:96) gives an interesting example of how Barundi perceive the conflict between German and British troops in east Africa during the First World War, and the subsequent transfer of Burundi from German to Belgian colonial status. These events are seen as a lethal quarrel between a man and his father-in-law about elephant hunting. The transformation, says Albert, occurs because of 'the requirement for literary embellishment, especially allusiveness and figures of speech, in the style of narration'.

Thus we see that the past, whether adequately documented or not, is a fertile source for the construction of symbolic assertions and pragmatic claims. Some of these assertions and claims are presented in good faith, irrespective of their historical authenticity. Others may be concocted deceptively, but since such assertions often relate to group or ethnic identity, their authors are likely soon to become ardent and even sincere defenders of the truth of their own lies. When this happens, we have the phenomenon of self-deception, mentioned in chapter 2 in connection with wartime propaganda and discussed more fully in chapter 7.

HARMLESS AND NOT-SO-HARMLESS LIES

Bok's category of 'white' lies ranges from what she describes as harmless lies, such as ending a letter with the phrase 'your obedient servant', to the giving of placebos and writing letters of recommendation in which 60 per cent of all students are said to belong to the top 10 per cent. In my view, 'your obedient servant' is not a lie at all. The writer does not intend to deceive, nor is the use of the phrase likely to be construed by others as attempted deception, even though it may well be regarded, when written by a well-protected bureaucrat to a powerless client, as insufferably hypocritical. Indeed, the use of the title *Your disobedient servant* (Chapman 1979) for a book by a former public servant about the inefficiency of the public service shows, I think, that the phrase is recognized as not meaning what it literally says. Since the expression is no longer deceptive, it is 'over-scrupulous', as Henry Sidgwick (1907:314) says, not to use it where it is customary to do so.

The use of a phrase which 'everybody' knows is not to be taken literally was discussed by Thomas Seaton in his book *The conduct of servants in great families* (1720:52–59). Referring to the porter who, when asked whether his lord is at home, replies 'He is not within', Seaton argues that the visitor will know that this reply carries the meaning: the lord is either not at home or he is at home but for some good reason does not wish 'to be spoken with'. If the lord is indeed absent, the statement is literally true. On the other hand, if the lord is at home, the statement is not a lie, for the visitor is not being deceived. Indeed, the visitor's own porter uses the phrase in the same ambiguous way. Therefore the porter has not sinned, and may still receive the sacrament of Holy Communion. Yet despite this freedom from the taint of sin, Seaton's 'Advice to Gentlemen' is 'to let their Porters tell the Truth', for this is 'much more becoming the Truth, Sincerity, and simple Undisguizedness of the Gospel'. Not surprisingly, Seaton does not discuss the possibility that the visitor might not be a gentleman, and therefore perhaps unaware of the correct interpretation of the porter's reply. Harmlessness in lying requires cultural consensus if the lie is to remain harmless.

Harmlessness may also depend on context, even on the time of day. Marcel Eck (1970:28) gives a good example of how a lie uttered during the daytime may lose its benign quality when used at night:

For reasons of discretion, my wife has developed the habit of answering the telephone with the words: 'This is the secretary'. One night at a late hour the phone rang and my wife answered it. The voice on the line said: 'Is this Mrs Eck?' 'No', she said in her semiawakened state, 'this is Dr Eck's secretary'. The reader can imagine the effect this had!

But what is there harmless about letters of recommendation that are full of glowing phrases about 'one of the best students I have ever known'? Although Bok locates these statements at the grey end of her category, she appears to class them as 'white', because, she says, to 'give extra praise to a friend, a colleague, a student, a relative', is a natural gesture. 'It helps someone, while injuring no one in particular', though it does injure those who do not benefit from this kind of inflated recommendation. She then goes on to show why the practice is more harmful than many writers of recommendations think and why, if possible, it should be avoided (Bok 1978:68).

In a homogeneous community it may be possible to reach consensus about how inflated expressions of praise should be discounted; the expression 'one of the best students I have ever known' might then come to be as well understood and vacuous as has 'your obedient servant'. Indeed, so I recall, the Royal Navy tries, or at least used to try, to make such a process of discounting a regular feature of its assessment procedures. Senior officers in the Navy were required to rate their juniors on a scale with the three mid-points labelled 'below average', 'average' and 'above average'. The first step in trying to prevent inflation was to remind officers that they 'should remember that in the Royal Navy there are exactly as many officers who are below average as there are above average'. The next step was to require admirals and other flag officers who scrutinized these reports to state for each reporting officer a correction factor which should be applied to all the assessments he had made, so as to ensure that for the Navy as a whole the truth of this statistical tautology was vindicated.

But whereas a procedure of this kind may be possible and worthwhile within an authoritarian and relatively homogeneous organization like the Royal Navy, it makes no sense to attempt the same quasi-objectivity in most contexts where power is disputed and words are weapons with problematic connotations. Nowhere is this seen more clearly than in the academic market-place, particularly when competition for jobs and research grants brings together applicants from many different countries, each with its own ill-defined conventions about what benevolent lies to tell. The 'top 10 per cent' into which virtually all applicants seem to fall might perhaps be a correct placement if the student population contained 90 per cent of zombies who never applied for jobs, but this is unlikely to be the case. Qualitative phrases such as 'a joy to teach' and 'outstanding among his peers' are just as difficult to evaluate without knowledge of personal and international inflation rates. Luckily there are other ways of assessing academic applicants than by reading references, and in general references are assumed to have been written in good faith, even when their assertions are drastically discounted. I have never encountered the legendary statement 'You will be lucky to get this man to work for you', but that other comment, made of a student with fewest marks, that 'He is able to hold his position in class with ease' seems more likely to have been actually used by a referee trying to do his best to help a weak job applicant. These are both examples of lies if the intention is to deceive, but they are phrased so that the liar can claim, if challenged, that the statements, taken literally, are perfectly true.

In warfare lies are taken for granted; in politics lying may be perceived as frequent, but occurs in the face of protests and is regretted; in bureaucracies protective lying is legitimate but other kinds of lies are not; academics usually assume that references, favourable and unfavourable alike, have been written in good faith even when doubting their validity. When people move from one domain to another, they may have to adjust their expectations of the truthfulness of others, as well as their own level of truthfulness. We all experience these shifts as we move from home to work and from private to public spheres of activity, and usually do so without great difficulty. Moving from one public sphere to another may be harder, particularly if the spotlight of publicity keeps step with the move. For instance, Harold Laski had the reputation of being 'something of a romancer' (Eastwood 1977:159); his biographer Kingsley Martin (1953:51) says that Laski's stories 'were not strictly true, but they were seldom wholly false, and they were never at all malicious'. Yet Martin admits that 'there were many who were ready to write him off as a liar and a charlatan'. Samuel Johnson (1963:363) would surely have called Laski's stories 'the Lye of Vanity' and it is interesting to speculate whether his reputation would have damaged his academic career if he had not been also a prominent political figure.

Thus in what I have called ambiguous domains we find expectations of honesty as well as expectations of untruthfulness. The criminal justice system has explicit procedures for enforcing honesty but otherwise truthfulness is treated as a default value, to be expected unless there are what Bok (1978:30) calls 'special considerations' that permit legitimate deceit. In chapter 4 we turn to examine a domain where consistent truthfulness is explicitly demanded.

4

Science

NATURAL SCIENCE

At first glance, science is the last place where we should find deceit. Contrasting science with other social institutions which endure despite endemic lying, Weinstein (1979:639) remarks:

The one institution that has the pursuit of truth as its dominant value is science.

Most philosophers and sociologists of science, notably Merton in his earlier writings, would have us believe that scientific inquiry is distinguished from other social domains by its openness and by the continual checking of the claims of colleagues. Yet the historians of science tell a somewhat different story, at least in the natural sciences. We now know that in the second century AD Ptolemy not only appropriated as his own data collected by someone else; he fudged his data as well to make them appear more supportive of his thesis that the sun moved round the earth and that the planets travelled in epicycles. Even after the notion of disinterested scientific inquiry had begun to be established in the West in the seventeenth century, Robert Boyle complained of 'fraudulent tricks' by experimental scientists, of which he could provide 'diverse instances' (Boyle 1744:205). Newton admitted amending his data so that it would be easier for the laity to see the support they gave to his theory of gravitation. Mendel did the same to provide stronger support for his views on genetic inheritance. Presenting data modified in this way as if they were the true outcome of observations might be deceitful, but is not necessarily so. The laity may be unable to see what the data mean until they are cleansed of the likely effects of measurement and other kinds of error. On the other hand, the trick played in 1726 on the physician and would-be palaeontologist Dr Beringer (1963) by his academic enemies, who manufactured spurious fossils to mislead him, was unmistakably deceitful and malicious. In recent times, though the identity of the perpetrators may still be uncertain (Daniel 1986; Langdon 1991; Spencer 1990a,b), it seems that the Piltdown hoax was a deliberate attempt to mislead everyone, scientists and laity alike, about the path of human evolution. In this case the crux of the deceit was not words but bones; the reports of the Piltdown finds were mainly, and perhaps entirely, produced by scientists writing in good faith. In this sense, we can say that although there was indubitably deceit, there may not have been any lying.

Perhaps Newton was right to make things easier for lay readers of his *Principia*. Babbage (1830:178) argued that 'trimming', as he called this process, was not so injurious as 'cooking' the data. Indeed, Gifford (1980:40) goes a step further, and queries the rightness of telling the whole story to the laity by asking

are we always justified in providing information, even if we know a framework for analysis of the information is not generally available outside a specialized community?

This argument cannot apply when 'the specialized community' is the clearly indicated and intended audience for the information; yet it has been claimed recently that 'Up to half of the scientific papers in the United States may be contaminated by data manipulation' (O'Neill 1991).

In the appendix to their book *Betrayers of the truth*, Broad and Wade (1982:225–232) list thirty-four cases of 'known or strongly suspected fraud' in natural and medical science. The earliest case is dated in the second century BC, and the latest ones occurred in 1981. The authors say that their list is not the result of an exhaustive search, but consists merely of those cases that had come to their attention; yet even so the concentration of twenty-five cases in the twentieth century reflects the enormous increase in scientific activity in the last hundred years, rather than a staggering increase in the proportion of claims by scientists that are fraudulent. Merton (1984) maintains that we cannot say from the available evidence whether or not scientific fraud has become more frequent in recent years, though the changes that have occurred in the social position of scientists since the days of the gentlemen scholars make an increase in the incidence of fraud seem highly probable (cf. Weinstein 1979:642–643). Four of the cases listed by Broad and Wade seem to have been instances of plagiarism, which is akin to lying, and though not all the others involved lying, they were all, if widely held suspicions are in fact justified, cases of deceit.

One reason why deceit occurs as frequently as it does in science is that although in many areas of natural science the replication of inquiries by other researchers is a possibility, it does not occur as frequently as the ideal vision of science might suggest (cf. Bridgstock 1982:373–375; Moomaw 1980:37; Weinstein 1979:645–646). Moreover in several branches of natural science, as in virtually the whole of the social sciences, exact, or even approximate, replication is impossible in principle as well as in practice, so that validation has to rest on other criteria or to be forgone entirely. The commitment of natural scientists to dominant paradigms, the emphasis on priority of discovery, and the importance of early publication for professional advancement combine to provide incentives for deceit as well as for scientific progress. As Bridgstock (1982:379) remarks: 'it is precisely the factors giving science its powerful dynamic that may in some cases promote fraud'.

Natural scientists compare themselves favourably with social scientists on many grounds (cf. Barnes 1990:11–12); one of them is that the natural sciences are more exact. Exactitude and precision are usually achieved by quantification, and those social scientists who seek to emulate the natural sciences practise quantification in their own research. But quantification leads all too easily to mystification, particularly when research findings are presented to lay audiences. The apophthegm about 'damned lies and statistics', mentioned in chapter 1, captures well this capacity to bamboozle the public with misleading quantified information. However it is not only the innumerate laity who can be misled by cunningly arranged statistical information. Long ago Devons (1950) showed how during the Second World War data on aircraft production and performance were manipulated for presentation to British politicians and military leaders so as to secure the adoption of one policy rather than another.

Deception in natural science, however regrettable, may be unavoidable in practice, but at least it is comparatively easy to detect, even if the process of detection takes time. Dominant paradigms may dominate but increasingly are seen as hypotheses and models, open to challenge, rather than revealed truth. Many findings can be checked by replication, and where this cannot be done, can be treated as tentative until supported by other evidence. Competitiveness in natural science may promote higher levels of deceit but it also stimulates greater efforts in the detection of deceit. Both deception and detection are certain to persist.

SOCIAL SCIENCE

In the natural sciences, despite the complications of quantum mechanics and Heisenberg's uncertainty principle, it is often possible to say with complete confidence that a certain assertion is false. In the social sciences assertions of falsity with the same level of confidence can be made much less frequently. Using conventional terms we can say that the data of social science are softer and therefore more difficult to interpret with certainty (Barnes 1990:133–149). Many of the data consist of statements made to investigators by other people about the state of the world and of their own minds. Discrepancies and contradictions abound, but for the most part these are evidence of falsity rather than of deception, to use Bok's terminology. Nevertheless deception does occur in the practice of social science, and does so in more than one mode. Informants, actors, members, respondents or subjects, as the human beings who provide data are variously designated, may endeavour to deceive the investigator, while the investigator may try to deceive them and, at a later stage, his or her colleagues as well as the general public. There is also the possibility of deceiving gatekeepers and other peripheral actors in the social science arena.

Social scientists, notably sociologists and anthropologists, make a distinction between two principal modes of data collection in the field, ethnographic inquiries and survey research. Each mode has its own pattern of opportunities for deceit. A distinction can be drawn between specific acts of deception carried out from time to time in the course of an inquiry, whether by the investigating social scientists or by the people who are being investigated, and more enduring deception that may form the basis of the relation between the two parties. The long-term deception I have in mind occurs mainly when ethnographic data are being collected, particularly when inquiries are carried out by what is known as participant observation, and when there is a wide cultural gulf between the investigator and the people being observed. Writing about the traditional praxis of social and cultural anthropology, Geertz (1968:151–152) refers to 'the inherent moral asymmetry of the fieldwork situation' and says that 'the relationship between an anthropologist and his informant rests on a set of partial fictions half seen-through'. Here he is referring to the disparity between the expectations and interests of the two parties. The anthropologist, says Geertz, 'is sustained by the scientific value of the data he is getting'. I agree, but I think he or she is likely to be sustained also by friendships made during the course of the inquiry. Often these are only friendships-for-the-time-being (cf. Barnes 1980:115–116), whereas for the informant there may be 'a sense of being an essential collaborator in an important, if but dimly understood, enterprise'. If the assumption to regard one another as 'members of the same cultural universe breaks down', then, according to Geertz, the relation 'either gradually expires in an atmosphere of futility, boredom and generalized disappointment or, much less often, collapses suddenly into a mutual sense of having been deceived, used and rejected'. Thus although the relation may have been begun with good faith on both sides, it may end with mutual feelings of deceit. Geertz (1968:154) characterizes the relation as a fiction, not a falsehood, 'that lies at the heart of successful anthropological research' and speaks of its 'moral tension' and 'ethical ambiguity'.

Although Geertz's comments refer to anthropological fieldwork in 'new states', rather than in the traditional world of pre-literate tribes, he has in mind situations where there is still a substantial hiatus between the culture of the investigator and that of his or her informants. Yet much of what he has to say applies just as forcefully to field investigations where there is no hiatus, where inquiries are carried out, using the technique of participant observation, by authentic members of the community under scrutiny. The constraints inherent in social science, as a science rather than as spontaneous cultural product, force some amount of dissimulation on even the most empathic observer. Even if some friends-for-the-time-being gradually become friends-for-life, there will be many more who do not. Even if the investigator steadfastly endeavours never to deceive informants, at the end of the day it is likely that some of them will feel that they have been deceived, particularly when reports of the inquiry appear in print. The history of empirical social research using participant observation is studded with examples of outraged ex-informants (Barnes 1980:70–72).

Against this background of ambiguous relations between even the most sympathetic investigators and the most cooperative informants, social research also has its acts of specific and deliberate deceit. Informants may lie to researchers and researchers may lie to informants. If there is trust between them, they may lie to protect one another, while if trust is lacking, malevolent lies are more likely. As early as 1909 Yerkes and Berry (1909) reported how some of their Harvard students had tried to trick them while participating in psychological experiments. Passin (1942) was perhaps the first professional anthropologist to discuss lying by informants, but little attention was paid to his paper for many years, perhaps because, as Salamone (1977:118) argues, fieldworkers during the 1950s and 1960s were reluctant to admit that their relations with their informants were not based on mutual trust. Salamone describes instances when his own informants lied to him, and other anthropologists have done the same. For example Chagnon (1974:91), reporting on fieldwork carried out among the Yano-mamö people of Venezuela and Brazil in the 1960s, says: 'I knew that my informants would lie under some circumstances and be truthful under others'. Chagnon (1974:92) encountered lying so widely that he advises anyone engaged in collecting genealogical information from Yanomamö always to assume that informants lie in respect of data about their own group.

The French anthropologist Marcel Griaule, working among the Dogon people in what is now Mali, paid particular attention to lying by inform-ants. Discussing how to make ethnographic inquiries (Griaule 1957:56–61), he details the different types of lies the field investigator can expect to encounter (Clifford 1983:137). For Griaule, lies told by informants were obstacles in the search for truth, so that for him an 'ideal' situation would be one in which informants could be manoeuvred into telling the truth. The positivist stance that Griaule, along with most other social anthropologists of his generation (cf. Freilich 1970:564–565), took towards the existence of ethnographic truth is rejected by many of their successors. In a postmodern intellectual climate, epistemological popularism, as I have dubbed it (Barnes 1981:15, 22; 1990:4–5), tends to flourish, and the statements that Griaule saw as lies become not obstacles but meaningful data in their own right.

Different kinds of deceit occur in survey research. Although information collected in survey research may sometimes be incorrect, the questionnaire-based survey remains a very powerful tool and indeed is used far more widely in social research than any other mode of inquiry. Survey researchers devote considerable effort towards ensuring that respondents provide sincere answers, by both phrasing questions with care and presenting them in a context conducive to cooperation. Sophisticated statistical techniques are used to determine the extent to which results may have been distorted by insincere replies. In general, the sincerity of individual respondents to surveys cannot be probed; the prolonged face-to-face interaction in mundane life situations between researcher and informant characteristic of participant observation is largely lacking. Nevertheless there is some evidence that in face-to-face interviews the answers given by survey respondents are influenced by the presence of a third person (Taietz 1962). Anecdotes suggest that if spouses are interviewed together, they may give answers intended to deceive the researcher and/or their partner. If postal questionnaires are used, little control can be exercised over the situation in which the respondent answers the questions, so that even greater care is called for in drafting the questionnaire.

Attempts to deceive or mislead the inquiring social scientist are encountered in all the social sciences, but in most cases the attempts are not reciprocated, at least not deliberately. However during fieldwork ethnographers may sometimes lie about such things as their own marital status or religious beliefs; social survey collectors may mislead their respondents about who is sponsoring them. In general, these instances of deceit do not form a critical element in the research design. Even Kloos (1983–4:134), an anthropologist more outspoken than most of his colleagues about his willingness to deceive, says only that for him

scientific research is a highly valued activity; when faced with a choice between doing research or refraining from doing research, therefore, I am perfectly willing to deceive in situations where honesty will not do.

His viewpoint was supported by a majority of Dutch anthropological field-workers who were polled in 1981. Kloos justifies his attitude by saying that

> the choice between telling a lie and telling a truth seems to be determined by differences in power. There are circumstances in which truth-telling may well be a luxury reserved to people in power. (Kloos 1983–4:135)

Van den Berghe (1967:185) also invokes differences in power when justifying lying to government officials in the Republic of South Africa, in order to study the regime (cf. Barnes 1980:151–152).

Deception as practised by investigators working in many branches of social science has been discussed extensively from an ethical viewpoint (Appell 1978; Boruch and Cecil 1983; Kelman 1967, 1968). I am not here directly concerned with ethical issues and note only that in all the examples I have discussed so far, deception has not been a central feature of the design, but only an incidental and generally regretted contingent feature. In some research designs, however, deception of the respondents by the investigator is an essential component, as for example in the study of an American apocalyptic sect by Festinger and others (1956), in which the investigators pretended to become believing members of the sect. In a study of male homosexual activity in a public lavatory, Laud Humphreys (1975:170–171, 230) acted as 'watchqueen', a role he carried out effectively. He argues that it was not deceitful to conceal that his interest in what went on around him was sociological, not sexual.

Sometimes a research design calls for deception but for little or no lying. An instance of this is the classic demonstration by LaPiere (1934) of the tenuousness of the relation between attitudes and behaviour. In the early 1930s he visited some 251 restaurants, cafés, hotels and auto-camps in the United States in company with a young Chinese student and his wife. Without disclosing his research objective, he matched the behaviour of hotel receptionists, waitresses and the like to the responses given by the management of their establishments to a postal questionnaire asking whether they would accept Chinese as guests. Whereas the great majority of managements stated that they would not accept Chinese guests, all but one of the establishments visited by the team did accept them. As far as I can tell from LaPiere's report, no lies were told during the inquiry. Yet the managements were deceived about why they were being questioned, and LaPiere himself seems to have acted deceptively toward at least some receptionists, for he says that he 'became rather adept at approaching hotel clerks with that peculiar crab-wise manner which is so effective in provoking a somewhat scornful disregard'. This example shows the difficulties of separating lying from other kinds of deceptive behaviour, at least in analysing research designs.

The efficacy of deceptive research designs in social science, as distinct from their ethical acceptability, has, as far as I know, been analysed only in the case of psychology. As is well known, psychological studies of deception have a fairly long history. The 'Bibliography of methods of detecting and measuring deceit' provided by May and Hartshorne (1928:245–248) contains items from 1902 onwards, and there are innumerable earlier non-experimental studies (e.g. Hall 1891). But in most of this literature, deceit is a phenomenon to be inquired into, not something to be practised by the investigator. The list of requirements provided by Hartshorne and May (1928:48) for a satisfactory test of deception contains the warning: 'The examiner should guard against being deceptive himself in order to test the subject'.

This 1928 precept was later abandoned by many psychologists, notably in the United States. Following Asch's (1956) experiments on conformity in the 1950s, deception came to be part of the accepted paradigm of research design in some branches of psychology, particularly in the study of personality. The ethical hazards of deception were noted as early as 1954 by Vinacke (1954). Other writers followed in his wake (e.g. Stricker 1967) but it was not until 1969, as far as I can tell, that the efficacy of deception was first evaluated (Newberry 1973; Stricker et al. 1969). The findings of Stricker and others reveal a pattern similar to that sketched for the field of politics. Initially most of the people being studied, the so-called subjects, believed that investigators were honest and meant what they said. Asch was an early free rider and was followed notably by Milgram (1974; cf. Miller 1986) and many less well-known experimenters. Eventually deception became so ubiquitous that even first-year psychology students could no longer be assumed to be naive and trusting. By 1962 Orne (1962:778–779) could write, with reference to the United States, 'that even if a psychologist is honest with the subject, more often than not he will be distrusted'. Suspicion, rather than mistrust, is sometimes in place; if we agree to enter a psychological laboratory to take part in an experiment and are not tricked, some of us are simply disappointed!

At about the same time, for reasons that had no direct connection with social research, university ethics committees, or institutional review boards as they are known in America, appeared on the campus. In Australia, and perhaps elsewhere as well, some of these committees interpreted their mandate naively as calling for the complete elimination of deception from all scientific inquiry. Yet it seems to me that, even without the arrival of ethics committees, there would have been a reduction in the prevalence of experimental deception, merely in an attempt to restore the initial assumption of sincerity required by most simple research designs. Nevertheless, it is salutary to remember that in 1977, when Kintz published the results of an inquiry into how various occupations were rated in terms of their acceptability of lying, top marks were awarded, not surprisingly, to politicians and bottom marks to clergymen, while psychologists were thought to be 'not too unfavorably inclined'. Kintz (1977:492) comments:

Whether this latter attitude stems from experience in the clinic, in the classroom, or from some other source is of considerable interest.

Unfortunately he does not reveal his own opinion on this matter.

Another kind of deception arises from assumptions necessarily made in the process of interpreting bodies of data. Most schemes of analysis in social science embody simplistic assumptions about the ways in which human beings think and act. Often these assumptions are recognized as merely heuristic devices, simplifications necessary because of the immense complexity of the real human and social world. Thus decisions may be assumed, for purposes of analysis, as substantially determined by a mere handful of 'factors', and the effects of these factors are assumed to act linearly and additively. We know that these assumptions are at best rough approximations to the truth, but they enable us to obtain results which, even if only approximately true, are thought to be better than no results at all. They are the best approximations we can get, and we may even be able to form some idea of just how approximate they are. No deception is involved, though we may be misled if we forget that the results are merely approximations. However, if heuristic assumptions are made that are incompatible with what we observe around us in the real world, and if practitioners cling to these assumptions despite this demonstrated incompatibility, the presence of deceit has to be considered. For example, Wolozin (1974) argues that Economic Man has become 'the *big lie*'. But in all instances we should ask who is being deceived, the social scientists who believe in the verisimilitude of the models they have constructed or the lay audience they seek to impress (cf. Granovetter 1985).

Thus, compared to the natural sciences, the social sciences exhibit a more complex pattern of deceit. Lying, when it occurs, is often a subsidiary part of some wider deception. Natural scientists occasionally discuss somewhat fancifully the possibilities of deliberate deceit in thought experiments but there are few if any analogues in their real experiments for the deceits practised by experimental psychologists. Likewise the inanimate nature of most of the objects studied by natural scientists provides room for neither trust nor deceit; natural scientists can trust or deceive only one another. Yet they share with their colleagues in the social sciences their commitment to science, and therefore to an attitude that is in general hostile to deceit. In this respect both moieties of scientists, in their professional roles, differ from politicians, propagandists, spies, police officers and all the other social types we have discussed in chapters 2 and 3. Yet though the contrast at the professional or occupational level may be sharp, we should not forget that all human beings live their lives in a variety of domains, and that personal involvement in science, with its emphasis on truthfulness, does not necessarily imply an intolerant attitude towards lying in other domains. Furthermore, attitudes towards lying vary along other dimensions as well as that of social domains, as we discuss in the next two chapters.

5

Cultural diversity

DIVERSITIES OF CULTURE

In 1900 the French anthropologist Topinard maintained that the various 'races' differed in their propensity to lie. He identified regions in France prone to lying, and also wrote of 'the cheating Italian, the hypocritical Englishman, the Greek without good faith, the Turk incapable of keeping his word'. Further:

The Asiatics, the Japanese, the Chinese, the Siamese, show bad faith, and are much disposed to make deceitful promises when they struggle with the English and the Germans. It is necessary to add that they can be of good faith when they feel that they are not threatened. (Larson 1932:51)

These evaluations tell us more about contemporary French stereotypes of other national characters than about the groups labelled so dismissively. Earlier Herbert Spencer (1892:400–409) made similar sweeping statements about the worldwide diversity in lying. There is no evidence for the causal link assumed by Topinard between propensity to lie and 'racial' type. His comments do however draw attention to the variations between one culture and another in attitudes towards lying and the incidence of telling lies. Although in the West, as well as in many non-Western cultures, deceit and lying are in general regarded as reprehensible, the evidence already presented shows how this generalization has many exceptions; for example, the San Blas Kuna, of northeastern Panama, are said to 'enjoy deceiving each other' (Howe and Sherzer 1986:684). Likewise Basso (1987:355–356) writes of 'the preoccupation with deception' in the culture of the Kalapalo, an Amerindian group living in central Brazil, and of how Kalapalo people even welcome being tricked.

One of the first field ethnographers to pay serious attention to patterns of lying was Bruno Gutmann, who worked among the Chagga people of what is now Tanzania (Gutmann 1926:702–725; cf. Steiner 1954). A more detailed study, in which institutionalized lying is prominent, was carried out among the Azande people of the southern Sudan by Evans-Pritchard in the late 1920s. At that time, he says, their princes maintained that the commoners 'are cheats and liars and practise every form of duplicity and deceit'. Zande commoners accepted the truth of this characterization, and its validity is demonstrated in Evans-Pritchard's (1956:179) descriptions of their culture and social life.

Most societies, however, resist the application of such assessments to themselves; they are more likely to denigrate their neighbours and enemies. Societies vary not only in their recognition of the ubiquity of lying and other modes of deceit but also in the way in which they evaluate different kinds of lies. Probably there is in every culture a recognition that some lies are comparatively malevolent and others comparatively benign. But though some recognition of difference may be universal, there is no cross-cultural uniformity in the content of these contrasting categories. A speaker or writer may make a statement in one cultural code without any intention to deceive even though, taken literally, the statement is untrue; if the hearer or reader interprets the statement as if it had been made in some other code, he or she may feel deceived. Thus for instance Bailey (1991:6) notes that when he began ethnographic research in India he

was puzzled and offended by polite young Indians who responded to a request by assuring me they would 'do the necessary', all the time (as I realized later) having no intention of doing so.

Since then many ethnographers have drawn attention to the diversity of modes of discourse current in different societies, and to the varying potentialities for deceit, both genuinely intended and mistakenly under-stood, that these modes possess (cf. Hendry 1989 and references therein).

Even between the industrialized societies of the West there are differences in the extent to which lying is considered justifiable. In surveys conducted in Europe and Australia in 1981 and 1983 respectively, adult respondents were asked to rate acts of lying in one's own interest on a scale ranging from 1 (never justified) to 10 (always justified). Average ratings were spread from a low of 1.95 in Italy to 3.37 in Belgium, with Australia scoring 2.7 (Harding and Phillips 1986:8–9; Jones 1989:113). An earlier study carried out on students at Harvard university in 1950 showed that the percentage of persons approving of lying in the interests of a friend varied widely according to the context; only 26 per cent approved of lying about speed in a car accident, whereas 51 per cent approved of 'shading the doubts in his favor' in a medical examination for insurance. More light is thrown on the ethical discriminations of these students in their responses to a question on what we would now call insider trading; 70 per cent approved of tipping off a close friend who would otherwise be ruined (Stouffer and Toby 1951).

In Russian culture a distinction is drawn between two kinds of lies, *vranyo* and *lozh* which do not have exact parallels in English. *Vranyo* has been claimed as uniquely Russian, and seems to consist of telling untrue but credible stories, a practice not condemned by those who recognize what is going on. Indeed, for success in *vranyo*-telling, there must be a listener who pretends to believe in the truth of what is being said. Hingley (1978:77–79, 85–86) suggests that

> *vranyo*'s continuing late twentieth-century vogue may well derive from its function of enlivening the drabness of modernity, since the official doctrine that totalitarian Russian life is somehow more exhilarating than life elsewhere is itself so extreme an example of creative fantasy.

Hingley, following Dostoyevsky, suggests that those who tell *vranyo* do not believe their stories when they begin to tell them. Later they become convinced by their own eloquence, though perhaps in retrospect they recognize their fabrications. *Lozh*, on the other hand, implies a conscious intention to deceive. Hingley associates *lozh* with the period of Stalin's rule, whereas when Khrushchev came to power *vranyo* began to flourish.

Cultures vary also in how entirely benign social lies are constituted. In Australia, for instance, an invitation to lunch is an invitation to lunch, particularly in rural areas. But Simpson-Herbert (1987:26) reports that in urban Iran, in the days of the Shah, invitations to a meal were extended frequently; these almost always insincere, and were recognized as such by those who were invited. She writes 'An invitation should be extended three times in a row with an insistent tone of voice before it can be taken seriously.' In this respect, Iranians followed the example of Lewis Carroll's (1910:3) Bellman, who insisted that 'What I tell you three times is true'. Among the Navajo the fourth time a lie is repeated it becomes deceitful (Hillerman 1986:177–178).

Differences between non-industrialized communities are as great or greater than those between the cultures of industrial societies. These differences reflect differences in the structure of social relations and in cultural expectations about how conversation and other social exchanges should be handled. With Grice's conversational maxim 'Be informative' in mind (cf. Levinson 1983: 100–102), Keenan (1976:69) observes:

> In some societies, meeting the informational needs of a conversational partner may be relatively unmarked or routine behavior. In other societies, meeting another's informational needs may be relatively unexpected or marked behavior.

She gives examples of some of the differences between conversational expectations in Malagasy society and in 'middle-class academic society of Europe and the United States'. For instance, suppose A asks B 'Where is your mother?' If B really knows where his mother is, it would be regarded in 'Europe and the United States' as deceptive to reply 'She is either in the house or at the market', for the reply would carry the implication, or implicature in Grice's terminology, that B did not know exactly where she was. Not so in Malagasy society, where people *'expect* the response of the addressee to be less than satisfactory' (Keenan 1976:70, her emphasis). Keenan links this expectation to features in Malagasy society but the same expectation is implicit in a line in Rudyard Kipling's (1965:251) song about smuggling: 'Them that asks no questions isn't told a lie'.

Trivers (1985:395) begins the chapter on 'Deceit and self-deception' in his textbook *Social evolution* by reminding his readers that 'systems of animal communication' are 'not systems for the dissemination of truth'. This comment might well lead us to assume (1) that human systems of communication, unlike their animal analogues, are mainly used for the dissemination of truth or (2) that, if they are not so used, they ought to be. Indeed, the earlier writings of Habermas (1970) seem to me to point in that direction. The evidence presented in previous chapters should have weakened any belief in the first, existential, assumption; we shall tackle the second, normative, assumption later, in chapter 11. Some writers, notably Marshall McLuhan (1962), have contrasted the restrictions on the communication of knowledge that, they say, characterized at least the early stages of industrializing societies with the free flow of information postulated for non-industrial societies, a free flow that is to be restored in the new world of satellites and electronic mail. Even a cursory glance at the corpus of ethnographic data on pre-literate societies is sufficient to refute the validity of this characterization. For example, Foster (1979:108–109), who studied the village of Tzintzuntzan in Mexico in the mid 1940s, reports that 'major and minor falsehoods are the order of the day'. Children, he says, 'are constantly told falsehoods' and lies are used in a pragmatic way to manipulate adults. As Michaels (1985:505) says, with pre-literate societies in mind:

Little evidence of this egalitarianism of knowledge was offered, however. In fact, the anthropological literature abounds with exceptions: secret cults, avoidance relationships, restrictions on access to ritual lore and ceremonial performance based on sex, age, kinship, and so forth.

In maintaining these restrictions, silence and deceit are the main weapons. But there is an important difference between industrial and pre-industrial societies. In large-scale industrial societies denial of access to information is achieved by policies of silence and disinformation that, roughly speaking, affect large categories of persons equally. In smaller-scale societies, access to information and denial of access are structured in terms of more particularistic criteria, such as kin affiliation, village residence, and the like.

When individuals from industrial and non-industrial cultures come into contact, each will tend to judge the other in terms of his or her own cultural expectations. Generalizing about his experience as an anthropologist in Papua New Guinea, Burridge (1960:36–37) writes that

> Manam islanders, for example, feel that white men are habitual liars and hypocrites. White men say much the same of Manam islanders. And, in their own lights, both sides are right. Both white men and Manam islanders would agree that without hypocrisy, without the 'white lie' and conventional courtesy where dislike is felt, social life would become impossible. The difficulty is that the situations which call for a conventional hypocrisy among Manam islanders are not those which call for precisely the same technique in any one kind of European. What might be obnoxious to a white man might be culturally enjoined for a Manam islander and *vice versa*.

Although in industrialized societies the truth of Bacon's (1861b:253) comment that 'knowledge itself is power' is demonstrated every day, those in power find themselves more likely to be regarded as liars than are the weak and powerless. In an Orwellian dystopia, thought control might become so effective that everything our government said would be accepted as true, and everything their government said treated as outright lies, but so far no modern system of repression has achieved this level of efficiency. Lindstrom (1990:xii, 162–163) describes a rural Melanesian society where power and truth are strongly correlated, but even in Tanna 'all alternative and resistant knowledge' is never completely silenced. Simmel, whose views we discuss in chapter 10, asserted that simple societies could tolerate lying more readily than could complex societies, but he had little evidence to support his view. As noted earlier, truthtelling is one of the norms recognized in the Kohlberg scheme of moral stages, but it is not associated with any one stage. A comparative analysis by Carolyn Pope Edwards (1981:521), using Kohlberg's scheme and based on evidence from peasant and tribal communities in Kenya, Turkey, the Bahamas and British Honduras, indicates that although cultures differ in the way in which lying is evaluated, the practice of lying occurs in most or all societies.

Patterns of lying may reflect features of economic life in tribal societies in much the same way as they do in industrialized societies. For example, Siskind (1973:7), an American anthropologist who studied the Sharanahua people of Peru, reports that as part of her fieldwork she learnt their art of lying. The meat of wild animals is highly valued as food; people like to be generous; direct refusals are perceived as insulting. Hence people often lie about their supplies of meat. As Siskind (1973:85) says: 'Lying and secrecy solve a conflict between widespread kinship obligations and a small amount of game.' For while direct refusals are insults, it is not insulting to be called a liar. In this society , 'lying is an essential social grace'.

The same association between lying and economic life is seen in the mountain state of LeSotho, in southern Africa, where fertile land is scarce and is often the subject of dispute. As in many traditionally oriented African societies, disputes are readily taken to court for settlement. With a dearth of written evidence and an adversarial mode of disputation, it is not surprising that lying is endemic. So widespread is lying in this context that Perry (1981:248) writes:

the use made of this particular form of lying about rights to allocation and use of a [plot of] land assumed the dimensions of a cultural form, so readily was it recognized and tested in court.

As mentioned in chapter 3, the same indifference to truth is found in the Mexican rural courts studied by Collier (1973), though there the emphasis is on acceptable compromise, even if based on lies, rather than on the aggressive confrontation, based on competitive lying, that characterizes court hearings in LeSotho.

A full survey of the available evidence for culturally driven diversity in patterns of lying would take up far too much space for our present purposes. In the remaining sections of this chapter, I present data from two societies where studies of lying have been carried out in greater depth, and look briefly at the significance of social class.

LEBANON

Michael Gilsenan (1976) has made an excellent analysis of lying, based on data collected in a Muslim village in the Bekaa valley of Lebanon during 1971–72, before the civil war had become acute. In this community liars are typically young men or children. Lies are told partly for fun, to trick one's friends. Success in lying depends on skill, but the final triumph comes when the liar reveals his lie to the dupe and claims victory; 'I'm lying to you, you ate it' (Gilsenan 1976:192). There is thus an attitude of playful competition towards lying, somewhat similar to the attitude towards the tricks played on the first of April in some countries. Lying is indulged in sometimes for its own sake, without an instrumental motive, and it is not surprising that lying is a symbol of the fantastic and unbelievable. Gilsenan (1976:193) illustrates this usage with the remarks of a taxi-driver from a

70

poor village who was describing what he had seen when he had driven some passengers to a New Year's junket in Beirut, then still a sophisticated city. The taxi driver said:

The streets were all hung in lights, decorations everywhere, ... the girls' dresses were up to here [graphic gestures!] ... People were kissing in the street, it was unbelievable, it would drive you mad, you can't imagine. it was – like *kizb* – absolutely – like *kizb*!

Kizb is the Arabic word Gilsenan translates as 'lying'. Yet as well as carrying the connotation of fantasy, lying is also perceived as the anti-thesis of truth, as revealed in the Holy Quran, and is associated with scepticism and pessimism about the world. Thus for example there is a Lebanese saying 'the world is a lie my friend, all of it's a lie' (Gilsenan 1976:194).

Gilsenan's data on lying are drawn mainly from the actions of members of what he calls the staff of the landlord of the area in which he worked. The staff belonged to a large immigrant extended family, some of whose members were socially well placed while others were little more than casual agricultural labourers. Nevertheless the so-called family had some corporate identity, at least in contrast to the true peasants on the one hand and to the landlords on the other. Gilsenan (1976:196) argues that the socially intermediate status of the family was 'riddled with contradictions' and that 'it is in this gray zone of contradiction that the lie comes into its own'. He notes that in the village men do not lie about things on which there is consensus, such as individual moral character, nor about objective evidence, such as mechanical ability, but only about matters that are essentially problematic, like social standing and prestige. Boys (Gilsenan says very little about girls) grow up in an environment in which social relations are perceived as competitive, and in which individual prestige fluctuates. Boys spar with words, and continually question one another's motives and intentions.

It is not surprising that in a cultural environment of this kind there are special devices to indicate that what is about to be said is true, and not a lie. These markers for code switching are phrases such as 'seriously', 'will you believe me', 'without joking', 'by your life', and 'by your father's life'. Gilsenan reports an incident when some young men rushed to his house to tell him that one of his friends had been shot. He refused to believe them until they said *wahyatak* (by your life); then he realized that what they said must be true. He remarks:

These cue words are particularly important among the young men, who carry on so much joking in their relations that without sign phrases it would be difficult to indicate the boundary between the authentic/real and the inauthentic/inverted-apparent. These cues establish a different domain of relevance and reference. (Gilsenan 1976:199, 215)

Gilsenan's material will be discussed further in chapter 6, in connection with relations between partners.

GREECE

In the Lebanon of the early 1970s, family honour was protected with violence but also by deceit. Introducing a symposium spanning several Mediterranean societies, Peristiany (1976:23) refers to 'the defensive use of deception and the offensive use of ridicule', with secrecy as the other major defensive strategy used by families jealous of their honour. Greek attitudes towards lying, conforming to this generalization, were mentioned in chapter 1, drawing on the findings of Ernestine Friedl. Such strategies are also reported by another social anthropologist, Juliet du Boulay, who studied a village on the Greek island of Euboea in the late 1960s. Comparing her findings with those of Gilsenan, important differences stand out. In rural Greece, family honour had to be defended, but the available level of violence was much lower than it was in the Lebanon; greater use had to be made of guile. On the other hand, individuals were able to mock and denigrate members of other families in ways which, in the Lebanon, would have been much more dangerous. In the Lebanon, the families whose honour had to be defended were large groupings with hundreds of members, whereas on Euboea the unit whose honour was at stake was more often the domestic family. Families competed with one another to gain a good reputation, but the stress on family honour was modified to some extent by the acceptance of another set of values supplied by Christianity. Thus

not only does a man not murder or steal in order to further the good of his family, but he does not lie, cheat, gossip, or infringe the rights of others either. (du Boulay 1976:392)

These were the accepted norms; but in practice 'eavesdropping, gossiping about neighbours, inventing scurrilous explanations of events, lying to destroy another's reputation' were common occurrences and were accepted as legitimate strategies to follow when defending personal secrets and uncovering those of others. But the victims of these ploys could appeal to the commonly accepted norms to condemn the deceit practised on them. Du Boulay comments, however, that the Greek word *psema*, which she, like Friedl, translates as 'lie', does not carry the overtones of moral failure that 'lie' does in English. Realizing that they might be lied to, people would test the propensity of others to tell lies by asking questions to which they already knew the answer.

In a village society of this kind discretion and secrecy are virtues, especially in relation to the affairs of one's own family. Du Boulay (1974:189) tells of being in a house when the kerosene ran out. The eldest boy, then aged eight, was sent to the café to get more. He was instructed 'If anyone asks you where you are going, say you're going to feed the animals. Say nothing else, see?' When the boy returned, he was asked 'Who was in the café?' The boy told his mother. She then asked 'Did anyone ask you what company you had tonight?' 'No', he replied.

Du Boulay (1976:399) also describes how a prospective marriage was kept secret. A priest who was acting for the bride's family as match-maker met the prospective bridegroom, a stonemason. In the village café they talked about prices and materials for repairing the church. After a while the priest said 'Come to my house and we'll discuss the matter further'. Later the priest commented to du Boulay 'So we deceived the community and they realized nothing'.

On the basis of the lies she encountered during the course of her fieldwork, du Boulay (1976:400–404) has devised a typology, distinguishing those lies used in defence and in attack. In the defensive category are lies told to conceal an inability to live up to the highest requirements of the social code, either by oneself or by one's family, and those told to conceal unintentional failures, such as being poor or being turned down in a projected marriage match. Then there are lies told to avoid trouble or quarrels. A typical situation for such a lie arose when two women, A and B, decided to criticize another woman C. Later, one of them, A, realized that B might well betray her. A therefore went to C and told C what had been said about her, imputing the slanderous report to B. Du Boulay describes as spurious loyalty the excuse A gave to C for making this report. A said something like 'I think you ought to know ...' C then went to B to confront her with the slander. If B did not want a quarrel, she would deny ever having said anything slanderous, or would claim that A had said it. According to du Boulay, the value of this kind of lie is that if everyone lied enough about what had been said, no-one would have to apologize and C would escape the necessity of having to quarrel with either A or B. Everyone's face would have been saved. Lies of this kind were often told when people found themselves in situations of conflicting obligations, as a way of avoiding trouble.

Another type of defensive lie arose out of the love of secrecy. For example, adults continually asked village children what their mothers were doing. It would have been insulting for a child to reply 'I won't tell you' yet to answer truthfully would be to reveal what should be a family secret. Children therefore learnt to reply to these inquiries by lying. As du Boulay (1974:74) says, 'a child is conditioned to deceit from a tender age, because deceit is necessary to safeguard the family from the curiosity and malice of the community'.

Then there are lies that are told of absolute necessity, to defend a friend or kinsperson. Du Boulay describes a lie she herself told. In the community where she worked, people in mourning and the relatives of a seriously ill person were not allowed to sing secular songs but could sing church music. For a parent, mourning lasted five years. Du Boulay walked with two sisters, both good singers, to the local market town to record some church music. Because of illness and death, the women had been unable to sing secular songs for fifteen years. While going to town, du Boulay heard them quietly singing secular songs. Back in the village, having supper with friends, du Boulay was asked where she had been. She replied truthfully that she had been to town to record the two women singing church music. At once her hosts asked 'Did they sing any secular songs for you?' Du Boulay replied 'Of course not, they are in mourning'.

Among the lies told offensively are those that attack others by making false allegations. Girls seeking marriage were particularly liable to be attacked in this way; du Boulay was told that no engagement could occur without someone slandering the prospective bride. Other lies were told for material gain. Community norms defined the contexts when lies of this kind could be told and when not. In a financial deal, cheating and deceiving were regarded as virtues, as legitimate ways in which a clever man outwits a stupid one; consequently everyone tried to cheat. On the other hand, to achieve material gain not through a formalized deal, but by acquiring something just by cheating without paying for it, was considered reprehensible. In this connection, contested court cases counted as formal deals. If the quarrel was about land boundaries, as many cases were, by the time the case was heard the issues, du Boulay says, would have become so confused that the contest was transformed into a vindication of the honour of the parties involved rather than an adjudication on the piece of land over which the quarrel started. Bearing false witness, therefore, in so far as it entailed a man laying claim to land that really belonged to someone else, was perceived as part of the wider struggle for prestige in the community and was continually indulged in, even though neither party to a dispute would admit to it. At the same time everyone agreed that it was sinful to make false statements in court, since a witness has to swear on the Bible to tell the truth. Yet du Boulay (1974:62) says that 'The villager does not feel that he is outraging his religious commitment by telling lies, ...' Indeed, because loyalty to one's family, one's 'house', overrides all other loyalties, the villager has 'a moral duty to quarrel with, cheat, or deceive the outsider in support of the house' (ibid.:74). In any case, as the saying goes, 'God wants people to cover things up' (ibid.:82).

Finally, there are lies told offensively simply to create mischief. The government was one of the main targets for this kind of lying, but du Boulay gives examples of such lies being used within the community as well.

Du Boulay's findings for the Greek island of Euboea are summed up in a phrase often used in the village: 'You can't live without lies' (ibid.:191; cf. Sciama 1981:102–105). But even in this community where the 'capacity for telling lies is highly developed', 'the incorrigible liar is no longer believed' (du Boulay 1974:77, 192).

A somewhat similar state of affairs has been reported for a community living under quite different ecological conditions in northern Greece, but following the same tradition of Orthodox Christianity. Here there were differences in the propensity and need to lie between men and women, between younger and older men, and between kinsfolk and non-kin. Campbell, who studied the sheep-herding Sarakatsani, notes the distinction they made between young unmarried shepherds and older men who were heads of households. Young men were pure and 'innocent in the sense of freedom from guilt or the need to use guile'. They were free of contamination from women who possessed 'the ability to deceive their men "forty times each day" '. For a household head, however, 'Deceit and lies are always needed'. As protector of his family and his flock, he should have 'the skill to plot with guile and craft'. He 'must continually use lies'. Indeed, Campbell (1964:278–283) says 'men lie as a matter of habit and principle to deny other people information'. In this respect, Sarakatsani household heads and Bailey's academic deans are in the same boat.

SOCIAL CLASS

Cultural diversity exists not only between territorially distinct societies but also within them, particularly within large-scale industrial societies. Members of a nation-state, or of some other social unit, differ in their life chances, access to resources, and culturally determined values, expectations and attitudes. Among these differences is a diversity of attitudes to lying and the kind of lies that are told. Communities also differ in how they classify statements as lies. For instance, Heath (1983:189) notes that in a working class community she studied in the United States certain untrue tales, being perceived as 'stories', were morally acceptable; yet the same tales, if told in a nearby middle-class community, would have been classified as lies.

An early example of a perception of class differences in these attitudes is provided by Madame Necker de Saussure (1839:164), who wrote on the education of children. She stressed the importance of parents and teachers being completely honest; their example would never fail to produce similar behaviour in the children. She goes on to say:

Nurses, especially, should be most carefully instructed on this point; though this is by no means easily accomplished, for perfect truthfulness, owing perhaps to their defective education and dependent situation, is very rarely to be met with in this class of people.

Her sentiments are echoed in the writings of the French developmental psychologist (as he would now be categorized) Gabriel Compayré, who published at the end of the nineteenth century. He implies the existence of lying on both sides of the class divide in writing that 'the child does not delay in perceiving that truth is not always respected in the conversation of his parents, nor in that of the servants'. He goes on to assert that there is 'no hereditary tendency to falsehood' and then to ask why some children demonstrate in court that they are accomplished liars. He explains (1902:198, 200)that these are children 'who have been spoiled by unhealthful surroundings, who have learned at the sad school of misery that knavery and deceit are weapons in the struggle for existence, ...' These vices, however, 'are developed only in appropriate mediums'; they are vices 'which Nature usually spares children that are well-born, ...'

These comments, and those of Madame Necker de Saussure, clearly reflect a middle-class view of working-class values that derives at least in part from popular assumptions rather than empirical evidence. Class differences are demonstrated more convincingly in the findings of a study of lower-class culture in a city in the eastern United States, carried out during the 1950s. One of the six focal concerns identified in this culture was 'smartness', which referred to

the capacity to outsmart, outfox, outwit, dupe, 'take', 'con' another or others, and the concomitant capacity to avoid being outwitted, 'taken', or duped oneself. (Miller 1958:9)

This 'smartness' was highly valued by young men who grouped themselves into gangs. It was acquired through participation with peers in 'recurrent card games and other forms of gambling, mutual exchanges of insults, and "testing" for mutual "con-ability" '. Those who demonstrated their greater smartness by making dupes of fellow group members were accorded higher status. While toughness was also valued, a smart leader gained more prestige than a tough leader, reflecting, says Miller, 'a general lower class respect for "brains" in the "smartness" sense'. Miller does not explicate, but takes for granted, the divergence of these sets of norms from those of middle-class Americans; writing before the rise of labelling theories he unproblematically labels the gangs as delinquent. In retrospect, what is interesting about his findings is that competitive deception was directed at fellow gang members. Gangs did not compete with one another in deception; they fought one another over women, gambling, claims of physical prowess, and territory. There was a high level of intra-group solidarity (Miller 1958:14), manifest in inter-gang contests, but it was a solidarity based largely on reciprocal insults and competitive deception, referred to by Miller as 'aggressive repartee'. The existence of strong intra-gang hierarchies is consonant with this kind of solidarity basis.

Class differences of another kind are demonstrated in a longitudinal study of children growing up in the English city of Nottingham during the 1960s. Mothers were asked about the extent to which they evaded or distorted the truth in their dealings with their children. The proportion of mothers giving a 'false account of where babies come from' varied with their position in the class hierarchy, ranging from 66 per cent for those whose husbands were unskilled workers (Class V), to only 8 per cent for those in professional and managerial occupations (Classes I and II). The mothers more likely to lie to their children, at least on this particular topic, were also those who more often reported smacking their children for telling lies (42 per cent of Class V mothers as against only 27 per cent of mothers in Classes I and II). The latter difference is in part explained by the somewhat greater use by mothers in Class V of smacking as a punishment for all kinds of misbehaviour, but these mothers were also less tolerant in their attitudes towards children's lies (Newson and Newson 1968:415, 419, 446, 471).

These scraps of evidence must suffice to suggest that social class is yet another dimension affecting not only attitudes towards lying but also the frequency with which lies are told, the content of lies and the contexts in which they occur. Inter-class differences within any one society may not be so striking as the differences that exist between societies, including those between some pre-industrial societies and industrialized states, which are certainly of great comparative cultural interest. But in a sense intra-societal differences are sociologically more interesting and socially more important, at least at the present time. Cultural differences between societies, including differences in patterns of lying, were certainly significant during the last two or three centuries during the process of expanding Western colonialism. In a post-colonial world marked by global cultural homogenization, many inter-societal differences still persist but they are less salient than before. Intra-societal differences have also diminished, but have not vanished; they still have to be taken into account in understanding how lying is used in intra-societal struggles. For in complex industrial societies lying is associated with the exercise of power, not in the negative sense reported by Lindstrom from rural Vanuatu but more often in a positive relation, sustained by the existence of mass media of communication. We shall look at what Simmel had to say on this topic in chapter 10.

6

Relations

DIVERSITY OF RELATIONS

We have seen that the content, frequency and evaluation of lying varies across different domains of social life; nevertheless the mainstream of ethical pronouncements on lying in the Christian West, at least from St Augustine onwards, has been universalistic, in the sense that the moral evaluation of a lie does not depend on the gender or social affiliation of either the liar or the dupe. This universalism may be said to have reached its apotheosis in Kant's Categorical Imperative. But there are other cultures and traditions which have not subscribed to this universalist principle and even in the Christian West many exceptions to it have persisted, notably in connection with warfare, as we have seen in chapter 2. Lay evaluations of lying depart radically from the universalistic tradition. Lies are evaluated differentially not only according to domain and culture but also with reference to the status of liar and dupe, their status both relative to one another and in the wider society. For instance, studies carried out during the 1970s showed that in the United States high-status persons and those in positions of responsibility were judged more harshly when they lied than were persons of equal or low status. Lies told to a friend were considered to be more reprehensible than those told to strangers and associates (Maier and Lovrakas 1976:577). Similar American studies carried out in the 1980s showed that lies told to benefit the liar met with greater disapproval from student respondents than did lies told to benefit the dupe (Lindskold and Walters 1983). In a recent survey in the northeastern United States of physicians' attitudes to the use of deception, many more respondents said they were ready to deceive medical insurance companies and the wives of their male patients than were prepared to deceive their own patients (Novack et al. 1989).

These findings suggest that one factor affecting the evaluation of lies is the extent of trust that exists, or should exist, between liar and dupe. However, perceptions of trust and expectations of honesty in other people's relations seem to differ from those in one's own relations. In particular, lying, especially defensive and protective lying, is not necessarily perceived by the liar as a betrayal of trust, though it may be seen in that light by the dupe or by third parties. Discussing how men and women responded differently in a study of the connection between perceptions of betrayal and trust, Blum (1972:222–230) remarks

Men are thus more concerned with lies about their activities, infidelity especially, and project that concern in the form of a belief that wives, too, are unfaithful and lie about it.

Most husbands and wives in the study, it seems, lied to one another, and realized that they were being lied to. Yet though there is some symmetry in their actions and perceptions, we cannot say that there was collaboration between them. There seems to be no evidence from Blum's study to suggest that the women accepted being lied to by their husbands; the lies they admitted telling to their husbands were not about infidelity but about protecting themselves in other contexts, or protecting their husbands and children. The men and women in Blum's sample differed significantly from the couples we shall discuss in chapter 7, where, although there was little collaboration between spouses, there was some mutual connivance.

These findings demonstrate that the type of relation existing between liar and dupe has a bearing on what lies are told and how they are perceived. In chapter 2 we contrasted lies told to national enemies and the lay public; at the level of interpersonal relations the main contrast in lying is between statements made to outsiders and those made to kin and friends. In this chapter we examine how the telling of lies is affected by inequalities in status between liar and dupe.

OUTSIDERS

The differential evaluation of lies told to allies and enemies is, in many cultures, extended to all outsiders, with the boundary between insiders and outsiders sometimes varying from one context to another. Likewise, insiders and outsiders are treated differently in how their truthfulness is perceived. In a handbook for interviewers and others in the world of business, the authors remark:

It is easy to suggest that someone is lying when he does not have to be confronted directly and when the relationship is impersonal. Deceit on the doorstep is much more difficult to deal with. (Comer et al. 1988:1)

As we shall see, deceit inside the house between spouses is even harder to deal with than deceit on the doorstep. The relative ease with which lying is attributed to strangers does not ensure greater success in making correct judgments about their truthfulness or deceptiveness (Miller et al. 1983), nor does the existence of a differential in the treatment of insiders and outsiders necessarily imply an enhanced tolerance of lying in general. For instance, Albert (1972:100–101) contrasts the Barundi, who valued highly certain kinds of lies even when told to insiders, with the Navajo, among whom, she says

the value of truth-telling is very high. A sharp line is drawn between in-group and out-group. Truth is for the in-group. Lying to outsiders or performing other negative acts toward them will either be given different names or different evaluations, or both.

As Alexander (1987:121) says, 'national boundaries most dramatically define the alien, the strange, the enemy'.

Yet while this may be true for the public sphere in well-established nation-states, the boundary between in-group and out-group with respect to telling lies is likely to be drawn much more closely in many other contexts. Where the nation-state is irrelevant, as with the Navajo, or in disar ray, as in modern states torn with ethnic or religious divisions, public transactions may be governed by narrow categories. In the private sphere, family members and close friends may be treated differently from outsiders. In general, liars consider they have no obligation to refrain from deceiving dupes who belong to what Bailey (1991:48) calls 'different moral communities'.In rural Greece, as we have seen, the moral boundary is defined in terms of kinship (cf. Campbell 1964:316). In industrial societies, the criterion of kinship is less salient in public life and the distinction between in-group and out-group is determined by other criteria. Writing about the United States at the beginning of this century, Cooley (1922:388) claimed that

the maxim, 'Truth for friends and lies for enemies', is very generally followed, not only by savages and children, but, more or less openly, by civilized people.

Enemies, for this purpose, included business rivals. The propensity to tell the truth arose, in Cooley's view, not so much from 'a need for mental accuracy' as from 'a sense of the unfairness of deceiving people of our own sort, and of the shame of being detected in so doing'. The insider–outsider boundary, the boundary of the moral community, can thus vary according to context. An individual who can be duped in one situation as an outsider may in different circumstances become an insider who must be treated truthfully. Not all fellow members of the moral community are treated alike; relative status within the community has to be taken into account.

PARTNERS

The close associates of liars may join them in their lying but may also be their dupes. In chapter 3 we mentioned how bureaucrats and other professionals may lie to their spouses to protect the confidentiality of their professional activity. This type of legitimated deceit is not confined to relations between spouses. Aubert (1965:307) describes how, during the German occupation, members of the Norwegian underground resistance organization used lies to conceal their activities from near relatives and friends, and in general from other resistance members as well. Aubert makes the point that these associates were 'those to whom one would reveal that one had secrets, but very little of the contents of the secrets'. Here then we have not straightforward connivance or collaboration in lying but rather a shared understanding that unspecified false statements, some of which would be intended to deceive, would be made and should not be queried or interpreted as evidence of distrust.

Alliances in deceit may be temporary or enduring or may give way under the pressures of changed circumstances. A good example of the complexities encountered in deceptive connivance is provided by Gilsenan (1976:205), in a sequence of events involving a 'vital lie'. He tells the story of a Lebanese man who returned home after working abroad. From what he had heard the man thought that his wife might have been having an affair with a highly regarded and forceful member of his extended family. Gilsenan comments that 'To acknowledge infidelity would be desecration of his total social self unless he killed his wife and challenged the alleged offender'. Instead of doing this, the man made a point of going regularly to the house of the supposed seducer and 'acting the part of friend'. The rest of the family connived at the deceit; husband and wife were treated as if nothing untoward had happened. However, one day Gilsenan visited a relative who had a grudge against the returned husband. The relative was drunk. He complained to Gilsenan about the husband's behaviour in some other context and then went on to say:

Why does he do this to me of all people? When he came back from abroad it was I who told him there was absolutely nothing to the talk about his wife and [the other man]. I pushed him off to [the other man's] house, told him nothing had happened, and supported him.

Gilsenan interprets this as an attempt to assure him that in fact the husband's status had been compromised. It was also, Gilsenan says, a way of ensuring that Gilsenan knew of the affair. Gilsenan goes on to report that

Two of the younger men of the [extended] family who were with me, both close friends, said not a word and I joined their tacit pretense that nothing had been said or heard by making no reply or sign of reaction, though I was in fact shocked by this breach of collective performance. No one mentioned the outburst after we had left the relative's house; we continued the vital lie of 'as if' and avoided the definition of the situation that our host had almost thrust upon us.

We shall have more to say about lies told to social equals in chapter 7, in connection with self-deception.

RELATIONS OF DOMINATION

In a hierarchical society, people tend to act in one way towards their superiors and in a different way towards those below them in the social hierarchy. Nevertheless, lies may be directed in both directions. In Albert's (1972:90) comments on the use of language in Burundi, she notes that 'No one is so high or low in the social scale, no one so secure in the affections of a superior or inferior, as to be able to afford the luxury of speaking the unedited truth'. This state of affairs has consequences for lying, particularly when someone is accused of some offence. What is needed, says Albert, is a 'rapid, graceful, and more-than-plausible falsehood'. It is considered safer to lie than to tell the truth, and men seem not to be anxious about the possible subsequent discovery of their deceit.

Whereas Lindstrom's evidence from Tanna, mentioned in chapter 5, associates lying with subordinate status, Albert speaks of lying to both superiors and inferiors in the Rundi hierarchy. As Bailey (1991:66) says:

Untruths provide weapons for the weak to resist the strong and for the strong to moderate the antagonism that their dominance provokes from the weak.

Many of the lies told by the powerful to deceive those who lack power have no smidgin of nobility about them but there are others that fall into the category which some translators of Plato (1935:99) have called 'noble lies' (cf. Bok 1978:165–170, 305–306). These 'lies for the public good', as Bok calls them, may emanate from a ruler, as with Plato's example, but many more issue from lower down in the hierarchy, though aimed downwards and outwards, at the public at large, rather than upwards.

The deception practised by some experimenters on their subjects may be seen as instances of deceit in a relation of superordination, even though the experimenter's superior status is usually severely limited in content and restricted to an hour or so in time. Deception, possibly long lasting, again of those who, for the time being, are in a position of subordination, occurs whenever a physician gives a patient a placebo. The physician's aim may be to gather evidence in a scientific trial of a new medicine, with the patient forming part of a control group; alternatively the doctor may hope that even a placebo will bring relief to the patient. In either case, for the experiment to be valid or for the relief to occur, the patient must believe that the medicine has genuine curative power. It is possible to imagine that a cool-headed patient might realize that deception was taking place and yet decide to connive at the deceit; but most patients are far from being cool-headed when they seek treatment.

How are we to classify encouraging comments made to bolster the self-esteem of someone else? Friends may make such remarks to one another, but they are often made in asymmetrical relations, by a parent to a child or by a physician to a patient. Sometimes such comments are true and are made truthfully, but often they are not. A parent cheers a discon- solate child who brings home a deplorable school report by saying 'I'm sure you tried very hard'; a toddler's scrawled drawing evokes the comment 'What a pretty picture!' These remarks may be lies, but are told because the liar hopes that falsely inflated estimates of their ability will make dupes happy and encourage them to do better next time. Similar statements of doubtful accuracy made by doctors to calm or cheer their patients are usually categorized as harmless or 'white', even though these are statements made by a person in a relation of dominance over the dupe. In Henderson's (1970 [1935]) classic account of the physician–patient relation, he discusses the complexities of the patient's likely reaction if the physician were to make a bland pronouncement 'This is a carcinoma'. Henderson justifies his prescription of 'do no harm' rather than 'tell the truth' by referring to the probable adverse consequences of attempting to tell 'the whole truth' to the patient, and to the obligation on the physician 'to act upon the patient so as to modify his sentiments to his own advantage'. Nothing, says Henderson, is more effective to this end than the physician arousing in the patient the belief that the physician is 'concerned wholeheartedly and exclusively for *his* welfare'. Here, then, we have a prescription for lying by the elite not for the public good but for the benefit of an individual citizen. Evidence indicates that some harmless lies do indeed have a positive therapeutic effect (Scheibe 1980:20–21); the case for telling encouraging lies to children and sick people is much stronger than for telling lies 'for the public good' to healthy citizens.

RELATIONS OF SUBORDINATION

Gourevitch (1990:100) glosses Rousseau's view of the connection between superordination and deceit by saying that 'only in a society of equals might men lead lives free of deceit'. He cites Rousseau's (1991:101) assertion that

it is the law of obedience which produces the necessity of lying because since obedience is irksome,... the present interest in avoiding punishment or reproach wins out over the distant interest of revealing the truth.

This claim is illustrated by the 'Marion' incident that occurred when Rousseau (1953:86–89) was a young man employed as a servant; he told a lie to escape punishment for a theft.

Rousseau's pronouncement is confirmed by the fact that in many cultures, it is considered rude and dangerous to contradict or say 'No' to anyone in a superior position. In some cultures the same constraint operates even among equals; there may be reluctance to disagree openly. For example, the Semai people of Malaysia 'dislike openly disagreeing with each other' and engage in various ploys to prevent disagreements coming to the surface. Dentan (1970:109), an American anthropologist who worked among the Semai in the early 1960s, had to adopt the same procedures to avoid quarrels. The semblance of agreement thus produced might be deceptive to an outsider but not to a member of the community. Nor is there necessarily any intention to deceive on the part of those who feign agreement while silently disagreeing.

Deference to superiors can be deceptive if the superior person mistakes deference for a response unconstrained by considerations of hierarchy. To an outsider the consequences of deference can sometimes be very amusing. A story, probably true, is told of a visit to Tokyo by a senior Indian academic. Invited by a Japanese colleague whom he had never actually met, he was greeted on arrival by a man who said 'Excuse me, but you must be Professor X'. The Indian, pleased to find himself recognized so promptly, replied 'Yes, and you must be Professor Y'. But alas, it was not Professor Y who had made the tiring journey out to Narita airport but one of his research students recruited to perform this chore. How could the student reply to Professor X's remark? It would have been unthinkable to say 'No' to such an eminent foreign guest. Yet to say 'Yes' was to open the way to endless confusion. The student resolved his dilemma by replying 'Probably'.

The widespread use of similar linguistic tools has been noted by feminists to explain what they see as some of the distinctive features of women's speech, shown particularly when women are speaking to men. Grice's conversational maxims, mentioned in chapter 1, have been criticized by Michell (1990:176) as being restricted to white, middle-class contexts. She argues that, when talking to men, women of necessity cannot conform to the maxim 'Do not say what you believe to be false'. Because of male dominance, women have to make understatements (and sometimes overstatements), to equivocate and to introduce 'red herrings'. Hence their statements are certainly not the whole truth, and are deceptive at least for hearers who assume that Grice's maxims are being followed. This way of speaking, labelled with Emily Dickinson's (1955:no.1129) phrase 'telling it slant', has been analysed by Michell (1990:188–189), who points out that the practice has benefits as well as costs for women:

the slant versions get the [female] speaker's point of view across in a way that the male hearer is likely to accept and attend to, while the straight versions do not.

On the other hand women may lose the habit of 'telling it straight' even in contexts where they are not being dominated, as with their female peers. Michell ties her discussion strictly to the domination of women by men but her arguments have a wider application. What Hartung (1988:171, 173–174) calls 'deceiving down' is a form of self-deception whereby a person lowers his or her self-esteem and thereby becomes better adjusted to occupying a subordinate status. Hartung, following Trivers, offers an evolutionary explanation for a tendency for women to self-deceive down and for men to self-deceive up, i.e., 'raising one's self-esteem in order to occupy a position for which one is initially underqualified'.

... since a man with ten wives can have more children than could a woman with ten husbands ... men have more often been in a position in which self-deceiving up has been to their reproductive advantage ... and self-deceiving down has more frequently been to the advantage of females ... (Hartung 1988:173–174)

In these terms, the women whom Michell describes as losing the habit of 'telling it straight' have deceived themselves downwards, thereby accommodating themselves more comfortably to a subordinate status. Many men do likewise.

In this chapter I have tried to show that, as well as differences arising from social pressures specific to various domains and cultures, there are other constraints on patterns of lying that are rooted in the structural relations prevailing between liar and dupe. To some extent these constraints cut across social and cultural differences, but their manifestation is usually coloured by them. For instance, lying may everywhere be a weapon that can be used by the weak, but whether the powerful avail themselves of 'Untruths ... to moderate the antagonism that their dominance provokes from the weak', as Bailey puts it, depends on social and cultural context. There is, however, one structural configuration that we have mentioned only in passing and which now needs attention. Liar and dupe are not necessarily separate persons. When these two positions are occupied by the same individual we have self-deception. This is the main topic of the next chapter.

7

Self-deception and connivance in deceit

SELF-DECEPTION AND SELF-DELUSION

Adrienne Rich (1980:188) comments that 'In lying to others we end up lying to ourselves'. Instances of this progression have been presented in chapter 2. But deceiving oneself is not always a consequence of continued deception of others. Lytton (1852:204) claims that 'the easiest person to deceive is one's own self' and Nietzsche (1911:212) says much the same: 'The most common sort of lie is the one uttered to one's self; to lie to others is relatively exceptional'. Yet serious semantic problems are raised when we speak of self-deception (cf. Trivers 1985:416). Grotius (1925:613) takes one extreme view and says bluntly that 'it is sufficiently clear that no one lies to himself, however false his statement may be'. Luckily, most other commentators have attempted to face the inherent difficulties in the notion of lying to oneself (Durandin 1972:405). Bok (1978:291) remarks that 'self-deception offers difficult problems of definition', and that whether self-deception is properly so called 'is a question discussed since Plato' (cf. Chisholm and Feehan 1977:158–159; Paulhus 1988a; Sackeim 1988). Demos (1960:588–589), indeed, argues that Plato's 'true lie' refers to lying to oneself.

Some of the incidents we commonly call self-deception are easily disposed of. When, for instance, I find that the road I expected would take me to A in fact leads me to B, I may well say 'I deceived myself'. But this is surely an instance of error, not of deceit; I was misinformed, perhaps, or made the wrong guess, but we cannot say that I was trying to deceive myself, unless perhaps I 'really' knew that the road went to B but for some reason was unwilling to accept this fact (cf. Trivers 1988:viii). Indeed the notion of self-deception hinges on the possibility of inner dialogue or many-sided conversation, in which the roles of liar and dupe are played by a single person, and in which some lies are thought in silence rather than spoken out loud. Hartung (1988:172) writes that only in humans does the self have 'social interaction with itself, controlling information transfer between the conscious and subconscious in order to manipulate its own behavior, ...' and Fingarette (1969:1) identifies 'man's enormous capacity for self-deception' as one of the most salient human characteristics.

Snyder and Higgins (1990:216) refer to an 'internal audience' but this reflexive engagement is unlikely to be a peaceful discussion; Raphael Demos (1960:588) speaks of 'inner conflict' (cf. Greenwald 1988). Fingarette postulates not so much a dialogue as a silent duet, in which two, or even more, parts of a single personality avoid speaking to one another. Kovar (1974:138) glosses Fingarette's thesis by saying:

> The self-deceiver willfully refuses to spell out for himself those engagements an awareness of whose clear meanings would threaten the integrity of his self as conceived and constituted at that time.

Kovar writes as a psychoanalyst, and indeed Becker (1973:51) sees psychoanalysis as being committed to the idea of self-deception. He says:

> The hostility to psychoanalysis in the past, today, and in the future, will always be a hostility against admitting that man lives by lying to himself about himself and about his world, and that character ... is a vital lie.

Goleman (1985:16, 22), writing from a more orthodox psychological viewpoint, says much the same, maintaining that with many people 'the mind can protect itself against anxiety by dimming awareness' through adopting 'vital lies', 'the family myth that stands in place of a less comfortable truth'. Likewise Dr Relling, in Ibsen's (1960:227) *The wild duck*, proclaims: 'Take the life-lie [*livsløgnen*] away from the average man and straight away you take away his happiness.'

In parenthesis, it is refreshing to come across the rare psychoanalyst who admits to having lied to his supervisor in entirely mundane terms. Farber (1974:132–133) describes how, during his psychoanalytic training, he pretended to agree with suggestions made by his supervisor so that they could get through the hour with something to say to one another. He says:

> mine was an expedient and deliberate deceit, undertaken to relieve us both and indulged in with the certainty that it would be received not only graciously but uncritically.

Here we have an instance of sophisticated and, it would seem, unstressful connivance, or perhaps even collaboration in deceit, occurring within the privileged context of a psychoanalytic training.

But while psychoanalytic theory raises expectations of stress and con-

flict, there is little suggestion of necessary conflict in the 'reality negotiation processes' postulated by C. R. Snyder (1989:130), a clinical psychologist, processes whereby 'people negotiate with reality in order to sustain
their personal theories of being "good and in-control" people'. These
processes entail the construction of illusions, and Snyder (1991;5) refers to
them as 'deceptive', even though the illusions generated by them, such as
'unrealistically positive statements about oneself' (Snyder 1989:145), are in
many instances adaptive (cf. Snyder et al. 1992). Indeed, Snyder's thesis is
that illusions can be beneficial not only to the individual who generates
them but also to society as a whole; he gives the example of Horatio Alger
success stories reinforcing 'the underlying, societally shared illusion about
how effort leads to success' (Snyder 1989:148). Snyder (1989:150–152)
points out that 'reality negotiation processes' can become counter-productive, but in a recent conference paper argues that in the present global
predicament, 'some self-deception at the planetary level may be required'
(Snyder 1991:10).

Yet though Snyder labels these processes of reality negotiation as deceptive, this adjective seems to me not entirely appropriate since the individual, and even the society, is not necessarily unaware of the mismatch
between perception and reality. The dupe becomes a collaborator, or even
a recognized co-author. Self-delusion rather than self-deception might
seem to be a more apt term for these 'reality negotiations'. This proposal
conflicts with Taylor (1990:36), who has drawn a distinction between delusions, which are 'false beliefs that persist despite the facts' and illusions, or
creative self-deceptive beliefs, which accommodate the facts, 'though
perhaps reluctantly'. The distinction Taylor draws has to be made, but I
prefer to maintain the established connotation of 'self-deception', referring
to the process whereby there is an inner dialogue in which one segment of
a personality deceives another segment, and where the lying segment
remains aware of the deceit. Self-delusion seems an appropriate label for
the state of affairs reached when a liar begins to believe that his or her lie is
not a lie at all but is true. The condition is described by Prospero in his
comment on his 'perfidious' brother Antonio in Shakespeare's *The Tempest*.

> ... like one,
> Who having minted truth by telling of it,
> Made such a sinner of his memory,
> To credit his own lie, he did believe
> He was indeed the duke, ...

(cf. Ewbank 1983:164).

The notion of reluctance mentioned by Taylor captures well the sense
of inner conflict that characterizes many instances of self-deception,

particularly with adults who are mentally healthy (cf. Paulhus 1988b). This inherent tension is well brought out in the distinction we make in ordinary speech between reasons and excuses. Durandin (1972:298) comments that 'lies of justification' in particular take the form of an inner dialogue. We can make excuses for ourselves to ourselves; we also sometimes have to make excuses for ourselves to others. Snyder and Higgins (1990:216–217) point out that we handle the two situations differently. When we are making excuses merely to ourselves, 'excuses take on the status of reasons in our own minds, and a state of self-deception may occur about the whole process'. I would add: also self-delusion. On the other hand 'when the external audience becomes involved there is less opportunity for self-deception. Indeed, the protagonist considers what excuse may work best ... and must continually remain somewhat aware of his or her excuses and the audience's reaction to these excuses'.

For people in public life it is doubly important for their self-esteem that excuses be elevated to the status of reasons not only in their own minds but also in the opinions of their audience. Snyder and Higgins look in detail at one of President Reagan's Irangate speeches and make the comment that for Reagan, as for others,

the problem is how to use excuses and yet appear not to use them. The self-deceptive solution, as shown in this important passage of the speech, is to elevate the President's explanations to the status of reasons and to assert simultaneously that there are no excuses involved.

They then make an important comment on the success, in this instance, of this tactic by adding: 'Perhaps this was more than mere *self*-deception, however, given the media reaction of "President makes no excuses".'

Drawing on data from a very different social domain, Werth and Flaherty (1986:299) provide striking evidence for the inner dialogue of deception. They report on a woman, identified as D4, who came to the conclusion that she did not love her husband and did not wish to be married to him. She deceived her husband by concealing her lack of love and her wish to leave him. Yet she tried to conceal from herself the fact that she was engaged in this deception. She said:

The beginning of the deception began when I flashed on the thought, 'I don't love this man. I cannot tolerate him', and turned off the thought, denied it completely ... If you are going to lie about something, eventually you have to believe it in order to live with yourself.

D4 eventually became aware not only that her husband had come to recognize that she was deceiving him but also that he was unwilling to recognize that he was being deceived.

In this situation husband and wife, despite their divergent interests, tacitly agree to treat as authentic her pretence of loving him, despite both knowing it is only a pretence; is this collusion? Many commentators would say it was. Ekman (1985:20) says, writing about collusion in general terms:

> By overlooking the signs of his wife's affairs a husband may at least postpone the humiliation of being exposed as a cuckold and the possibility of divorce. Even if he admits her infidelity to himself he may cooperate in not uncovering her lies to avoid having to acknowledge it to her or to avoid a showdown.

Ekman, in this context, refers to the dupe 'collusively helping' the liar to maintain the lie, and Bailey (1991) entitles one of his chapters 'Collusive lying' (cf. Kovar 1974:148–149). Nevertheless I think collusion is the wrong term to adopt; the configurations Bailey and others discuss usually do not constitute instances of collusion in the narrow sense, as when we speak of 'the collusion of husband and wife to deceive the court and thus obtain a divorce'. The word 'collusion' has acquired a range of meanings, even within the restricted confines of legal discourse, but the clearest definition, for our present purposes, is:

> The arrangement of two persons, apparently in a hostile position or having conflicting interests, to do some act in order to injure a third person or deceive a court. (Bird 1983:78)

In the situations outlined by Ekman, and in the case described by Werth and Flaherty, there is no third party who is the target of deceit, other perhaps than the public at large. What we have, at least initially, is better described as connivance, with X deceiving Y and Y deceiving X by pretending not to have recognized X's deceit, compounded in some instances by X's self-deception. We shall look later at situations where collusion does seem to be the appropriate description. In the case we are discussing, connivance is a better term than collusion; D4's husband connived at her attempt to deceive him:

> I think he was probably on some level quite aware of what was going on and didn't want to believe the truth ... He accused me and I lied.

As with a woman who was deceived by her husband, discussed later in this chapter, the deceit came to pervade D4's everyday life:

> You take one piece of deception and the layer upon layer that you have to add to it to protect it to keep it from coming to the surface ... just fabricating a whole existence.

She experienced contradictory emotions and a mixture of motives for continuing with the deceit:

I couldn't tolerate my sense of guilt at being that dishonest. So I began to say, 'Well, if he weren't such a bastard. If he didn't yell all the time'. I kept on rationalizing in order to make it okay for me to be doing what I was doing.

In the beginning ... I didn't even start to think about [deceiving]morally. I just felt that I was not telling him [the truth] to protect him.

This instance, like others reported by Werth and Flaherty, shows a woman sustaining a deceit in order to maintain a relation that, despite its imperfections, she still valued. Without this evaluation, there would be no point in keeping up the deceit. Another woman who deceived her father about her lesbian orientation made this point well:

Deceiving is a lot of work. You always have to be on your toes and it is exhausting. (Werth and Flaherty 1986:303)

Nietzsche (1968a:158) goes a step further; he says 'lying is very exhausting'.

Holding contradictory beliefs, or in Festinger's (1957) terms cognitive dissonance, is characteristic of the process that Orwell (1984:186, 342) in *1984* calls 'doublethink'. 'Doublethink' is holding 'simultaneously two opinions which cancelled out, knowing them to be contradictory and believing in both of them' and is a process that is conscious and unconscious at the same time. Yet despite these similarities, there are significant differences between the mental processes postulated fictionally by Orwell and the inner conflicts experienced in real life by the women interviewed by Werth and Flaherty. Orwell asserts that 'the essential act of the Party is to use conscious deception while retaining the firmness of purpose that goes with complete honesty'. Firmness of purpose is far removed from the anguish experienced by the women, whereas their internal struggles are absent from the fully brainwashed Party member who has shed any sense of guilt at practising conscious deception. Likewise Branch (1982), writing about homosexuality among politicians and bureaucrats in Washington, presents convincing evidence for the anguish experienced by his main subject, Dan Bradley, who, he says, 'had long since accepted the idea that homosexuality was powerful enough to twist a person into any shape and to make him lie to himself and anyone else, as necessary'. Bradley eventually declared publicly that he was homosexual, but many of the other secretly gay men discussed by Branch showed more of that firmness of purpose envisaged by Orwell. Where it occurred, it took the form of active support for the repression of homosexuality; as Branch puts it, they 'flew broomsticks to the witch-hunt'.

Nietzsche (1911:212) sees the process in generational terms; 'what was a lie in the father becomes a conviction in the son'. With Orwell's Party members, as with Arendt's Vietnam War policy makers, the generational gap disappears.

As we have seen, success in lying may lead liars to believe in the truth of their own lies; perhaps they need to deceive themselves in order to preserve their sense of self-esteem. Indeed, Arendt (1968:253) asks: 'Why has self-deception become an indispensable tool in the trade of image-making? For the authors of the Pentagon Papers, she says (Arendt 1972:35), 'it is as though the normal process of self-deceiving were reversed; ... The deceivers started with self-deception.'

Part of her explanation is that nowadays lies in the political realm tend to be bigger than they were in the past, and are aimed not at hiding real secrets from rival elites but at reconstructing or obliterating facts that 'are known to practically everybody'. Arendt (1968:252) gives as examples de Gaulle's assertion, or 'evident non-fact' as she describes it, that France belonged among the victors of the Second World War, and Adenauer's (1966:89) claim that 'the barbarism of National Socialism had affected only a relatively small percentage of the country'. These, in her view, were lies, but necessarily believed in by their authors. Latter-day statesmen are contrasted with 'the restricted circle of statesmen and diplomats' who, in former times, 'could deceive others without deceiving themselves'. Her contrast may be overdrawn, but I think she is correct in her comment (Arendt 1968:254) that 'Only self-deception is likely to create a semblance of truthfulness, ...' and that 'the more successful a liar is, the more people he has convinced, the more likely it is that he will end by believing his own lies' (Arendt 1972:34).

A somewhat similar process can affect dupes who connive at lies they are told. Epstein (1989:217) gives the example of the building of the German battleships *Bismarck* and *Tirpitz*. These ships should have conformed to limits specified in the Anglo-German treaty of 1935; British aerial reconnaissance showed that they exceeded them. The Germans were trying to deceive the British, but British naval officers did not wish to admit that they were being duped. Consequently they dismissed the evidence as ambiguous and tended 'to become advocates of the integrity of the persons of whom they secured the agreement'. Epstein comments: 'The British thus gradually became active allies of their German deceivers.'

The contrast between the professionals who do not need to believe their own lies and the amateurs who do can be restated in terms of the main characters in the television comedy *Yes, Minister*. Sir Humphrey Appleby is an old-style professional bureaucrat who can deceive others without believing his own lies, whereas Jim Hacker, the 'amateur' politician, has to believe them. Yet the authors of the Pentagon Papers, whom Arendt (1972:9, 11) describes as 'much better men' and, following Neil Sheehan, 'professional problem-solvers', and thus seemingly closer to Sir Humphrey than to Jim Hacker, were the people who 'lied not so much for their country ... as for its "image" ... they also believed that politics is but a variety of public relations, ...' Though they conformed to the model of Sir Humphrey in one respect, the Pentagon problem-solvers, like British naval officers of an earlier generation, were unable to distance themselves from the myths they were engaged in creating.

Where is the inner dialogue in these instances of self-deception, and where is the intention to deceive? In the case of D4, she may well have intended to deceive her husband, but that she had also an *intention* to deceive herself is far from clear. She certainly came to pretend that she believed what she told her husband to be true, but her continued unease at what she was doing indicates to me that she was only pretending. Likewise, if Arendt is right and the Pentagon planners really did *begin* by believing their own statements about the progress of the war in Vietnam, did they ever have an intention to deceive? Rather, they were engaged from the start in trying to persuade the public to concur with the truth of what they were saying. If, on the other hand, they came to believe in the truth of their lies only gradually, then initially they were engaged in deceiving the public. In these circumstances, to continue to speak of sustained deception is confusing. Some, at least, of the definitional problems can be avoided if we use here the term 'self-delusion', rather than 'self-deception', as suggested earlier. Where belief in the truth of what was previously recognized as a lie is not whole-hearted, as with D4, we have not exactly self-delusion but rather a pretence of self-delusion. This refinement in the use of self-deception and self-delusion clashes somewhat with Demos' (1960:590) proposal to use the term 'delusion' to refer to a false belief held by a person for which he or she is not responsible, such as, for instance, the belief that he is sick held by a healthy man who has been hypnotized. On the other hand, it tallies with Demos' usage when he comments that:

An important difference between what I call delusions and self-deceptions is that the person having delusions experiences no conflict; there is no countervailing belief, as there is with self-deception. (Demos 1960:590)

A tightening of vocabulary also seems to be called for when we describe the responses of dupes. It is misleading to continue to speak of dupes being deceived after they have recognized the liar's attempt to deceive them. The attempt has failed. Dupes who connive at the deceit may pretend to remain deceived but this is only a pretence. The dupe becomes an unacknowledged partner with the liar in a *folie à deux*. Here we should make a distinction between conscious and unconscious connivance, between recognition that one is being targeted as an intended dupe and an unconscious accommodation to this situation.

Trivers (1985:417), who characterizes self-deception as entailing 'keeping information from the conscious mind', argues that 'deception is a natural ally of parental domination' and that 'the child may be selected to acquiesce'. In this situation, selection pressures favour self-deception, 'rendering some facts unconscious on both sides the better to deceive others' (Trivers 1985:165). Trivers associates the favouring of self-deception with the improvement, by natural selection, of 'powers to deceive and to spot deception', for

> Self-deception renders the deception being practiced unconscious to the practitioner, thereby hiding from other individuals the subtle signs of self-knowledge that may give away the deception being practiced. (Trivers 1985:395)

This characterization of the notion of self-delusion, as we would term it rather than self-deception, clearly applies more appropriately to the Pentagon policy makers than to the anguished women studied by Werth and Flaherty.

Self-delusion and, even more so, the pretence of self-delusion, are facilitated and sustained by collaboration. For the self-deluding authors of the Pentagon Papers, Arendt (1972:35–36) has this to say:

> The internal world of government, with its bureaucracy on one hand, its social life on the other, made self-deception relatively easy. No ivory tower of the scholar has ever better prepared the mind for ignoring the facts of life than did the various think tanks for the problem-solvers and the reputation of the White House for the President's advisers.

It would be interesting to know whether policy makers, under these conditions, experience the same inner conflicts as those endured by the women interviewed by Werth and Flaherty. Were they really self-deluded or merely pretending? Trivers (1985:416) mentions the 'shifty eyes, sweaty palms, and croaky voices' that may accompany 'conscious knowledge of attempted deception'. In the Pentagon case, there was no danger of these and other involuntary signs of stress being spotted by face-to-face interrogators or even by lie detecting machines; television producers and public relations officials shielded the liars, if that is what they were, and ensured that their lies were presented to the public and the Congress with all the outward signs of authenticity. If Arendt is right in saying that Pentagon policy makers *began* by deceiving themselves and then told their lies to the public, then there was no pretence; the self-delusion was real. Perhaps the ability to succeed in public life is linked to an ability to believe one's own lies without continual inner conflict. A connection of this kind would explain the sour comment: 'memoirs – in our century the most deceitful genre of literature' (Arendt 1972:10).

Autobiographies constitute another category of statements where it is not clear who, if anyone, is deceiving whom. H. L. Mencken (1924:270) says simply that 'Honest autobiography is ... a contradiction in terms'. Adams (1990) analyses in detail how several modern American autobiographers deviated from the truth in their writings. An autobiography, he says, is created out of the author's 'private mythologies' (Adams 1990:169), myths formed in the author's memory 'by a complicated pattern of psychological self-deceptions and constructions'. Adams, however, endorses Goleman's (1985:96) categorization of autobiographers, along with 'most of us some of the time', as 'innocent self-deceivers'. Innocence and guilt are attributes that can be readily applied to attempts to deceive others but become problematic with reference to self-deception. Some biographies are written deceptively, for example in an attempt to whitewash a rogue. To make the same attempt with an autobiography is risky. As Adams (1990:167) remarks: 'Writers who have an overwhelming wish to conceal their personal lives do not turn to autobiography.' Given this convenient postulated absence of rogues, Adams (1990:173) is able to end his critique by saying that 'autobiographers are not telling lies but telling their lives'.

Adams' study is limited to American autobiographers; he therefore does not comment on George Bernard Shaw (1970:1), who begins his autobiography with: 'All autobiographies are lies. I do not mean unconscious, unintentional lies: I mean deliberate lies.' Perhaps only someone as accomplished with words as Shaw would dare to make a Cretan of himself so uncompromisingly. Yet the outcome conforms to Adams' generalization, for his editor, Stanley Weintraub (1970:xvi), comments: 'Here is Shaw as he wanted the world to remember him ... perhaps the most likeable and entertaining G. B. S.' There is no self-delusion here, and adequate warning is given for the enjoyable deceptions that lie in wait for the duped reader. By framing his autobiography in this way, Shaw is in effect claiming for it the privilege of confabulation accorded to fiction, as discussed in chapter 9.

Should we try to avoid deceiving ourselves? We discuss the wider question of the social merits and demerits of lying in chapter 11, but the special characteristics of self-deception, when liar and dupe are the same individual, call for separate notice. The symposium edited by Lockard and Paulhus (1988) presents a cafeteria of observations and opinions on the advantages and disadvantages of self-deception. What is advantageous to an individual is not necessarily advantageous to his or her society or to the survival of the human species, and vice versa. Surveying the range of assertions made by contributors to the symposium, Paulhus (1988c:254) comments that 'only a Pollyanna would claim any consensus here'. He summarizes the 'mixed blessings' of self-deception by saying:

Self-deception promotes short-run psychological health and adaptive decisions. It also helps maintain the societal status quo, thus promoting political stability. Long-run psychological health and beneficial social change, however, are thereby constrained.

Simmel (1958:258) also recognizes the positive value of self-deception. He coined the term *Lebenslüge*, translated by Wolff as 'vital lie', to refer to the condition of the individual who is

so often in need of deceiving himself in regard to his capacities, even in regard to his feelings, and who cannot do without superstition about gods and men, in order to maintain his life and his potentialities. (Simmel 1950:310)

Simmel is here referring to self-deception and self-delusion, and maintains that 'we obtain the exact amounts of error and truth which constitute the basis of the conduct required of us . . .' Unfortunately, he does not spell out how this desirable mix is secured. Clearly, the optimal position is somewhere in the middle; but just where? There cannot be much of a case for self-delusion, for then a deceived person becomes unaware that he or she has been deceived. There is, however, a case for some self-deception, neither too little nor too much. Unfortunately, in the absence of accepted scales of measurement, all prescriptions for golden mean positions are vacuous. We shall encounter the same difficulty when we come to tackle the wider task of specifying an individually and socially optimal level for lying.

I have argued against the use of the term collusion for what is better described as collaboration or connivance in deceit. However, when a liar has associates who, despite their divergence of interests, are willing to help him or her deceive an enemy, we can speak of collusion in its more usual conspiratorial sense. Thus in our terminology we make a tripartite distinction between connivance, collaboration and collusion. If a dupe detects the deception but pretends that the lie has been successful, we have connivance. Connivance is inverted deceit; the dupe, no longer deceived, deceives the liar into thinking that the lie has succeeded. This is one-sided connivance. When a third party joins the dupe in the pretence, the connivance is shared. If the liar realizes that the lie has been detected and joins the dupe in the pretence that it has not, we have mutual connivance; both parties shut their eyes to the deceit attempted by the other. If their mutual connivance is more or less openly acknowledged by both parties, neither party is deceived; they join in a pretence. If they start to treat the pretence as authentic, they become self-deluded. Although this may be said to be a form of collaboration, a clearer and perhaps more stable form occurs when we have not an uneasy alliance of liar and dupe but cooperation by several liars. Basic and collusive lies, in Bailey's terms, are lies told by a plurality of liars, who are likely to be self-deceived or self-deluded. Finally we have collusion when several people with divergent interests combine to deceive a dupe. Friendship is sometimes said to be characterized by the ability of friends to tell one another the truth about themselves; friendship may also entail a willingness to collaborate in deceiving a common enemy.

This suggested terminology works reasonably well in sorting out patterns of deceit in those domains of social life where truthfulness is expected. On the other hand it might sound odd to speak of one side in a war conniving at the deceits attempted by the enemy, though this seems a reasonable way of describing what occurred with the German battleships mentioned earlier in this chapter.

CONNIVANCE

Connivance sometimes develops gradually and without any explicit acknowledgment that it is occurring. This possibility is discussed by Werth and Flaherty in a case involving a woman, identified as R2, who was deceived by her husband who had become sexually involved with someone else. R2 described her growing realization that she was being deceived:

It was like an atmosphere more than blatant evidence ... It is so hard to grab on to something and say, 'This is deceit', because it is just so much like a feeling you get when there is something amiss, something is wrong. It is in the atmosphere. It's just, and it might be ... an uneasiness from the other person that you just, you know something is wrong, that it can't be the truth, and it might just be sort of a sensation you get from nervousness or fidgetiness or uneasiness or it is like they can't hide it. A person who is deceiving can't hide that he is deceiving. There is a lot he can hide but he can't hide everything even if he is a master. (Werth and Flaherty 1986:297)

R2 also described her feelings about being deceived:

I felt sick to my stomach, nauseous. He was giving me this sense of something and it was going right to my gut ... It was funny things that just didn't, well, they seemed fishy. But when I think about it there was part of me that didn't want to believe they seemed fishy, so I wouldn't believe it. (Ibid.:296)

Here we see how the realization that she was being deceived by her husband was accompanied by a realization that also she had been deceiving herself by refusing to believe that she was being deceived. At least, this is how Werth and Flaherty characterize what happened. But clearly the labels 'deception' or 'deceit' are here being used in two distinct ways. The husband, we can assume, intended to deceive R2 about his involvement with another woman; he may well have told her lies. But we cannot reasonably assume that R2 *intended* to deceive herself in quite the same sense. We have to regard the wife as a multivocal personality, with one segment aware of the husband's deceit while another segment resists recognizing it and endeavours to believe it was not occurring. R2 described her internal struggle in graphic terms:

> Little by little things were happening that didn't make sense, but I can remember making excuses for them myself ... I didn't want to believe there was anything to find out ... so I was being deceived from two angles ... I was deceiving myself ... I didn't sit there when it was happening saying, 'I am just fooling myself'. You know, I, I, as I said, I made up a lot of excuses, and really believed them ... I didn't confide in anyone, too, because I was afraid of what they would tell me. I wanted to believe everything was going to be fine and I wasn't being deceived. If I told someone else they might tell me I was being deceived and I didn't want to hear that ... But as much as I wanted to be a detective and find him out, I didn't want to either. Because the truth, I was afraid more of the truth than living in the lie kind of. (Ibid.:296)

If we retain the notion of a multivocal personality, then R2's 'excuses' might perhaps be seen as lies told by her lying segment with the *intention* of deceiving her duped segment. I doubt if this perception adds much to our understanding of what is going on in R2's mind; intention and self-deception are concepts that fit together only with a dose of casuistry. For consistency, but at the cost of being pedantic, perhaps we should speak of 'pseudo-lies' when referring to inner-directed pretences whereby we come to deny what we believe, or used to believe, to be the truth.

More significant is R2's statement that she did not want to hear from other people that she was being deceived, and that therefore she did not confide in anyone. Kovar (1974:148) maintains that self-deceivers require the assistance of others to succeed but here we have an instance of a self-deceiving liar, some of whose lies were thought rather than spoken, who does not conform to this generalization. Was she afraid of being told that (1) she was being deceived by her husband, or (2) she was deceiving herself in refusing to admit to her husband's deceit? Perhaps both. In any case she was not expecting that other people would support the duped segment of her personality and join with her in pretending that her husband was not deceiving her. In this respect R2's situation differed sharply from that of the returned Lebanese migrant, referred to in chapter 6, whose relatives connived at his pretence that his wife had not been unfaithful to him during his absence overseas.

The absence of friends and relatives who might have shared her connivance may help to explain R2's feeling of powerlessness:

I felt totally out of control of the situation ... What was going to happen was in his hands ... Fear was there all the time, and anger and hurt ... I felt as if I was being experimented on, as part of the apparatus. I felt so used to achieve his ends. I was a means to his ends ... Because it was so degrading and so hard on my self-esteem I felt I wasn't in any position to do anything about it. I didn't trust my own power, my own ability. I began to really feel was I really worth it. (Ibid.:305)

Later, R2 came to accept that her husband was deceiving her. This brought a sense of relief:

It was like a weight, you know, had been taken off my shoulders. As much as I feared finding out the truth, when I did it was a release. It was like, whew, the worst is over ... It wasn't just a question any more. (Ibid.:306)

In other words, whereas before there had been two deceptions, now there was only one; the inner conflict had been resolved. However, more deceit lay ahead for R2. Her husband's lover tried to deceive her about the existence of the extra-marital relation:

She was pretending there was nothing going on also ... She would call him. She even called me a couple of times ... to find out things about him but never said that was her intention. She said she just wanted to say 'hi' and then she would get off the phone and report to him about how self-righteous I was. (Ibid.:300–301)

R2 responded to this attempt at deceit by retaliating in kind. She tried to give the impression to her rival that her marriage was more rewarding than it really was. This led to a state in which she and the other woman jointly connived at the man's deceit:

I had words with her and it was like we both knew this was going on and we didn't let on that we knew ... We were talking about the weather as far as our conversation was going, but there was a lot more going on. And I was aware of it and she was aware of it ... Although we never talked right on the subject, I talked about how much I cared about him ... giving her messages that I was not about to give him up, for her or anybody else, although never actually coming out and saying it, nor she asking. (Ibid.:301)

Yet despite the shared connivance, R2 did not feel that she was being deceived by her rival:

... I didn't feel deceived by her, at least I didn't feel the emotional impact of being deceived ... (Ibid.)

Nor did R2 feel at the time that she was herself engaged in deceit:

And I was deceiving her but it wasn't something that I was consciously aware of, at all ... At the time I didn't feel I was deceiving her. (Ibid.:302)

Unfortunately we have only R2's account of her relations with her husband and the other woman; maybe they had a clearer picture at the time of what was going on. Nevertheless, even if the testimony is one-sided, it illustrates vividly how inadequate an analysis of deceit would be that ignored the dialectical relation between liar and dupe, and which assumed that at all times individuals have clearly defined intentions to deceive and unambiguous perceptions of being deceived. Lies told in the public sphere may perhaps be used more readily to achieve defined goals, without the complications of feedback and internal conflicts, but where intimate interpersonal links are infected with deceit, self-deception, connivance and shared connivance are likely to occur.

One interesting feature of the above account is that R2 seemed not to place a high value on her relation to her husband, except in the context of appearing to compete with the other woman for her husband's affection. She said: 'But I got very competitive with her, very competitive', even though 'around [my husband] I had no feeling of self-worth and I had low self-esteem' (Ibid.:301).

Data such as these lead Werth and Flaherty to postulate several propositions about deceptive relations. I have mentioned their notion that dupes, on discovering that they are being deceived, initially respond to the discovery by denying that the deceit exists. In the second phase, the deceit is acknowledged and appropriate action may follow. Deception in a dyadic relation may ramify to involve other people, whether as joint connivers or collaborators in lying or as the initiators of separate deceits. The deceptive relation also expands in a different sense, encompassing the whole of the lives of the dupes; 'it was as though it was a twenty-four-hour-a-day thing', said R2 (Ibid.:302). The feelings generated by the deception are often intense, and sometimes conflict with one another. A variety of reasons may be given by dupes to explain why they continue in relations in which they are being knowingly deceived, or, to put the matter more pedantically, why persons maintain relations with others whom they realize persist in trying to deceive them and at whose deceit they connive.

In general, connivance, whereby the dupe pretends that he or she has not been deceived and behaves as if the lie was true, is a deceitful act, for the liar is deceived about the success of the lie. Nevertheless the dupe's response may be welcomed by the liar, since it conveys the message that the lie has succeeded. One-sided connivance may cause anguish in the dupe, and this may persist even if the connivance becomes mutual, with the liar merely pretending that the lie has succeeded.

Open collaboration may be welcomed when liar and dupe are in a relation of equality but is less likely to be the case in relations of inequality, as for example in relations between parents and young children. Here connivance occurs more often than open collaboration, though children may collaborate with their parents in deceiving someone else. Parents may perceive the lies they tell to children as unsuccessful if the children connive at the deceit and merely feign being deceived; parents may then consider that it is the children who are liars, not the parents, because the former are trying to deceive the latter about the success of their deceit. Eck (1970:71) tells the story of one of his patients, an adopted child. The adopting parents deceived the child by telling him that he was their natural son. He eventually discovered their deceit but did not reveal his discovery to them. When, in Eck's presence, the child did tell the parents, they exclaimed angrily: 'What! you little liar! You knew we weren't telling you the truth and didn't tell us!'

In discussing self-deception and self-delusion we have focussed our attention on two very different instances of lying, by policy makers in the Pentagon and by some distressed American women. These complex phenomena do not occur only in these two disparate contexts, and these data should alert us to the likely conflation of liar and dupe in many other situations. John Locke's comment, mentioned in chapter 1, that 'men find pleasure to be deceived' applies not only to lies told by others but also to the lies told by oneself. Furthermore, one way of enhancing the likelihood that a lie will not be detected is for the liar to believe the lie to be true. There are thus good reasons why many liars should succeed in deceiving not only their dupes but also themselves. Our examples show that this outcome may entail serious costs, for liars and dupes alike.

8

Telling and detecting lies

SOCIALIZATION AND PERSONALITY

The ability to tell lies and the complementary ability to detect them, which so far in our discussion we have taken for granted, do not appear fully fashioned in every newborn child. They develop gradually as part of the process of growing up, along with the socially based knowledge of when to make use of these abilities. In this chapter we look at how children grow into adults capable of telling lies, and at how the dissemination of success-ful lies is facilitated by certain characteristics of language.

Children do not always spontaneously speak the truth. In many cul-tures, though perhaps not in all, a considerable amount of effort is put into training children to be honest, or at least in teaching them *when* to be honest. In some communities, moral and physical pressure is augmented by threats of supernatural sanctions against lying, such as being struck dead by lightning, the growth of a tree on one's tongue (Vincenzi 1977:40) or the elongation of one's nose, like Pinocchio. Rather less cultural empha-sis is placed on the desirability of parents being honest with their children, and many commentators regard some of the lies told by adults to children, such as that storks bring babies, and that Father Christmas brings presents, as excusable and even desirable. Comparing the extent of parental inter-vention in two areas of children's behaviour, and writing presumably with reference to practices in the United States, Aronfreed (1969:308) writes that:

Punishment may be used more intensively on conduct that is relevant to honesty or responsibility than it is in the area of achievement.

This allocation of parental effort is not found in all cultures. Ackerman (1990:3) reports that among the Quechua-speaking mestizo group in Peru among whom she worked:

Teasing is a form of play which uses lies as an exercise of the imagination and which tests the credulity of the listener. Teasing plays an important part in the socialization of children, and I never heard of children being punished for lying.

Ackerman (1990:2) says that in the course of her research she encountered numerous instances of lying, Yet, she says,

people seldom complained about being lied to. It was constantly emphasized that when lying involved two parties, the burden of finding the truth fell on the person lied to.

Its somewhat unusual customary assignment of responsibility may perhaps explain the absence from Quechua society of sanctions against lies told by children. Most of the evidence available on children's lying comes, of course, from cultures where these sanctions are applied; the absence of sanctions is probably under-reported. In many cultures, some of children's lies are regarded as bad, while others are regarded as harmless or acceptable. Explicit injunctions for children to lie are probably also under-reported, though this seems to have been the case in ancient Sparta (Hall 1890:63). There is, however, a widespread understanding that children should be actively discouraged from always spontaneously blurting out the whole truth, from telling 'Aunt Martha that she is fat, or Uncle John that he has bad breath', as Alexander (1987:198) puts it. If he has only adults in mind, Ekman (1985:279) may be right to claim that 'a school for liars would not make sense', but children have to learn how to lie acceptably if they are to develop into fully encultured adults. As Lewis and his colleagues (1989:442) say: 'Although parents tell their children not to lie, they also inform them both directly and indirectly that deception is socially appropriate'. These authors claim that their experimental evidence of cheating and lying by three-year-olds in a psychology laboratory supports the role of socialization in developing the ability to mask emotional expressions. This may well be the case, though it seems unlikely that middle- and upper-class Caucasian parents in New Jersey, the site of the investigation, socialize their children into thinking that deceiving experimental psychologists is 'socially appropriate'.

Children may well have to learn how to lie effectively, but the ability, and probably the propensity, to deceive seem to develop spontaneously. As Eck (1970:4) says, 'the very young child is capable of deceptive behavior long before the development of language'.

The acquisition of speech brings many new possibilities. One of the ways in which children learn to make full use of the potentialities of language for deception is through verbal fantasy. A hundred years ago Compayré (1902:197), commenting on the young child, wrote that:

> In the first awakening of his imagination he delights in fiction, and he plays with words as he plays with sand, ... he makes sentences without thought for reality, ...

Similarly Dunn (1980:205) describes how in the speech of young children in England and America, verbal fantasy is 'one of the dominant aspects'. Through engaging in fantasy, children learn that words can be liberated from 'the here and now', as Rappaport (1979:180) puts it, and hence can, if this is what is wanted, be used to deceive. If this linguistic potentiality is combined with that 'delight in transgression and confrontation evident early in the second year' the stage is set for telling lies, for 'playing with names or with the truth' (Dunn 1988:160, 163). Perez (1885:87) comments that: 'A child of two years who says to me: "I have just seen a butterfly as large as a cat, as large as the house," is telling for fun what he knows to be a falsehood.'

Is this deceit? The same question can be asked of an incident reported by Valentine (1938:286) in which a child of fourteen months pretended to be hurt in order to get a kiss. Rather than seeing them as attempts to deceive, it seems more plausible to regard these actions by young children as invitations to adults to join in a fantasy. Valentine calls the child's action 'pretence play', a categorization validated by the child's action a month later of bumping 'her doll's head and bringing it to be kissed'. De Villiers and de Villiers (1978:164–165) report as typical a child aged three or four rushing forward as his mother arrives and saying determinedly 'I didn't break the lamp' before anyone claimed that he had done so, thus revealing that he was the culprit. This incident they regard as an example of an 'immature' form of lying.

LaFrenière (1988:251) has constructed a developmental taxonomy of deceptive behaviour in pre-school children, based partly on observations, presumably made in Quebec, and partly on other inquiries; deceit becomes more complex as age increases. Experimental evidence from the United States indicates that about half American three-year-olds can tell lies with enough control of their facial muscles to avoid detection (Lewis et al. 1989). Thus the evidence indicates that, beginning early, children gradually increase in efficiency as liars.

The link between lies and fantasy, to which Ferenczi (1955:77–80) draws attention, can be seen in adult life in the lying competitions sometimes organized for amusement and/or to raise money; we refer to these in chapter 9. Recognition of the connection between fantasy and deceit is not restricted to liberal-oriented developmental psychologists; the link is also seen by members of subcultures in which the exercise of imagination is met with disapproval. John and Elizabeth Newson (1968:189) note that among a sample of English urban working-class mothers in the 1960s, a minority distrusted 'an imagination which, they believe, might later lead the child into plain dishonesty'. One woman in this category, who almost certainly was unaware of Plato's (1966 Books 2 & 10) condemnation of imaginative writers, said that she tried to stop her four-year old son from telling imaginary stories 'because I didn't want him to go from an imaginary story to a downright lie – because there's not much difference between the two'. The opposite point of view is presented in a recent book about lying designed to be read by young children. Joy Berry (1988) distinguishes carefully between fantasies (untrue stories told for fun), mistakes (things you thought were true when you said them but which you later discovered were not) and lies; fantasies and mistakes are allowable but lies are not.

The evidence I have cited on processes of childhood socialization comes from England and America; similar processes of learning when to lie and when not to presumably take place everywhere. Yet though the development of the abilities to lie and to detect lies may be more or less uniform for all human groups, there are likely to be significant variations between one culture and another in how these abilities are used. In England there are marked differences between social classes in regard to fantasy, with Nottingham middle-class mothers in the Newson study more supportive of their children's fantasies than working-class mothers; these findings were repeated a decade later in Leeds by Dunn (1980:210–211). Whether attitudes to lying also differ is not clear. Parental responses to children's fantasies are not the only aspects of child-rearing that influence children's lies. Ammar (1954:138–139), in his study of the socialization of rural Egyptian children, echoes Rousseau in attributing the tendency of children to tell lies to the 'techniques of fear' used by their parents, particularly their fathers, to discipline them.

There may be differences between boys and girls in the training they receive in honesty and deceit. In a study of schoolchildren in Iowa City, USA, Castaneda and others (1956) found that girls scored higher than boys on a scale designed to measure the tendency to falsify responses to a questionnaire about anxiety. Likewise Albert (1972:77) reports that in Burundi upper-caste girls used to be trained in 'artful silence and evasiveness', qualities significantly absent from the socialization of their brothers.

Training in deceit is not confined to 'artful silence' either in Burundi or elsewhere. Albert (1972:84) mentions that 'The Rundi technique for avoiding an unwanted visitor is familiar: a child or servant is sent to announce that nobody is at home'. This technique is familiar indeed; in chapter 3 we noted its use in early eighteenth-century England. As formerly in England, maybe an announcement of this kind deceived no-one in the highly formal culture of pre-revolution Burundi which Albert studied. But similar announcements nowadays must surely be often made deceptively by children who have been trained or ordered by their parents to do so. They may even be told to cross their fingers behind their back when telling the lie. Social lies may well be perceived by all adults for what they are, but children have to learn which lies are harmless and social and which are not.

Dunn and Wooding (1977:46) draw attention to the evidence that imaginative play by infants begins earlier at home than it does in psychological laboratories. Whether similar differences exist between the propensity of children to lie in laboratories and their behaviour in the real world of home and peer group awaits inquiry, since few, if any, of the studies of children's lies carried out by developmental psychologists have been conducted outside laboratories. There are ethical constraints on the extent to which children, for experimental purposes, can be tempted to tell lies, and considerable ingenuity is called for in designing ethically acceptable inquiries. The lies that are elicited are usually little lies rather than big, in the sense that their consequences for the dupe are not serious; indeed if the apparent dupe is the investigating psychologist, he or she may well be regarded as fair game. When 40 per cent of Hopi children cheated on an academic task, the experimenters commented: 'Academic achievement tests may have low salience in their Hopi moral system' (Burton and Reis 1981:685). In any case, lying at the behest of the experimenting psychologist must surely often be perceived as what DePaulo and Jordan (1982:169) call 'sanctioned deceit', as is called for in many children's games, and therefore may be handled differently from authentically deceitful lying. A hundred years ago Hall (1890:59) drew attention to what he called 'certain current and more or less licensed forms of juvenile dishonesty connected with modern school life', but the continued existence of these permitted deviations from official norms is often overlooked.

Although a good deal of research has been carried out, mainly in the United States, into the development in children of the ability to tell lies successfully (Feldman and Custrini 1988 and references therein), we have very little systematic evidence about how children learn the social skill of telling the right lie at the right time and place. For instance, DePaulo and Jordan (1982:176) note that 'when children get old enough to be accountable for courtesy, ... it is costly for [them] *not* to tell lies'. Evidence on how children become aware of social constraints on honesty would be welcome. My guess is that many of them learn more from their peers (who teach them how to be acceptably bad) than from their parents (who tend to teach how to be acceptably good). But research is needed to discover how lying skills are acquired, along with such common childhood tricks as crossing one's fingers behind one's back (so that the action is not seen by the dupe), or putting one's left hand on one's right shoulder (Hall 1890:68), thus to gain immunity from the secular and religious consequences of having lied. We need more observations like that made of American children by G. S. Hall over a century ago, that 'To nod is less sinful than to say yes; to point the wrong way when asked where someone has gone is less guilty than to *say* wrongly' (Hall 1890:69). Is this because the meaning we attribute to a nod is imprecise and ill-defined, or is it that we attach to words a quality of commitment that hearing individuals, unlike deaf signers, do not associate with gestures?

Psychologists interested in lying have concentrated their attention on children and adolescents and have published relatively little on the connection between lying and the psychological attributes of adults. An exception to this neglect is a recent study by Sandi Smith and others (1990:101) of qualitative differences in lying between individuals who vary in how much they monitor their own thoughts and actions. They found that under certain conditions high self-monitors in their sample were more able to deceive other people than were low self-monitors.

HOW TO TELL LIES

Given the available evidence on socialization, it seems reasonable to assume that children develop their potential for lying as they grow older more or less automatically. To assume that they automatically achieve success with their lies is much less plausible. How do children learn to lie successfully? Presumably they do so as a part of the wider task of learning to handle language with increasing skill and confidence. Indeed, de Villiers and de Villiers (1978:164) make what they describe as a scandalous claim, that the ultimate achievement of a child's progressive mastery of the intricacies of discourse is 'to lie effectively' (cf. DePaulo and Jordan 1982:167). As noted earlier, there are reports of very young children telling lies, in some cases failing dismally to achieve deception.

Learning to lie has to be seen as part of the wider process of learning to deceive. This involves, among other things, learning to transcend contextual cues, whether or not any lies are uttered. Thus to gain maximum benefit from an exceptionally good hand at cards, a player has to learn to inhibit expressions of excitement and delight that might arise spontaneously. Poker faces do not arise naturally but have to be acquired by self-discipline. In the language of the psychologists, 'the deceiver must be able deliberately to encode disappointment' (DePaulo and Jordan 1982:168). Furthermore, would-be successful liars have to learn to 'monitor the listener's responses for signs of skepticism and then [to] modify the message accordingly'. DePaulo and Jordan go on to suggest that 'children perhaps begin by mastering certain fairly rigid deceptive routines within certain contexts; subsequently, they may learn a variety of deceptive techniques, which become increasingly adapted to the characteristics of their listeners'.

These are suggestions as to what happens, rather than empirical findings. Indeed, the same authors comment further that children may also learn to simulate expressions that they do not feel either in a natural manner or with exaggeration; alternatively, they may learn to feign a neutral expression. In other words, children may learn to deny, distort, evade, fail to respond, make things up, introduce irrelevancies and omit important information. DePaulo and Jordan suggest that because denial is 'the most cognitively simple' of these tactics,it may be acquired early in the process of development but for the rest all they can say is that 'The order of development of the other strategies is best left to empirical testing'.

As far as I know, this empirical testing has not yet been undertaken. A likely candidate for early inclusion in the child's repertoire of strategies, at least in Christian cultures where guilt is salient, is the ploy mentioned earlier of crossing one's fingers, thus making the sign of the cross and avoiding God's displeasure at the sin of lying. Others are those that Pascal condemned when they were employed by casuistic Jesuits in the seventeenth century (Pascal 1967:140). These include equivocation and 'mental restriction' or 'mental reservation' (Kerr 1990:116), whereby the liar qualifies the spoken statement with an unspoken clause, or uses an ambiguous expression, that turns falsehood into truth. Ruskin (1905:352) calls statements of this kind 'false lies' and draws attention to the execration directed in classical Greece at Euripides' alleged advocacy of this mode of deceit (cf. D'Israeli 1791 (1):203). Bailey (1991:2) regards 'mental reservation' as the adult equivalent of crossing one's fingers, but its use is not confined to adults. 'I didn't take the biscuit' is all that is said aloud but this apparent lie is converted into a true statement by the addition of an unspoken thought: 'before breakfast'.

Variation in the extent and subtlety of lying is however, not determined solely by the ability of the growing child. The prevalence of lying varies with the social context, as we have seen earlier with our discussion of lying in different domains. Analogous variations for children were demonstrated in the classic studies of 11,000 American children carried out by Hartshorne and May in the 1920s. The children, aged from eight to sixteen years, were studied mainly for their propensity to cheat, but two of the tests measured lying. The data (Hartshorne and May 1928:94–103) indicate that lying and other morally charged actions are highly situationally specific (cf. Burton 1976:174–176).

Along with the development of these skills there is likely to be some change in the 'affects and attitudes that are associated with deceit'. The fear of getting caught might come early, to be followed later by feelings of guilt or shame or what DePaulo and Jordan (1982:169) refer to as 'evaluation apprehension'.

The Mach scale of personality characteristics was constructed in the late 1950s to provide psychologists with a way of classifying children in terms of how they manifest feelings of this kind. The scale purports to measure the extent to which, in his or her interpersonal relations, an individual follows the precepts of Machiavelli, operationalized, roughly speaking, as a lack of affect in interpersonal relationships, a lack of concern with conventional morality, a lack of gross psychopathology and a low ideological commitment (Christie 1970:3–4). Experimental psychological studies carried out in America in the 1960s show that children with high Mach scores engage in deceptive manipulative acts with 'an aura of emotional detachment' (DePaulo et al. 1985:341; cf. DePaulo and Rosenthal 1979:1717–1718; DePaulo et al. 1980; Exline et al. 1970). Low scorers are distinguished from high scorers by their ineptness but not by their moral unwillingness to deceive.

There are also gender differences in the deceits of high Mach children. In the experiments little girls with high Mach scores tended to tell omissive lies by withholding information and evading questions, whereas high Mach boys tended to tell commissive lies by distorting information. Commissive lies told by boys were more often successful than were the commissive lies told by girls. A somewhat similar gender difference has been detected in adults. When they are lying, women tend to make comments that are more evasive and noncommittal than those they make when telling the truth, whereas with men the difference is not so great.

One of the many contexts in which these skills and associations are gradually acquired is play, particularly games in which the rules invite or require the practice of deception. Even a game as simple as a staring contest may provide practice in the control of non-verbal behaviour. DePaulo and Jordan point out, however, that 'deception in children's games is sanctioned deceit' and that therefore any feelings of guilt or shame, or even of 'evaluation apprehension', that are present are probably not as important to the child as joy at fooling others. In his paper 'Button button who's got the button?' (1980) Sacks analyses vividly the complexity and significance of the lessons children learn in games. Important differences exist between games and the ordinary world; for example, games are usually played with friends, whereas outside the context of games deceit may be attempted on and experienced from non-friends as well. Another difference is that, in a game, all the players are aware that deceit is ubiquitous, whereas in real life an initial presumption of honesty and authenticity is more likely to hold. A further point of difference noted by DePaulo and Jordan (1982:169) is that 'in most games, the probable object or content of the deceit is also usually known'. By this they mean that, for example, in the button game the focus of the deceit is the location of the button; in other games the deceit is focussed on the location or identity of a playing card. In real life, deceit can focus on anything whatsoever.

Given these differences, we might expect that skills used in game-based deception cannot be transferred easily to real-life situations. Alternatively, games might be seen as a sheltered training ground for real-life deceit. DePaulo and Jordan favour the latter view, and outline what part games would play in a hypothetical programme for teaching skills in deception.

One way a liar can hope to reduce both the chances of being detected, and any feelings of guilt that may arise from lying, is to tell what Max Black (1983:133–134) calls a 'virtual' lie. These are statements that, taken at their face value, may be true. They are deceptive because of the implicatures, in Grice's (1989:24–26) terms, that they carry and which, the liar can confidently assume, will be attached to them by those who hear them. For instance, during the Second World War, the British Admiralty said in a communiqué that, following an airborne torpedo attack, the German battleship *Tirpitz* left the scene of the action 'under a thick pall of smoke'. In that context, the implication of the communiqué is clear: the battleship had been damaged by the torpedoes and was on fire. The communiqué was a virtual lie, since in fact no torpedo reached its target. Likewise, on another occasion, the Admiralty announced that a Mediterranean convoy, after being attacked by German and Italian aircraft, had reached Malta safely. The statement carried the implication that the attack had been unsuccessful. The statement was true, but only in the sense that those ships in the convoy that reached Malta were then safer than they had been while en route. The statement was also deceptive, concealing the fact that two-thirds of the vessels in the convoy had been sunk, a fact indubitably already known by the enemy.

The most secure way of avoiding the danger of detection is, however, to put the lie into an innocent, or at least unwitting, mouth. This is lying by proxy. It is illustrated with admirable clarity by Vice-Admiral Poindexter (*Washington Post* 1987) in his testimony to the US Senate committee investigating the Irangate affair:

I made a very deliberate decision not to ask the President so that I could insulate him from the decision and provide some future deniability for the President if it ever leaked out.

Q. And when you say 'deniability', are you saying that your decision was not to tell the President so that he would be able to deny that he knew of it?

A. That's correct.

Thus, assuming that Reagan was ignorant of the plan to funnel money received from arms sales to Iran to the Nicaraguan Contras, a statement from him that he did not know of the existence of a plan would be true but would carry the false implication that there was no such plan. The implication was strengthened by the belief, held by Poindexter and doubtless many others, that if Reagan had heard of the plan, he would have approved of it. Thus 'deniability' is essentially an attribute for facilitating lying by proxy. In bureaucratic terms, we have a form of division of labour which entails a very unequal division of moral responsibility.

But suppose Reagan did have a vague notion that some such plan was being contemplated by his officials, though he did not know whether or not a definite plan had been drawn up? Or suppose he had even suggested something like the plan and then had heard no more about it from his staff? We would then have the situation in which Reagan, by saying that he did not know of the plan, would be engaged in deceit along with Poindexter and his crew. The only excuse for Reagan in these circumstances is to make the somewhat improbable, but not inconceivable, assumption that he would not have realized that his statement carried the implication most people would attach to it. But making that assumption merely opens the way to saying that Reagan was not to be believed, whatever he said. The quip contrasting Reagan with Washington and Nixon, noted in chapter 2, would be confirmed.

Common understandings about when to expect lies, even though we may sometimes by mistake treat as a lie a statement made without any intention to deceive, constitute part of the culture of the community and are learnt in the normal process of socialization. Children delight in playing games in which they are expected to trick one another; they argue about how to signal whether or not these expectations are in force. Problems arise when we try to interpret a new situation. However homogeneous the community, and however well we have absorbed its culture, there are bound to be, from time to time, occasions when we are in doubt about whether the principle of veracity has been suspended, and about what special code applies in its place. The incident reported by Gilsenan, mentioned in chapter 5, when he was told that his friend had been shot, is an excellent example of this uncertainty. In this incident, the uncertainty was resolved when the young men bringing the news swore 'by your life', thus providing the cue that signalled which code they were using.

In Tarski's (1956:167; cf. Jakobson 1981:25) terminology, such cues belong to a metalanguage used for indicating the code that is in use. When several different codes are available, deception can take the form of speaking authentically in one code, in the expectation that it will be misheard as a message in a different code. In Gilsenan's case, we have an example of a special area, in this case an island of veracity in a sea of deception, defined linguistically. Verbal cues take the place of spatial markers, such as the four walls of parliament and the courts, or temporal markers, such as the proclaimed dates of an election campaign or the calendar defining April Fool's Day.

In a society where deception is expected, telling the truth can be a way of lying. For example, a man A asks another man B where he is going the next day, in a context in which A expects that B will try to deceive him. B does indeed hope to deceive A; but he also knows that A expects to be deceived, and takes advantage of his knowledge. This he does by replying truthfully to A's question. He says 'I am going to X', confident that A will interpret this message wrongly as really meaning 'The place I am going to is not X; I am only trying to deceive you by saying that I'm going there.' This configuration of expectations forms the basis of a traditional Jewish joke, presented by Freud (1960:115) as the paradigm of what he called the sceptical subclass of tendentious jokes. As told by Freud:

Two Jews met in a railway carriage at a station in Galicia. 'Where are you going?' asked one. 'To Cracow,' was the answer. 'What a liar you are!' broke out the other. 'If you say you're going to Cracow, you want me to believe you're going to Lemberg. But I know that in fact you're going to Cracow. So why are you lying to me?'

Max Black (1983:133) calls this 'the classical Minsk–Pinsk joke'.

Saint Augustine (1952:57–59) presents a similar hypothetical situation, discussing casuistically whether or not telling the truth deceptively constitutes lying. Siegler (1966:130–132) gives other examples of lying by telling the truth, and discusses their logical significance; Vincent and Castelfranchi (1981) look at the phenomenon from the point of view of linguistics, and discuss how Iago deceives Othello in Shakespeare's play. Roberts (1972:92) gives further examples from literature. Mark Twain (1899:266) says simply: 'Often, the surest way to convey misinformation is to tell the strict truth.'

Even more complex examples of metadeception can be found in many detective and spy novels. In these situations, the literal truth of the message provides a sure indication neither as to whether the speaker intends to deceive nor as to whether the hearer will perceive the message as a lie.

On the other hand, in situations when people expect not to be told the truth, the intention to deceive may be absent even when false statements are made. Douglas (1976:67) describes how 'in any casual sex scene, such as a nude beach or pick-up bar', there is 'widespread lying' about last names, occupations and addresses. But is this lying? The members, or participants, have, says Douglas, 'the shared goal of concealment' and therefore 'support each other's lies', and joke about them. Thus it seems that in these contexts untrue statements about personal identities are expected and that no-one is deceived by them; any intention to deceive, if it exists at all, must necessarily be very faint-hearted.

Another problem arises when the community is not homogeneous, or when strangers arrive. If the understandings about truthtelling and lying are not shared, there are likely to be accusations of bad faith and of attempts to deceive. These misunderstandings are a recognized hazard of field research in cultures other than one's own, exemplified by Bailey's Indian experience cited in chapter 5. Such problems are certainly not the monopoly of the social scientist; many a tourist has felt cheated and deceived when promises made by local inhabitants are not fulfilled because, in the minds of those who made them, they were never intended to be taken literally. Herbert Passin, an American anthropologist who worked among a group of Mexican Indians in the 1940s, has provided a full account of the lies he was told. There was, he says, a systematic denial of the ownership of economic goods, and yet, in other contexts, he also encountered exaggerated claims about the extent of a person's wealth. Like many other societies, the group he studied had a well-elaborated belief in sorcery. Yet his informants often denied involvement in the network of sorcery accusations, or even denied the very existence of sorcery. Passin comments that we can understand these deceptive responses by speculating upon the responses we would get in our own culture if we were to ask someone 'Whom do you hate? Who hates you? Whom would you like to kill?' He also mentions the lies he was told about activities the Mexican administration treated as illegal but which the local Indian community regarded as right and proper; again we can see analogies in other cultures (Passin 1942).

The possibilities for successful lying are indeed numerous and diverse. We have looked at some of the variations in tactics and techniques and at some of the constraints imposed by context and culture. Within these parameters, there are likely to be significant differences between one individual and another. Yet, apart from the special case of pathological liars, little work has been done on discovering why some people tell more lies and have more success in lying than do their neighbours. The effectiveness of diverse pedagogical recipes for honesty awaits testing. For instance, earlier in this chapter we mentioned that some mothers in Nottingham posited that tolerance of fantasy in childhood leads to lying in adulthood. It would be helpful to discover whether this is true.

LANGUAGE

Success in telling lies depends in large part on exploiting the possibilities inherent in natural languages. Refusing to call a spade a spade is not necessarily an attempt at deception, but if we substitute for one phrase another which carries connotations which mislead, then we may well be engaged in deceit. A rose by any other name may smell as sweet, but a war may seem less sour if it is called an 'international armed conflict', the Pentagon term for the carnage in Vietnam. That war saw the use of numerous other euphemisms used to reduce the impact of its horrors: for instance, 'take out' for 'kill and destroy', and 'new life hamlet' for 'refugee camp'. Terms such as these anaesthetize us more selectively than the simple use of traditional metaphors. Wat (1988:174) describes this process as 'a vast enterprise to deform language' and says that it is 'deeply and subtly oppressive'. In chapter 3 we referred to the use of 'neutralizing vocabularies' by civilian bureaucrats; the same process was a key element in the system of oppression sketched by Orwell (1984) in *1984*. For the real world Max Black (1955:289) comments:

> the vocabulary of chess has its primary uses in a highly artificial setting, where all expression of feeling is formally excluded: to describe a battle as if it were a game of chess is accordingly to exclude, by the choice of language, all the more emotionally disturbing aspects of warfare.

An alert reader, listener or viewer is not necessarily deceived by the use of metaphor, nor do those who use anaesthetizing metaphors necessarily intend to deceive. Nevertheless, when many members of the audience are likely to be deceived, it is also likely that metaphors will be used by those who wish to deceive. The nightly use by the BBC, in its bulletins during the Falklands fighting, of a format similar to that used for analysing chess tournaments is a good example. Was the format chosen by default or with conscious deceptive intent? In the case of the Vietnam War, euphemisms were employed by policy makers or their subordinates; were they trying to deceive and, if so, whom? During the Gulf War linguistic anaesthetization was supplemented by a close control of visual imagery shown on television, aimed at 'the erasure of the human body from the picture' (Mitchell 1992:7). The domestic use of television screens for playing videogames further enhances the ease with which the reality of high-tech warfare is transformed into just another game.

But because some people are deceived by these euphemisms and dysphemisms, we cannot infer that those who employ them necessarily intend to deceive. Our ailing pet animals are 'put down' rather than 'killed' or 'murdered', yet we do not perceive these descriptions as deceitful. Some of the linguistic usages of bureaucrats seem to arise spontaneously in the cloistered environment in which these officials conduct their business, and their pronouncements become deceptive only when these are mistaken for ordinary discourse. Indeed, one of the aims of Orwell's Newspeak project was to eliminate the possibility of 'ordinary' discourse. Yet though bureaucrats may not be self-deceived and may not intend to deceive others, their use of euphemisms facilitates the deception of the general public.

Similarly no deceit may be involved in making statements that, taken literally, are untrue if in fact no-one does take them literally. For example, Albert (1972:82) reports on Burundi that:

If an underling quietly accepts an order, there is a good chance that he is showing respect but has no intention of carrying out the order. On the other hand, if he gets his resentment out of his system by shouting protest and refusal and by drawing his superior into a noisy quarrel, he is almost certain at the end to do as he has been told.

From Albert's account, it appears that both parties understand the conventions and no deceit is involved. Likewise when someone says 'I went to X's house but there was no beer', everyone understands that there was beer but not enough for the speaker's liking (Albert 1972:95).

In Western culture, examples galore of deceitful manipulations of language are to be found on the pages of newspapers, in the statements of radio newscasters, and in other mass communication media; the politicians and public relations officials discussed in chapter 2 have many emulators. William Randolph Hearst is said to have been the inventor of yellow journalism at the end of the nineteenth century, but the tradition that he developed and popularized goes back a long way. Nevertheless the lies told in the media do not, I think, differ significantly from those we have already examined in other contexts. Presenting a bouquet of lies from the media might add to our amusement but would not advance our analysis.

> A page of *The Times* the Devil read,
> And he flung it down – 'Ahem'!
> 'I'm the father of lies, I know', he said,
> 'But I'm damn'd if I father them'.
>
> (Smith 1973:92)

This piece of verse by William James Linton, published in the *Red Republican* in 1850, can serve as an adequate comment on lying in the mass communications media.

HOW TO DETECT LIES

Given the prevalence of lies, it is obviously an advantage to be able to detect them. Does skill in lying imply skill in detecting lies? The evidence suggests that it does not. On the basis of a laboratory experiment with forty adults, DePaulo and Rosenthal (1979:1717) come to the conclusion that 'the ability to get away with one's own lies seems to be completely unrelated to the ability to catch other people in their lies'.

Children start to tell lies at an early age; what about their ability to detect lies told them by other people? DePaulo and Jordan (1982) summarize the findings of psychological research, carried out almost exclusively in laboratories, by saying that the results are not very flattering; maybe the studies underestimate children's ability to detect lies because of their laboratory provenance. The laboratory findings do not sit well with the experience of most parents in the home. There are two distinctions that children have to learn to make. They have to distinguish between fact and fantasy, and between truthfulness and deceit. The former contrast seems to be recognized first. From an early age most Western children, at least, have to learn to distinguish cows that jump over the moon and dishes that run away with the spoon from cows and dishes that do neither of these things. Discussing the development of the imagination, Repina (1971:263) reports:

Investigations of Soviet, as well as a series of foreign authors, indicate that no matter how clear or emotional the child's imaginative images, he nevertheless distinguishes quite clearly the imaginary from the realistically perceived.

Yet if most children succeed in making this distinction, how is it that so many parents are able to sustain well into school age their children's belief in Father Christmas, flying reindeer and chimney descents? Is it that children soon learn to connive at this pretence? Or is it that Christmas gifts, unlike moon-leaping cows, do actually arrive and require some sort of explanation. Father Christmas can be seen many times over in department stores, giving support to the deceit; similarly babies appear and real storks fly in the sky, even though none appears to be carrying a baby, whereas dishes and spoons remain obstinately static. Unfortunately most of the research conducted by psychologists into the ability of children to detect deceit, to distinguish truthfulness from deceit, has been done with deceits constructed for the occasion in the laboratory, rather than with material drawn from the ambient culture. In these experiments the ability to discern that deception is being attempted (deception accuracy) is distinguished from the ability to identify the true but concealed state of the liar's mind (leakage accuracy). Like adults, children look for compatibility between what is said and how it is said when deciding whether a speaker is being sincere or is lying, using what is referred to as a 'verbal–nonverbal consistency principle' (Rotenberg et al. 1989). Use of this principle increases with age. Children in the laboratory, it seems, do better at detection when both verbal and vocal cues are present; they are probably better at recognizing vocal non-verbal cues than at understanding facial expressions. They are likely to do better at detection when contextual cues are available as well as message cues, when the deceptive communication is truly interactive and extends over time, when the task of detecting deception is very involved and is a task at which children have had extensive practice, and when the deceivers are persons familiar to the children rather than strangers. DePaulo and Jordan (1982:169) note that these favourable conditions are present in many popular games and sports.

At secondary-school age, skill in detecting deceit may have some adverse consequences, for both boys and girls. Students who were particularly skilled at reading covert clues were rated by their teachers as less popular and less socially sensitive than their fellows who conformed more to the canons of politeness, i.e., who were better at reading overt cues than covert ones or were better at concealing their detection of covert cues. Similar results were obtained in psychological experiments carried out with college students.

What are the personal and interpersonal consequences of detecting lies? Some evidence suggests that women are more likely than men not to notice, or to pretend not to notice, cues that liars would prefer to remain unnoticed. For example, women are better than men at differentiating honest liking from honest disliking, but in detecting deception females are not at all superior to males. This difference between men and women probably increases with age; old women are even more polite than old men (DePaulo et al. 1985:361).

DePaulo and Jordan (1982:175–176) comment that these results seem to show that skill in uncovering deceit may cause social friction. Taking messages at face value may have its advantages. Seeing only what you are supposed to see may be simpler not only cognitively but also emotionally. Skilled detectors may feel guilty about their suspiciousness and lack of trust; they may even find out something about another person's true feelings towards them that they might be much happier not to know. DePaulo and Jordan seem to consider misplaced trust unproblematically preferable to unpleasant facts, an assumption that I find surprising but which perhaps reflects a feature of American culture. They do, however, go on to admit that sensitivity to true but concealed feelings may have some instrumental advantages in 'certain professions, such as psychiatry and medicine'.

In this view, skill in detecting deceit can be socially hazardous; it is left to the naive child to call out 'The emperor has no clothes'. Skill in deceiving, by contrast, may carry fewer hazards. DePaulo and Jordan (1982:176) note that while children are sufficiently young, naive forthrightness 'is usually excused as innocent or even adorable'. But as they get older, the excuse falls flat; forthrightness becomes socially embarrassing and, as noted earlier, it becomes 'costly for children *not* to tell lies'.

Much of the advice offered by psychologists and ethologists on how to detect lies focusses not on the content of what is said but on the body language of the liar, his or her facial expressions, body posture and the like. The underlying premises for this focussing are that 'lying is accompanied by specific perceptible physiological or behavioral alterations' (Orne et al. 1972:743) and that it is harder to simulate false messages in body language than in speech.

Gregory Bateson (1968:615) puts this state of affairs in evolutionary perspective:

It seems that the discourse of nonverbal communication is precisely concerned with matters of relationship – love, hate, respect, fear, dependency, etc. – between self and vis-à-vis or between self and environment and that the nature of human society is such that falsification of this discourse rapidly becomes pathogenic. From an adaptive point of view, it is therefore important that this discourse be carried on by techniques which are relatively unconscious and only imperfectly subject to voluntary control.

Bateson makes the point that those people who are able to control their non-verbal communication effectively, such as professional actors and confidence tricksters, have more difficulty in acting sincerely than do others, and have even more difficulty in getting others to accept that they are acting sincerely. As with the ordinary language of speech, too many lies in body language are counter-productive. Yet Bateson (Ibid.:614, 622) also argues that since human body language, or as he puts it, communication by kinesics and paralanguage, has not decayed following the evolution of verbal language, the two systems must serve different functions (cf. Burling 1993). The need for honesty in personal relationships is ensured by the survival of body language. In discussing how cooperation might have evolved, Patrick Bateson (1988:28) makes the point that, once 'highly functional cooperative behaviour' had been established, 'Signals that predicted what one individual was about to do and mechanisms for

responding appropriately to them, would have become mutually beneficial'. Body language constitutes one such signalling system.

Facial expressions and body posture may be harder to control than
speech and writing, but heartbeat and blood pressure are harder still.
Defoe, in a tract written in 1730 and entitled 'An effectual scheme for the
immediate preventing of street robberies . . .', noted that 'there is a Tremor
in the Blood of a Thief that, if attended to, would effectually discover him'
(Moore 1955; cf. Lykken 1984:484). Deceptographic technology, exemplified by polygraph machines (Gale 1988) and voice stress analysers, is based
on the premises that some physiological processes, including the electrical
conductance of the skin, are not to any significant extent subject to
conscious control but are subject to change when anyone engages in
deceit. Both premises are open to challenge, particularly in the light of the
large proportion of false positives (innocent people declared to be guilty)
given by polygraph machines. As one reviewer puts it, 'the only people
who can be confident of being found innocent in a lie detector test are
thoroughly trained liars' (Collins 1988). Whereas the polygraph may give
false positive readings, another detection device, the voice stress analyser,
may give false negatives. A sample of students at an American university
were tested with an analyser; presumably they did not include many
'thoroughly trained liars'. Some subjects in the experiment were asked to
lie in response to a specified question but were also given the opportunity
to lie spontaneously in response to another question they had not been
briefed on. The analyser detected differences between truthful responses
and prepared lies but not between truthful answers and spontaneous lies
(O'Hair and Cody 1987).

Nevertheless some countries, notably the United States, support a large
lie-detection industry. In some other parts of the world, for example New
South Wales, the use of lie detectors in connection with insurance and
employment is forbidden by law. The attempt to achieve a technological
fix for securing trust is open to ethical objections even if both premises
were true and there was no measurement error. Yet even if lie-detection
machines are significantly inaccurate, as seems to be the case, Richard
Nixon's comment still rings true:

I don't know anything about polygraphs, and I don't know how accurate they are,
but I do know that they'll scare the hell out of people. (Marx and Reichman
1984:434)

Almost everything that has been published about ability to detect lies,
other than by mechanical means, relates to detection by dupes. In the real
world, however, many lies are detected and exposed by third parties. In
the political domain, most lies are generated with the intention of fooling

everybody, so that even investigative journalists might be regarded as potential dupes who have seen through the attempted deceit. But in other domains where lies are targeted more narrowly, the dupe may be alerted to the existence of the lie by someone who is not directly affected by it. Indeed, a dupe who is conniving at a lie may seek to avoid the possibility of a third party exposing the connivance. As noted in chapter 7, the self-deceived woman interviewed by Werth and Flaherty said: 'I didn't confide in anyone, too, because I was afraid of what they would tell me. I wanted to believe everything was going to be fine and I wasn't being deceived.' Indeed, a third party may be better placed to detect a lie and possibly expose it because connivance would not bring any great advantage.

Thus we see that even if certain potentialities for telling lies and for detecting them develop without special effort during the normal course of human maturation, the ability to achieve success in lying is a learned skill; some people do better than others. In the same way some children and adults are better than others at detecting lies. Success in both enterprises depends at least in part on sensitivity to the ambiguities of ordinary language. If the polygraph is a dubious technical aid in the detection of lies, the telephone and the audiotape are more reliable aids to success in lying, with the written word also available as an uncertain aid. In general, just as the occurrence and impact of lying vary according to social, cultural and structural context, they vary also from one individual to another.

9

Benign untruths: the discourse of fiction

In chapter 8 I cited a joke analysed by Freud to illustrate how true statements can, in certain circumstances, be used to deceive. Likewise, in other circumstances, statements may be untrue without being deceptive. The presence or absence of an intention to deceive does not always conform to the falsity or truth of what is said. The contrast between falsity and falsehood, or between truth and truthfulness, manifests itself in many contexts but is nowhere seen more clearly than in connection with what we call 'fiction'. The linguist John Searle (1975:325) notes:

It is after all an odd, peculiar and amazing fact about human language that it allows the possibility of fiction at all.

With a sufficiently wide definition of 'fiction' this possibility can be seen as a universal attribute of human society. In any given society, however, fiction, and what Searle (1975:326) calls 'the conventions of fictional discourse', take forms that are socially constructed. Literary theorists have examined the concept of fiction at great length (e.g. Pavel 1986, Smith 1978) but my concerns are somewhat different from theirs; I limit my discussion to the possibilities for deception in fiction and to the ways in which authors have asserted or denied the veridicality of their texts. Furthermore I confine myself to selected evidence from one group of literate societies.

In general, the readers of a work of fiction nowadays recognize it for what it is. For at least the last two centuries a distinction has been maintained in Western cultures between historical accounts and works of fiction. In current jargon, they constitute distinct discourses. We expect histories and news items to be 'true', in the pedestrian sense of 'corresponding to the state of the world', whereas we are content for fiction to be true, if at all, only in the much weaker sense of being 'true to life' (cf. Allon 1985:53). Samuel Johnson (1905:271), writing in 1779, pronounced that: 'the legitimate end of fiction is the conveyance of truth', but the truth he had in mind was moral rather than historical.

Many of the statements in works of fiction are true in the stricter sense but many others are not, even though we are ready to concede that they might well have been historically true if events had taken a different turn. There are of course also statements that, however many contortions history might have taken, could not possibly correspond to any state of the real world; works of science fiction are filled with this third class of statements. Many novels call for what we might term second-order suspension of disbelief; here the author introduces events and characters which are imaginary even within the main imaginary framework of the text. The point I wish to emphasize is that although we readily recognize the lack of correspondence between what we read in fictional writing and the events of the real world we do not consider that we are being told lies. Patricia Waugh (1984:87–114) devotes a chapter of her book *Metafiction* to answering the rhetorical question 'Are novelists liars?' and shows in what sense they (or at least the many modern novelists whose work she cites) are not. In general we do not regard works of fiction as attempts by authors to play tricks on their readers. Whether or not readers feel that they are being deceived in some other sense, distinct from being told lies, is an open question. Roberts (1972:23) maintains that 'many writers of fiction by intention are trying to deceive us' but goes on to say that an author of fiction gives signals 'to alert his readers that his book should be taken as neither factually a lie nor as factually a mistake but as something different from either'. These signals are of various kinds: the simplest is simply the statement that the book is a novel. The reader then knows what to expect and what rules apply. As Pleynet (1968:95; cf. Culler 1975:136; Pavel 1986:123) says:

It is indeed this word (novel, poem) placed on the cover of the book which (by convention) genetically produces, programmes or 'originates' our reading.

Roberts calls 'fiction by intention' works with these signals and notes:

If the writer then proceeded to use every device at his command to make the reader *forget* the warning he had been given, this does not affect the text's status for the critics as fiction by intention. (Roberts 1972:24)

Signals of this kind have become established by convention. For instance, the opening phrase 'Once upon a time' is not a claim for the historical truth of what is to follow (cf. Macdonald 1954:169; Scriven 1954:195); perhaps it never was. It is a recognized disclaimer and is interpreted 'Never upon a time'.

Although with many works of fiction no ontological queries arise, the separation of the artificial universe of the novel from the world of real people and real events is not always obvious. For example, many historical novels contain accounts of some real events and some real people, along with statements which, though plausible and 'true to life', do not correspond to the real world. Some readers become irritated if they cannot easily decide whether an event or a character is real or invented, while others are intrigued. For example, Drusilla Modjeska, in her *Poppy*, ostensibly a biography of her mother, states that she has included in the book many incidents that are imaginary, and has disguised the attributes of some of her characters. 'Nothing is to be taken simply as literal.' But she also says that her book is not a work of fiction but 'a mixture of fact and fiction, biography and novel' (Modjeska 1990:317). This statement is made in the acknowledgments section of the book, not in the main text, and therefore can be taken as authentic. But given that some unspecified incidents reported in the text are truly biographical, the reader tends to wonder continually which are true and which are imaginary. In her critique of Australian novels, Helen Daniel's Reader says in a dialogue with Liar: 'it's so hard being a reader these days. Writers can't be trusted any more' (Daniel 1988:7–8). Yet even those readers who like to keep their feet on the ground and to know for sure what is true and what has been invented do not deny the right of authors to invent.

Some fiction achieves success with its readers by generating fantasies that cannot be realized; science fiction is the obvious current genre of this kind, but the medieval romances that preceded the development of the modern novel also belong to this class. Successful realistic fiction, on the other hand, may be successful because it is 'true to life', or, more likely, 'larger than life'. As Horace (1929:479) said of poetry long ago: 'Fiction meant to please should be close to the real, ...' Both kinds of fiction, realistic and fantastic, seen in contrast to the discourse of history, are distinguished by the absence of the otherwise pervasive obligation that statements should be true, or at least truthful. In this sense fictional statements are privileged; their readers grant them a privilege and collaborate with their authors in indulging in a guided non-deceptive fantasy, or even in a nested hierarchy of fantasies. But the granting of this privilege does not always go unchallenged, and the suspension of disbelief entailed by the fantasy has not always been regarded as benignly non-deceptive. In any case, the concept of 'fiction', now well recognized, has itself a long non-fictional history.

Bok (1978:207n) oversimplifies the position when she states that 'fiction and lying are in themselves quite separate, ...' She goes on to qualify this statement and is on firmer ground when she notes that 'The confusion of fiction and deception has long antecedents'. Here Bok is using the concept of fiction in a relatively narrow sense. Steiner (1975:224), on the other hand, seems to use the term in so wide a sense that it covers all forms of verbal deceit. Referring to the development of language, he explains the origins of fiction by the survival value of deceit. He says:

Fiction was disguise; from those seeking out the same waterhole, the same sparse quarry, or meagre sexual chance. To misinform, to utter less than the truth was to gain a vital edge of space or substance. Natural selection would favour the contriver.

But when Steiner, a few paragraphs earlier, speaks of 'the creativity of falsehood' and endorses Nietzsche's claim for the divinity of lying, he attracts the judgment of writing 'nonsense on stilts' from a debunking, or rather de-humbugging, Max Black (1983:135). In any case, the leap from the waterhole to, say, Lilliput is dauntingly long. Yet Steiner's assertion makes sense when we note that he fills in the gap with Loki, Odysseus, Robin Hood and other characters of myth and folk tale. Bok's linkages are more conventional. She refers to Plato's disapproval of artists and play-wrights, and goes on to discuss 'borderline' cases where fiction and lying meet. That they do meet is not surprising, for the success of a novel depends, in part, on our ability as readers to imagine ourselves trans-ported into the environment constructed by the author.

The concept of fiction as a distinctive type of discourse is largely an outcome of that development in the eighteenth century which has been described by Lévi-Strauss (1981:652) as the time when 'the literary narra-tive' changed 'from myth to the novel'. Although the concept of the novel was not yet firmly in place even at the beginning of that century, accept-ance was already much nearer than it had been in classical Greece, where falsehood

was accepted on low or modest levels where it could not seriously be mistaken for truth, as in animal fables ... amusing and rather scurrilous anecdotes ... and parodies of every-day life, ... (Forsdyke 1956:158)

The same distinction is found today. In Britain, if advertisers claim falsely that their product has desirable attributes that it might conceivably have but in fact does not possess, they are in danger of prosecution under the Trades Description Act. On the other hand, if the claim is fantastic, as, for example, that a glass of a certain beer will give one the strength to set the Leaning Tower of Pisa upright, the Act turns a blind eye. Because the claim is fantastic, it cannot have been intended to deceive.

Closely related to the phenomenon of fantasy is the concept of allegory. In early English literature we speak of the 'political allegory' of Piers Plowman, and earlier still we have the parables of the New Testament and the plays of classical Greece. These productions were not intended to deceive; we judge and enjoy them now, as did their contemporary audiences, by the validity of the message they convey rather than by their correspondence to events in the real world. Nevertheless, even with allegorical works, the possibility of misreading them as historical accounts was always present. For example, Isaac D'Israeli (1793 (2):23) reports that when Thomas More's *Utopia* was first published in 1516, some of its readers took the existence of the ideal island republic sufficiently seriously to discuss the feasibility of sending missionaries to convert the population to Christianity.

Most of the time allegories have been recognized as products of the imagination rather than of history. Arguments about the literal truth of the Bible hinge on the accuracy of its account of the earth's creation and the age of Methuselah rather than on the historical existence of the Prodigal Son and the Good Samaritan. Even John Bunyan's seventeenth-century Baptist colleagues, Puritans though they were, seem to have been willing to accept that *Pilgrim's progress* was an allegory rather than an untrue story. Yet some of his Baptist critics were suspicious of what Sharrock (1954:139) calls 'the dangerous freedom of fiction'(cf. Newey 1980:27). We should remember that 'throughout the eighteenth century reading fiction was regarded as an inferior and oftentimes dangerous activity' (Uphaus 1988:vii). These sentiments were certainly already current in Bunyan's time, particularly among his Puritan readers. In his opening 'Apology for his book' Bunyan (1967:5) defended his use of an allegorical mode against a critic by saying

> May we but stand before impartial men,
> To his poor One, I durst adventure Ten,
> That they will take my meaning in these lines
> Far better than his lies in Silver Shrines.

The hazards of the 'dangerous freedom' offered by Bunyan are unambiguously set out by his critic Thomas Sherman, a member of the General Baptists. In 1682, two years before Bunyan's own Part Two appeared, he published his proffered sequel to Part One of *Pilgrim's progress*, which, he said, would

deliver the whole in such serious and spiritual phrases that may prevent that lightness and laughter which the reading of some passages therein [in Bunyan's Part One text] may occasion in some vain and frothy minds. (Sharrock 1954:139; cf. Bunyan 1967:338–339)

Categorizing *Pilgrim's progress* as an allegory is easy to defend, for the work is not realistic. Yet despite Bunyan's claim, some readers, in his own day as well as many years later, must surely have taken his story as literally true. McKeon (1987:296–297) draws attention to an account of a mid-

Victorian childhood, in which Thomas Burt (1924:115) refers to *Pilgrim's progress* by saying:

Not as a dream or allegory, but as solid literal history did it present itself to my boyish mind. I believed every word of it.

The more realistic novels that started to appear in Europe in the eighteenth century were typically presented to the public with an emphasis on their truth, even when they contained material that sceptics might regard as clearly unrealistic. Sometimes they were alleged to be old diaries recently unearthed, or reminiscences of persons recently deceased. The use of this conceit had already been employed earlier by Cervantes at the beginning of the seventeenth century.

We might say that in these early novels there were often two sets of false statements. For instance, Jonathan Swift's *Gulliver's travels* contains on the one hand an account of Lemuel Gulliver's adventures in Lilliput and other fabulous places, and on the other an introduction to this account, describing how Swift, or rather his fictitious character Richard Sympson, acquired Gulliver's manuscript. Many of the statements in the main text are not only false; they are also incredible, at least for sane adults. In this respect, Swift therefore cannot be said to be trying to deceive his intended audience of 'young Noblemen'.

But the statements in the preliminaries to the text, though we now find them false, are highly credible, and were presented to the public without any anti-libel caveat, so that at first glance we might be inclined to say that Swift was engaged in deceit. For example, Richard Sympson is introduced as Gulliver's cousin and editor of his manuscript. Sympson is made to say that he has omitted from the published version at least half the manuscript, removing 'innumerable Passages relating to the Winds and Tides' and 'the Account of Longitudes and Latitudes' (Swift 1941:xxxvii–xxxviii). This assertion can have been made only to give greater verisimilitude to the main story, and thus to fool at least the naive reader.

But if the falsity of eighteenth-century travel accounts is easy to establish, their deceptiveness nevertheless remains open to question, as shown by the experience of Defoe who published *Robinson Crusoe* in 1719 as the work of a mariner 'born in the year 1632, in the City of York', although the book was based on the real experiences of the Scottish sailor Alexander Selkirk. In the preface Defoe wrote: 'The Editor believes the thing to be a just History of Fact; neither is there any Appearance of Fiction in it' (Defoe 1927:vii). A year after publishing *Robinson Crusoe*, Defoe was accused by Charles Gildon of being a liar. He defended himself by maintaining that the work was an allegory of his own life (Allen 1954:38), but presented this defence not in his own name but as if it were written by a real Robinson

Crusoe. Adams (1990:34–35) characterizes this tangle of inventions by saying: 'Thus we have an imagined literary character, based on an actual person, who claims that his life is a metaphor for the author who created him in the first place ...' As with Cervantes and *Don Quixote*, a character is made to comment on his author, partly to advance moral arguments but also to provide additional evidence for the pretence of historicity. Defoe, like Cervantes before him, may not have intended his disguises to be deceptive, but certainly some of his readers were deceived. Indeed, he has been described as 'the greatest liar who ever lived' (Backscheider 1989:xii).

Baker (1924:12) maintains that fictions of this kind, as used by Defoe and others, were 'deliberately framed to deceive'. And indeed what are we to say when, at the beginning of *Gulliver's travels*, Swift, in a section entitled 'The Publisher [i.e. Sympson] to the Reader', writes:

There is an Air of Truth apparent through the whole; and indeed the Author was so distinguished for his Veracity, that it became a Sort of Proverb among his Neighbours at *Redriff*, when any one affirmed a Thing, to say, it was as true as if Mr. *Gulliver* had spoke it. (Swift 1941:xxxvii)

Is he not overplaying his hand? Would anyone other than the most naive of readers take him seriously? Their naivety might well have been shaken by the complaint in Gulliver's letter to Sympson that some 'Yahoos ... are so bold as to think my Book of Travels a meer Fiction out of mine own Brain' and by his reference to 'that infernal Habit of Lying, Shuffling, Deceiving, and Equivocating, so deeply rooted in the very Souls of all my Species; especially the *Europeans*' (Swift 1941:xxxvi).

It seems clear that Swift was able to write for an audience of readers readily able to recognize his work as satire, not to be taken literally, even though they would not have seen a letter, ostensibly from the fictitious Richard Sympson to his publisher, in which Swift writes that 'some parts of this and the following volumes may be thought in one or two places to be a little satirical' (Williams 1941:xxiv). Unlike Defoe, Swift did not have to defend himself against the charge of lying; nor was he writing for an audience of Baptists, as Bunyan was.

Taking a long view, we can look on the arrival of the novel as an achievement that advanced the freedom whose first steps had been taken many millennia earlier with the birth of language, a freedom grounded in the ability of discourse 'to transcend the here and now' (Rappaport 1979:180). Discourse could now transcend historical truth as well without being stigmatized as deceitful.

But if most of us have no qualms at classifying these two books as fiction rather than historical narrative because they are implausible and/or incredible, how are we to deal with Defoe's quite credible (at the time it was published in 1725) but also quite false *A new voyage round the world*, which he wrote without leaving London, or his *Journal of the plague year*, presented as 'Written by a CITIZEN who continued all the while in LONDON' (1928). Defoe and Swift were not alone in disguising their authorship in this way. Farb (1973:133) argues that Defoe and other writers of travel narratives 'lied simply because their speech communities expected it of them', by which he means that they provided material to bolster the ethnic and religious prejudices of their readers. But were they lying? Despite the accusation made against Defoe, it seems more likely that they expected their readers to recognize the type of discourse presented to them. They did not necessarily make the right judgment, nor did the literary critics who followed in their wake. For instance, Defoe presented his *Journal of the plague year* to the public in 1722 as an historically authentic account of events that took place in 1665. Nineteenth-century critics praised the work as an imaginative piece of fiction which was 'a masterpiece in its verisimilitude' but warned against accepting it as history. Nicholson (1919:1–3), however, argues that it is the critics, not Defoe's contemporary readers, who have been misled; ignoring Defoe's spurious statement about authorship, he demonstrates that 'there is not a single essential statement in the *Journal* not based on historic fact.' In other words, Defoe lied so often that his critics disbelieved even his true statements.

Rousseau took a somewhat different view of the relation between fiction and deceit. He seems to have held that the depictions of fictional characters that distort our moral perceptions, such as that of Molière's *Misanthrope*, are lies (cf. Gourevitch 1980:94). Writing in 1777, he made the same judgment about Montesquieu's anonymously published *The temple of Gnidus*, a work which Rousseau condemned because of its 'licentious details' and which the author presented to the public in the guise of a translation of a Greek manuscript. He maintained that

If *The temple of Gnidus* is a useful work, the story of the Greek manuscript is no more than an innocent fiction; but it is a reprehensible lie if the work is dangerous. (Rousseau 1979:73)

Rousseau appears to base his classification not on an intention to deceive as diagnostic of lying, but on the causing of harm. Thus he distinguishes, on the one hand, 'the educated public' who would regard the false claim about translation of a Greek manuscript as 'a foolish piece of childishness', and, on the other

the many simple and credulous readers who have been genuinely deceived by this manuscript story told in apparent good faith by a serious author and who have unsuspectingly drunk from what appeared to be an ancient goblet the poison of which they would at least have been wary if it had been presented to them in a modern cup. (Ibid.:70)

Rousseau certainly treats Montesquieu as a liar, particularly since the latter's account of his discovery of the alleged manuscript is described 'in the manner most calculated to persuade his readers of the truth of his account'. On the other hand, if the book had not contained so many 'lascivious images', and had not been poison for the laity, Rousseau (1979:72) might well have treated the pretence as one of those 'occasional lies about things of no importance' that he was prepared to tolerate.

Later in the eighteenth century the concept of the 'novel' as a recognized and legitimate type of fiction became established (Watt 1957:10), fiction itself being a type of discourse which 'allows for any imaginable kind of confabulation without constraint' (Pavel 1986:2). Even so, some Christians continued to be suspicious of all forms of fiction. For example, Edmund Gosse (1949:20) grew up in the late nineteenth century in a household from which 'story-books of every description' were excluded by his mother, a member of the Plymouth Brethren, who held that to 'tell a story' was a sin. Furthermore the contrast between truth and fiction has never been completely uncontested, as shown by the continuing awareness of the possibility of libel actions based on works presented as fiction (e.g. Hardy 1971; cf. Roberts 1972:91). This possibility prompted some twentieth-century publishers to insert in the preliminary matter of their novels a brief statement of their claim for the privileged status of fiction. I do not know of any existing technical term and 'disclaimer' seems an appropriate designation for a written statement of this kind, matching the usage of 'disclaimer' for analogous oral statements (Hewitt and Stokes 1975). Disclaimers, stating that none of the persons mentioned in the text has any connection to any real person, living or dead, were put there to emphasize that the separation between reality and imagination was intended to be complete, and to provide some slight protection for authors, publishers and printers against suits for libel. The simplest disclaimer is the bald statement 'All characters are fictitious' (e.g. Gordon 1957:6). Sometimes more details are added to drive home the message. For example:

This is a novel and each place and situation is wholly imaginary. Each character is imaginary too; and whatever the chance similarity of a name, no reference is made or intended to any living person. (Bush 1949:vii)

In these and similar disclaimers we see the appeal to concepts such as 'fiction', 'allegory' and 'novel' which are assumed to provide legitimate releases from the otherwise ubiquitous obligation to tell the truth, the obligation that Grice (1989:27) labels a supermaxim: try to make your contribution [to a conversation] one that is true. Sometimes a writer of fiction extends his disclaimer beyond the more usual rubric of people and places; privilege to invent is claimed for other classes of facts as well. For example Martin Amis (1975:ix) prefaces a novel with this comprehensive disclaimer:

Not only are all characters and scenes in this book entirely fictitious; most of the technical, medical and psychological data are too. My working maxim here has been as follows: I may not know much about science but I know what I like.

An author may defend his invention of imaginary large-scale events by arguing that these are appropriate to accompany fictitious characters. Thus Picton-Warlow (1967:5) prefaces a novel, in which 'Except for some self-portraits all the characters ... are fictitious', by noting that

several years of Australian social and economic development are ignored. I must ask Australia to forgive me taking this liberty with it. I do not think a fiction can in itself displease any reader of fiction, ...

On the other hand, an author may claim authenticity for a central character while asserting that others are fictional, as in O'Grady's (1964) novel *The sun breaks through* about an Australian convict. Other authors point the way to texts that correspond more closely to reality than their own. Thus Banville (1976:vii) accompanies his novel about Nicolaus Copernicus with suggestions for 'further reading for anyone seeking a fuller and perhaps more scrupulously factual account of the astronomer's life and work', thereby announcing his own wandering from the facts.

A disclaimer of a somewhat different sort appears with Nathaniel Hawthorne's (1900: xxi–xxiv) *House of the seven gables*, written in 1851. Hawthorne spends four pages insisting that his characters 'are really of the author's own making, or, at all events, of his own mixing' but bases his right to proceed in this way by labelling his work a romance and not a novel. A novel, he says, 'is presumed to aim at a very minute fidelity, not merely to the possible, but to the probable and ordinary course of man's experience'. A romance, on the other hand, is not constrained in this way. Though it must not 'swerve aside from the truth of the human heart', it 'has fairly a right to present that truth under circumstances, to a great extent, of the writer's own choosing or creation'. Thus embellishing his disclaimer with a somewhat idiosyncratic distinction between novels and romances, Hawthorne supplies under the rubric of 'romance' a convenient description of the contemporary novel. His distinction has, however, recently been followed by A. S. Byatt (1990) who calls her work *Possession* a romance.

The contrast between fact and fiction has been eroded not only by postmodernist notions of what I have elsewhere (Barnes 1981:22) called epistemological popularism but also by the emergence of the genre of 'faction' where, so it seems, the author says: 'Some of the things I say are true, and some are false, and you can guess which are which, but I won't tell you.' Presumably Modjeska's *Poppy* belongs in this category. The uncertainty inherent in faction is used dramatically in the British weekly newspaper the *Sunday Sport*, where manifestly fictional items (e.g. 'Uncovered: evidence of Super League in 3100 BC') are juxtaposed with plausibly authentic statements (e.g. 'Nigel Mansell has to beat Ayrton Senna in todays's Belgian Grand Prix'). The status of other items (e.g. 'I thrashed forty bank managers' bottoms') is thereby left open to the imagination and credulity of its readers (*Sunday Sport* 1991).

Even the conventional disclaimer can be used to attack common notions of the relation of truth, facts and fiction. For example, in a 'Prefatory note', the novelist Oakley Hall (1973:5) says:

But any relation of the characters to real persons, living or dead, is not always coincidental, for many are composites of figures who live still on a frontier between history and legend. ... The pursuit of truth, not of facts, is the business of fiction.

Presumably Dr Johnson would agree. Currently, emphasis on the separation of the novel from the real world is not always confined to a prefatory disclaimer; it is carried a stage further in what Patricia Waugh (1984:2) calls 'metafiction':

fictional writing which self-consciously draws attention to its status as an artefact in order to pose questions about the relationship between fiction and reality.

It is a pity that Defoe is not with us to comment on this modern development.

For most fiction, however, membership of the genre is not in doubt, whether or not the once customary disclaimer about 'no connection with any living person' appears at the beginning of the book. As Scheibe (1980:21) says: 'The frame provides license. A lie revealing itself as a lie is not called a lie but a fiction.'

Realistic novels must be true to life, but not too true. Even when a disclaimer is printed, any novel that mimics the real world is potentially a ground for an action for libel. Libel laws vary significantly from one jurisdiction to another, so that truth, which may be an adequate defence in one legal system, may be an aggravation of the offence in another. But whatever legal calculus may be invoked, a libel suit is an attempt to abrogate the privileged fictional status claimed for the novel. The main thrust of most literary libel actions is the demonstration of defamation rather than deceit, but accusations of deceit may arise, particularly if truth is accepted as a valid defence. Thus in a recent Australian legal case it was argued that an odious character in a novel was unmistakably intended to be identified with the plaintiff, and that the novelist had deceitfully attributed to this character reprehensible actions which the plaintiff had not performed. Sutherland (1978) discusses some of the issues that arise from the vulnerability of novelists to charges of libel, and mentions various artifices they have adopted in self-defence. The danger persists, particularly when political comment is cast in the form of a novel. As Sutherland says, 'The novel ... touches the living great at its peril'.

The relation between fact and fiction is problematic not only in connection with novels and other literary forms; it has become a matter of controversy also in some branches of social science, notably ethnography. Indeed, Edmund Leach is reported to have said to his fellow social anthropologists that they should criticize themselves for being poor novelists rather than incompetent scientists (Abrahams 1987:15). Leach (1987:1, 9, 12) says that '*all* ethnography is fictional' (his emphasis), that 'most ethnographic monographs are fiction' and that even when 'the algebra of structural transformation' is substituted for 'missing sequences of recorded history' 'the past becomes a fiction invented by the ethnographer' (Leach 1987:11). The association of ethnography with lying has even become fashionable, as seen by the inclusion of the claim that 'All anthropologists are liars' in the title of a journal article merely, so it seems, as a rhetorical postmodernist flourish (Michaels 1987). The claim is never examined in the article (cf. Bailey 1991:103–114).

Leach's rhetoric is in line with Lévi-Strauss' (1970:6) well-known remark that 'this book on myths is itself a kind of myth'; but neither Lévi-Strauss nor Leach would condone the deliberate fabrication of ethnographic evidence.

The attempt to conflate the domains of fact and fiction has been carried further with reference to the writings of Carlos Castaneda. Here we are not dealing with a simple instance of alleged fraud. The authenticity of his graphic descriptions of Yaqui shamanism (Castaneda 1968, 1971, 1972, 1974, 1977, 1981) has been queried so widely that, according to Marvin Harris (1979:323):

> We cannot rule out the possibility that Castaneda never interviewed any Yaqui Indian shaman, and that the apparent authenticity of his shamanic experiences derive entirely from his own shamanic gifts and literary and imaginative powers.

Instead of trying to determine whether or not Castaneda is trying to deceive the public, and his academic supervisors in the University of California, some postmodernist commentators (cf. de Mille 1980) have argued that this question is irrelevant. Silverman (1975:xi) says: 'It does not matter to me in the least whether any or all of the "events" reported by Castaneda ever "took place".' But in what capacity does Silverman make this assertion? Presumably as a reader of Castaneda's book rather than as an examiner of his doctoral dissertation. Fooling the reading public may be tolerated or even encouraged, but most academics would consider fooling the examiners reprehensible. Doctoral dissertations, term papers and the like do not enjoy the privileged status accorded to fiction. In Silverman's view, presumably, Castaneda's books are to be seen as texts, and studied in their own right, whether or not the events described in them actually occurred. Here, then, is a claim that we cannot ever know the truth, and therefore cannot distinguish between truth and falsity; deception is a logical impossibility, for if truthfulness is meaningless, so likewise is deceit. This position is, in Harris's judgment, an 'invitation to intellectual suicide'. It is, we might say, a claim that all data, or at least all the data of social science, are irretrievably soft, and that all attempts to discover what does 'really', or 'in fact', go on in the world are bound to fail.

When we contrast fiction with fact we usually have in mind fiction as a written text. The same contrast can, however, be drawn in pre-literate cultures, between those oral stories that are taken to be true and those that are recognized as not corresponding to any state of the real world. There is no deception unless a fabricated tale is presented as if it were true. In all cultures, literate and pre-literate alike, people indulge in fantasy and can share their fantasies with others without being deceptive, provided they do not try to disguise their fantasies as facts. On the borderline between fantasy and deceit are the activities of professional impersonators who merely amuse most members of their audience but certainly deceive the more gullible members, notably young children, at least temporarily (Macdonald 1990).

Ironically, one of the culturally accepted modes of sharing fantasies is labelled as lying. Lying, not for real but for fun, can be promoted cooperatively, as in the activities of liars' clubs, or competitively, as in contests to see who can tell the biggest lie (Ludwig 1965:19–20). The formation of a society of political liars was proposed satirically by Arbuthnot (1712:17–18; see also Pollard 1897:118–120) but his ideas have been implemented in a more plebeian form. For example, in 1987, a toastmasters' club in a Canberra suburb arranged a charity fund-raising dinner at which the main attraction was a competition to see who could tell the biggest 'lie'. Clearly these competition entries are not lies according to our definition, for there was no intention to deceive; furthermore I doubt whether any diner was deceived. Lying clubs, so called, are said to have existed in Britain in the eighteenth century. In the nineteenth century, Henry Labouchere, the independently-minded member of the British House of Commons whom Queen Victoria called a liar, described in his journal *Truth* a flourishing lying club in the north of England:

There were different grades of proficiency. If a man could not lie at all he was expelled. If he lied rather badly, he was given another trial. I never knew anyone expelled.

Labouchere claimed that when he had been proposed for membership of the club, he had been blackballed (Thorold 1913:107). But how can we tell whether this claim is not just another lie? And in our own time, how can we tell whether the reports our fishermen friends give of their catches are lies or fantasies? Indeed, a recent collection of Australian 'tall stories', designated by their author as 'very true' (Egan 1991), poses precisely this question for the reader with its main title *Would I lie to you?*

The evidence marshalled in this chapter should be sufficient to demonstrate not only that, just as true statements can sometimes be lies, so can untrue statements be made without intent to deceive and without anyone being deceived. More importantly, the historical evidence shows that a discourse in which falsity is freed from its usual link with deception achieves recognition only as the outcome of an historical process. Writers innovate and audiences learn, but only over time. Furthermore the separation of deception and falsity is never entirely uncontested. This is evident from the continuing threats and actual instances of libel suits arising out of fictional works that follow Horace's maxim too closely. Some authors of fiction have been punished by governments which have rejected the claim that no connection exists between the text and the real world. Finally, the emergence of 'faction' and similar amalgams of fact and fiction shows that the autonomy of the discourse of fiction is challenged by its own practitioners.

In this chapter we have diverted our attention from intended lies to look, necessarily somewhat superficially, at untrue statements intended not to be lies. My aim has been to emphasize the absence of any necessary connection between truth and deception, and between truthfulness and falsity. Just as the context has an effect on the content, frequency and effectiveness of the lies that are told, so too does it have an effect on how untrue statements are perceived. Fiction constitutes the antithesis of the lie.

Having thus commented on the negative as well as the positive face of lying, we can turn to a couple of wider topics. In chapter 10 we look at how various writers have evaluated lying, morally and sociologically, and finally in chapter 11 we ask why do we have to have lying at all.

10

Evaluations

In this chapter I try to address two separate but related topics: the evaluation of lying in moral terms and the assessment of lying in sociological terms. The separateness of the topics is obvious; for centuries moralists have felt themselves able to write at length about the moral rights and moral wrongs (mainly the wrongs) of lying without saying much or anything at all about its sociological significance. The laity have been even less inclined to wait for sociologists to tell them whether they should condemn or applaud lying. Yet though the topics are distinct they are also related; the primary objective of sociological analysis, a better understanding of how the social world operates, should serve as a reliable stepping stone towards a second objective, the attainment of a social world which works better.

Although most philosophers and religious moralists have, for most of the time, condemned most lies as morally bad, this condemnation has varied considerably from one writer to another and from one kind of lie to another. As mentioned earlier, in antiquity Plato, who condemned the lies told by imaginative writers, discussed the rights and wrongs of what philosophers have called noble lies, told by the ruling elite to deceive the masses with the aim of preserving the social order (Bok 1978:165–170). Whether or not he approved of 'noble lies' is open to dispute (Arendt 1968:232, 298 n.5; cf. Bok 1978:305–306; Toynbee 1935:93; Voegelin 1957:104–108).

The same ambivalent attitude towards lying occurs in the myths and folk tales of most, perhaps all, cultures; stories of deceit and trickery abound. Moreover, the perpetrators of these acts are not all depicted as villains. Odysseus is only one member in a long line of heroes admired for their cunning and deceitfulness (Homer 1974:291–295; cf. Wax 1986:4). Plato (1966:53–54) attributes to Socrates the opinion that the gods do not lie, but in the Bible, the Old Testament contains several instances of Jehovah deceiving mortals. Recently it has been suggested as a possible argument for creationism that the apparent evidence for the immense age of the universe was fabricated by a god 'smart enough to cover his tracks' after creating the universe in 4004 BC (Denness 1988; cf. *Nature* 1989).

Scheibe (1980:16) asserts that:

Viewed in the context of our animal and ancient cultural heritage, the moral requirement that we must always tell 'the truth' must be seen as a very recent accretion to our ethos.

Scheibe's view is supported by Arendt (1968:232) who argues that none of the major religions, except Zoroastrianism, included lying, as distinct from 'bearing false witness', in their catalogue of grave sins, and that only with the arrival of Puritanism and organized science did lies come to be considered serious offences.

Both claims have been challenged (Bok 1978:302). Theravada Buddhism includes an uncompromising injunction not to tell lies (Gombrich 1971:65, 255). The first Druze commandment enjoins truthtelling among believers, but allows lying to outsiders to protect the secrets of the faith, in accordance with the doctrine of *taqiyah* (cf. Patai 1987; Patton 1920:458). For a blanket Christian condemnation of lying, we can turn to Saint Augustine, in his attack on the Priscillianists (Deferrari 1952; cf. Forrester 1989:152) in 420 AD, and in his earlier short thesis *De mendacio*. Augustine condemned the Priscillian doctrine that it was permissible to lie about religious beliefs in order to protect them from outsiders. He later had doubts about the clarity of his thesis but nevertheless it became established in the orthodoxy of medieval Christianity as an eight-valued calculus of lying (Augustine 1952:60–66, 86–88, 146–170; cf. Bok 1978:34–37). In Augustine's scheme, all lies are sinful, though some are not as bad as others.

The causal link posited by Arendt between the burgeoning of science and the enhanced condemnation of lying has still to be demonstrated. Arendt associates science with a stress on 'absolute veracity and reliability', but these values are better linked to Puritanism and the philosophy of Kant (1949; 1964:92–96, 155) who, at least in his later writings, followed St Augustine in condemning all lies (cf. Bok 1978:37ff., 295 n.15; Kant 1930:224–229), than with the beginnings of modern science, still closely associated with alchemy and astrology (cf. Uberoi 1978).

Twentieth-century moralists tend to write approvingly of benign lies and social lies, while condemning malevolent lies. The blanket condemnation of all lies made by Kateb (1980) is unusual for this century. Most commentators nowadays acknowledge that some lies are justifiable and even desirable. Likewise few lay people would condemn all lies, and even fewer, if any, would condemn none. There are differences from one culture and subculture to another in how lying is viewed, and within communities some people are more condemnatory than others. Having a clear understanding of one's own position, irrespective of how it compares with the views of others, may be recommended as a first step towards getting rid of guilt feelings (e.g. Larsen 1979:179). Many scholarly texts give the results of surveys of attitudes. One of the earliest examples is a collection of instances of lying, provided by 673 college students and schoolchildren and analysed by Leonard (1920). In more recent inquiries greater attention has been given to the representativeness of the sample, and empirical findings have taken over completely from the mixture of reporting and moralizing typical of Leonard and his contemporaries. For example, in a study of schoolchildren in England and New South Wales, the proportion of those who 'think that telling a lie is always wrong' was about 19 per cent for twelve-year-olds but only 4 per cent for fifteen-year-olds (Corson 1984). We have already mentioned in chapter 5 the attitudes of European and Australian adults towards lying in one's own interest. Information of this kind is relatively easy to collect, but only if the collection is done systematically over the years does it become possible to establish reliable connexions between replies to questionnaires and decisions taken in the real world.

Other empirical inquiries show that variation in attitudes to lying can be associated with attributes like age and gender. For example, in a recent study of children aged four to eleven attending middle-class suburban schools, presumably in Australia, Bussey (1992) found that older children had stronger feelings of pride in truthfulness than did younger children, though there was no significant difference between boys and girls in their evaluation of protective lies. Gender differences have, however, been found later in life in some North American inquiries. Two of the studies by Lindskold and Walters (1983), mentioned in chapter 6, showed that female university undergraduates were less tolerant of lying than were male students. However in another of their studies they found no significant difference between the attitudes expressed by male and female undergraduates living on campus; both groups were less tolerant of lying than were older evening-school students. A more striking difference of another kind is revealed in the survey of attitudes held by American physicians mentioned in chapter 6. Seventy-four per cent of the respondents said that they considered that deception was utilized by physicians 'occasionally' or 'often', but only 19 per cent admitted to doing so themselves (Novack et al. 1989:2984).

This intermediate view of lying, in which some lies are bad and others acceptable or even good, is the attitude held by the laity, not only in industrial societies but, as far as we can tell from the ethnographic evidence, by members of most non-industrial societies as well. Albert

(1972:98) speaks of 'the high cultural evaluation of clever lies and evasions' of the Barundi people among whom she worked, but also mentions that one of her informants gave her false assurances that he did not lie; this suggests that even the Barundi sometimes express disapproval of some kinds of lying.

Some discussions of practical ethics include advice on what kinds of lies are permissible. For example, handbooks of medical ethics often include a section dealing with lies that may be told to patients who are dying, who are being given placebos or are taking part in clinical trials. But perhaps it is significant that in at least one instance this section is camouflaged under the title 'Truth-telling' (Veatch 1978).

How do we decide which lies are bad and which are good? As noted earlier, common experiences from travel abroad in unfamiliar cultures teach us, sometimes rather painfully, that lies acceptable in one society may not necessarily be acceptable in another. Phillips (1965:79), discussing social interaction in a village near Bangkok, writes:

> The typical Bang Chaner excels in the art of indicating agreement with people – responsiveness, cooperativeness, and compliance with their verbal requests and orders – and then once the situation has been concluded, doing precisely what he wants, often exactly the opposite of that to which he had agreed.

This behaviour, devious as it appears to Western eyes, is not, says Phillips, evidence of an intention to deceive; rather, it is a manifestation of the unsurprising cultural evaluation that 'People are much happier when you agree with them and tell them what they want to hear', combined with the assumption that plans and intentions can be changed 'with impunity at the slightest provocation' (cf. Bilmes 1975:66, 68).

As mentioned in chapter 1, Bok (1978:20) considers two perspectives on lying, that of the liar and that of the dupe. Ford and Hollender (1988) comment that 'the lie is often perceived by the recipient as an aggressive assault'. Whether or not we feel sympathetic towards liars, we all realize that we ourselves may become dupes. Hence it is in our interest that lying should be avoided as far as possible, particularly when we adopt the viewpoint of the deceived. Bok (1980:7) gives a good illustration of the difference between the two perspectives. She recalls the actions of Frederick II of Prussia who, as Crown Prince, wrote a book attacking the doctrines of Machiavelli, and then later, when he had become king, instructed his employee Voltaire to see that all copies of the book were destroyed.

In Bok's view there is an essential asymmetry in the relation of lies to truth. 'Lying', she says (Bok 1978:30), 'requires explanation, whereas truth ordinarily does not'. Likewise there is asymmetry between lying and secrecy. For: 'Lies are part of the arsenal used to guard and to invade secrecy; and secrecy allows lies to go undiscovered and to build up'; yet: 'Whereas every lie stands in need of justification, all secrets do not' (Bok 1984:xv).

Thus although Bok takes what we call an intermediate position, her point on the continuum is nearer to the pole of complete prohibition. She bases her moral philosophy on what she calls the principle of veracity, namely 'that truthful statements are preferable to lies in the absence of special considerations' (Bok 1978:30). In her book she devotes most space to discussing what these special considerations might be, and rejects many of those that have been put forward by other writers. She is particularly suspicious of excuses advanced by liars themselves, notably by members of the medical profession. Her principle of veracity is easy to accept; the crunch comes when we start to specify the special considerations. Furthermore, in pursuing veracity, we should not lose sight of intent. Writing nearly two hundred years ago, William Blake (1982:491) reminded his readers that:

> A truth thats told with bad intent
> Beats all the Lies you can invent.

A few writers have taken a more positive view of lying, and have argued for its importance and inevitability. We have referred earlier to Nietzsche's condemnation of religion as a 'holy lie'. This condemnation is however an atypically clear statement of Nietzsche's views, and does not sit well with his more general statements on lying, which are somewhat confused. For example, he says (1968a:204): 'The powerful always lie' and

We have need of lies in order to conquer this reality, this 'truth', that is, in order to *live* – That lies are necessary in order to live is itself part of the terrifying and questionable character of existence. (Ibid.:451)

In these statements Nietzsche seems to say that lying is inevitable if we are to avoid depression or perhaps even if we are to remain sane. He says that with the help of lies 'one can have *faith* in life'. But when describing his 'great man' he is clearly in favour of lies:

A great man – a man whom nature has construed and invented in the grand style – what is he? ... He rather lies than tells the truth; it requires more spirit and *will*. (Ibid.:505)

In much the same vein is the taunt in his *Genealogy of morals*:

Our educated people of today, our 'good people', do not tell lies – that is true; but that is not to their credit! A real lie, a genuine, resolute, 'honest' lie (on whose value one should consult Plato) would be something far too severe and potent for them: ... All they are capable of is a *dishonest* lie ... (Nietzsche 1968b:573)

Statements such as these might seem to point to a simple dichotomy: lying is to be admired in great men but deplored in priests and philosophers. But there are numerous other references to lying in Nietzsche's writings that do not tally with this dichotomy. His longest treatment of the topic is in his posthumously published unfinished essay 'On truth and lies in a nonmoral sense'. Here he describes the liar as someone who uses words 'to make something unreal appear as real'. He speaks of man having 'an invincible inclination to allow himself to be deceived' and of lying as 'an artistic pleasure'. The drive to lie, he says, is 'fundamental' (Nietzsche 1979:81, 89, 96, 97). Bok (1978:7, 29) gives little space to Nietzsche's views. She labels him and Machiavelli as advocates of deceit and violence. Nietzsche's advocacy was, however, differentially directed and was coupled with a stress on the weakness of ordinary mortals and their propensity for being deceived. His ambivalent attitude is well put in one of his 'Maxims and missiles':

There is such a thing as a hatred of lies and dissimulation, which is the outcome of a delicate sense of humour; there is also the selfsame hatred but as the result of cowardice, in so far as falsehood is forbidden by Divine law. Too cowardly to lie ... (Nietzsche 1911:6)

Compared with the amount that has been written about the concept of truth, the corpus of literature on lying, viewed morally and philosophically, may be small but the body of sociological writing on lying is meagre indeed. Rousseau (1973:86) was one of the first writers to suggest a sociological explanation for the spread of lying, with his contrast between, on the one hand, archaic societies where there was no surplus, and hence no envy, and on the other market societies with competition for relative superiority:

It now became the interest of men to appear what they really were not; and from this distinction sprang insolent pomp and cheating trickery, with all the numerous vices that go in their train.

Spencer (1892:400–409) includes a chapter on 'Veracity' in his *Principles of ethics* and presents an array of snippets of ethnographic comment from all over the world, including a remark about Indian hill tribesmen made by a Brahman: he 'is such a fool that he will tell the truth without any reason at all'. On the basis of this evidence, which by the standards of today would not pass muster, Spencer argues that hunting-and-gathering peoples are untruthful, as are 'members of larger societies consolidated by conquest under despotic rulers'. The ancient Greeks had little regard for veracity, whereas the Hebrew people, on adopting a settled way of life, became more truthful. Spencer claims that there is no association between

141

bloodthirstiness and the telling of lies, and his firmest conclusion is that 'it is the presence or absence of despotic rule which leads to prevalent falsehood or prevalent truth (cf. Forrester 1989:153; Koyré 1943:100–101).

Spencer ends his survey by contrasting the 'universal and loathsome treachery' of statesmen in Elizabethan England 'when monarchical power was still but little qualified' with the 'veracity of statesmen in recent days', i.e. in late nineteenth-century England. I think he would not have written so confidently had he lived a hundred years later. His interest is focussed on reports of the incidence of lying and truthfulness, rather than on whether or not there are sanctions against lying. He does not discuss, for instance, the fact that among the Inca, lying was a crime punishable by imprisonment (Guáman Poma 1980:286; cf. Ackerman 1990:1).

In the twentieth century, psychologists, rather than sociologists, have made innumerable investigations of lying and its detection, mainly involving children and mainly carried out in the laboratory rather than in the field. More recently social anthropologists have published several valuable studies of real-life lying, mainly by adults rather than children. For a convincing sociological analysis of lying, however, we still have to go back to the work of Georg Simmel, first published over eighty years ago. He wrote only four pages explicitly on lying. His short discussion is closely related to his more extended treatment of secrecy and the circulation of knowledge. Simmel, more than his contemporaries, stresses the ubiquity of conflict in social life and entitles one of his essays 'How is society possible?' He argues that for social interaction to take place between two persons, each must know something about the other. Reciprocal knowledge is, he says, 'the positive condition of social relationships' (Simmel 1906:448). But it is not the sole condition. Relationships, he says,

actually presuppose also a certain nescience, a ratio, that is immeasurably variable to be sure, of reciprocal concealment.

Indulging in what may now sound as unjustified reification, he says:

The strenuous organizing forms which appear to be the real constructors of society, or to construct society as such, must be continually disturbed, unbalanced, and detached by individualistic and irregular forces, in order that their reaction and development may gain vitality by alternate concession and resistance. Relationships of an intimate character, the formal vehicle of which is psycho-physical intimacy, lose the charm, and even the content, of their intimacy, unless the proximity includes, at the same time and alternately, distance and intermission.

To obtain 'reciprocal concealment' people lie, though

The lie is only a very rude form, in the last analysis often quite self-contradictory, in which this necessity comes to the surface.

Lying with the object of achieving the limitation of the knowledge of an associate is, says Simmel,

only one of the possible means, the positive and aggressive technique, so to speak, the purpose of which in general is obtained through sheer secrecy and concealment. (Simmel 1906:448–449)

He then goes on to discuss, at much greater length, the characteristics of secret societies, which make extensive use of this defensive technique.

There are two points about Simmel's discussion of lying that are worth noting. First is the emphasis he places on deception not about the state of the world but about the state of mind of the liar. He says:

the liar hides his true idea from the other. Its [the lie's] specific nature is not exhaustively characterized by the fact that the person lied to has a false conception about the topic or object; this the lie shares with common error. What is specific is that he [the dupe] is kept deceived about the private opinion of the *liar*. (Simmel 1950:312)

The second point is the contrast that Simmel draws between 'primitive man, living in communities of restricted extent' (1906:445) on the one hand, and on the other 'modern civilized life'. Writing in 1908 he argues that

in very simple circumstances the lie is often more harmless in regard to the maintenance of the group than under more complex conditions. Primitive man who lives in a small group ... surveys and controls the material of his life more easily and completely than does the man of higher cultures. ... the practice of his life is guided in the main by those few facts and circumstances of which his narrow angle of vision permits him to gain directly a *correct* view. In a richer and larger cultural life, however, existence rests on a thousand premises which a single individual cannot trace and verify to their roots at all, but must take on faith. Our modern life is based to a much larger extent than is usually realized upon the faith in the honesty of the other ... Under modern circumstances, the lie, therefore, becomes something much more devastating than it was earlier, something which questions the very foundations of our life ... modern life is a 'credit economy' in a much broader than a strictly economic sense. (Simmel 1950:313)

We now know a great deal more about the complexity of contemporary pre-industrial societies, a complexity that has been present, as far as we can tell from the archaeological record, for the last ten thousand years. Simmel's contrast, which was plausible in the light of the ethnographic evidence available to him when he wrote, looks less plausible today. He does not cite any evidence for his statements about 'primitive man', nor indeed for any of his claims about 'modern civilized life'. He does not mention Herbert Spencer's generalizations about lying in non-industrial societies, noted above. Yet Spencer (1902:219) supports Simmel's view when he maintains that as voluntary cooperation and 'the activities of industry' increase, so does truthfulness. However, from what we now know about modern pre-industrial societies, there would be, I think, little support for the proposition that in these societies lies are comparatively harmless for the reasons given by Simmel. It is scarcely true that 'primitive man' 'surveys and controls the material of his life more easily and completely than does the man of higher cultures' (Simmel 1906:445). On the contrary, it could well be argued that 'the material of life' can be controlled easily neither in pre-industrial nor in late twentieth-century industrial societies. Simmel was writing at a time when pre-industrial societies were envisaged by scholars in the industrial world as much more balanced, consensual and stable than subsequent empirical research has shown them to be. In these societies, lies may be judged as relatively harmless only in the sense that they are unlikely to lead to changes in the form of social organization; they have little revolutionary potential. But when Simmel claimed that lies were 'more harmless in regard to the maintenance of the group', I think he had in mind not merely the continuance of the *form* of organization but rather the continued existence of the group as a cohesive entity with unchanged membership. The ethnographic evidence, particularly for hunter–gatherer societies, indicates that in general it is easier for groups to break up or lose members because of internal quarrels when the level of technology is low.

Simmel (1950:314) does, however, suggest that lies told in 'primitive circumstances' have a potential for change; they have, he says, a 'positive *expediency*'. Social change, he asserts, takes place 'by the subordination of the weak under the physically and intellectually superior'. Successful lying is one process whereby this subordination is achieved. Yet social goals may also be achievable by means that are ethically more acceptable than lying; in Simmel's view these should then be preferred. He comments that 'Historically this process is by no means completed'. It is as part of this uncompleted process that Simmel bases his dubious contrast between wholesale and retail trade with reference to advertising, discussed in chapter 3.

Simmel also refers to the differential effect of lying according to the social distance between the liar and the dupe. He says (1950:313–314):

> The farther removed individuals are from our most intimate personality, the more easily can we come to terms with their untruthfulness, both in a practical and in an intimate psychological sense – while if a few persons closest to us lie, life becomes unbearable.

He then generalizes this proposition by saying:

it shows that the measures of truthfulness and mendacity which are compatible with the existence of certain conditions, constitute a scale on which the measures of intensity of these conditions can be read off.

I find this passage somewhat obscure but I think I grasp what Simmel is driving at. Some people become sorely distressed when they discover that someone they have trusted has in fact been deceiving them, but are less likely to feel so distressed by discovering that, for example, a politician on whom they do not depend has been shown to be a liar. But there is also evidence, for example the interviews with American women reported by Werth and Flaherty (1986) presented in chapter 7, that sometimes people are more ready to make allowances for, or to forgive, close associates than they are deceivers who are not so close to them affectively. Likewise many people are reluctant to 'come to terms', as Simmel puts it, with politicians whom they do not know personally.

Simmel (1950:312–313) is on firm ground when he states that 'Sociological structures differ profoundly according to the measure of lying which operates in them'.

Simmel (1950:316) rounds off his discussion of lying by saying that, though lies have an ethically negative value, they have also 'sociologically quite positive significance for the formation of certain concrete relations'. I hope that I have shown something of this positive significance, even though the concrete relations Simmel had in mind were, I think, not those on which I have focussed my attention. In his discussion of lies he seems to be talking about dyadic relations which are being constituted piecemeal, whereas the fully institutionalized relations that come under his scrutiny are, as he says, more often sustained by secrecy and concealment than by positive lying. Nevertheless I fully agree with Gilsenan (1976:191), in his gloss on Simmel, when he says:

The lie is a technique for the restriction of the social distribution of knowledge over time, and is thus ultimately woven into the system of power and control in society.

I suspect that Lt.-Col. Oliver North would also endorse this proposition.

Some commentators argue that studies applying games theory to arms races point towards the necessity of deception as well as secrecy in international relations if the likelihood of war is to reduced, so that neither side can be sure that its estimate of the enemy's strength is accurate. Without deception, says Alexander (1987:239–240) 'there would be times (not entirely predictable) when the temporarily more powerful adversary might simply *use* its advantage before it is lost'. Given the human capacity for self-deception, together with the abundant instances of self-deceived policy makers in twentieth-century international conflicts, Alexander's argument, if he has only outwardly targeted deception in mind, is open to question. Nevertheless, even if Simmel would have preferred modes of interaction that are ethically preferable to lying, I think he would have conceded that in delaying or avoiding war, lying does sometimes have 'quite positive significance'.

In general, then, Simmel may be said to have drawn attention to an important aspect of social life which few earlier writers had looked at sociologically, and which subsequent generations of sociologists have curiously neglected. Later research has shown him to have been mistaken about pre-industrial societies, and further developments in industrial societies, notably the emergence of mass media and the growth of disinformation generated by governments and pressure groups, have undermined his projection for the future. Nevertheless, Simmel's contribution to understanding is well worth having.

Unfortunately Bok, in her treatise on lying, does not mention the work of Simmel. Discussing her principle of veracity, she says that 'trust in some degree of veracity functions as a *foundation* of relations among human beings; when this trust shatters or wears away, institutions collapse' (Bok 1978:31). I think that Simmel would have agreed with Bok that veracity is an essential constituent of many of the 'relations among human beings', but I doubt if he would have endorsed the second half of her statement. On the contrary, it is clear to me that he would maintain that some institutions of 'modern civilization' thrive on the absence of trust, however regrettable this may be. Indeed, that institution which is arguably the dominant social institution of the twentieth century, warfare, flourishes precisely because trust is so often shattered or worn away.

11

Do we have to have lies?

EVOLUTIONARY PERSPECTIVES

Lies, we have seen, are a mixed blessing. If we wanted to, could we stop telling them? If we cannot do away with our ability to lie, and/or we prefer to continue to lie, how much lying should we aim at? In this final chapter I put forward a decidedly woolly answer to the second question and, I hope, a rather more definite answer to the first.

We can all agree that lying has been a human activity for a long time; but just how long has it been with us? We might argue that the more recent its first occurrence, the easier it might be to eradicate it. We know that lying was a recognized phenomenon in classical Greece three thousand years ago. We can only guess what happened earlier but if, suppose, lying was an innovation arising out of the agricultural revolution some ten thousand years ago, it would then be not an ineradicable human characteristic; it would be rather the product of a change in economic life and hence potentially open to modification or even eradication with further economic changes. On the other hand, if lying has been possible for humans for many more thousands of years, the prospects for curbing the propensity to lie are much dimmer.

In the past many writers assumed that the contemporary way of life of pre-literate communities, particularly those of hunters and foragers, provided evidence for how all humans, including our own ancestors, lived in prehistoric times. Nowadays this evidence is used much more cautiously, for we recognize that even the most isolated present-day human communities have histories of millennia of development behind them, during which they have indubitably changed significantly. Recently, many scientists, particularly sociobiologists and ethologists, have begun to use evidence from contemporary animals, particularly from non-human primate species, to make inferences about the human and hominid past. Here, I think, we are on much firmer ground. If the way of life of a species

147

is governed mainly by genetic inheritance rather than by inter-generational teaching, it is likely to change more slowly. We should still be very cautious about the inferences we make but that is no reason for refraining from making them; what better evidence have we got? Scientific interest in this topic has increased in the last two or three decades, and has affected current perceptions of many phenomena, including deception. For example, at the 1991 annual meeting of the American association for the advancement of science a symposium was held with the title 'The evolution of deception: a biocultural approach'.

The evidence presented in the preceding chapters should suffice to establish the ubiquity of lying as a human activity, as well as its diversity and antiquity. We know that some plants and many animals deceive their predators. We may therefore well ask when, and perhaps how and why, in the long story of animate evolution, did deception, and later lying, appear on the scene? In our present inquiry we are of course mainly concerned only with the latest stages in the evolution of deception but some reference to earlier stages can form a useful preliminary to the next, and pragmatically more important, question: what are the advantages and disadvantages of possessing the ability to deceive? In the light of a discussion of these two questions, we can go on to consider how this ability can best be used.

The processes, social as well as mental, whereby human liars deceive human dupes are much more complicated than those involved in, say, the deception of predatory birds by the presence of misleading markings on the wings of butterflies. Only humans, and possibly some other primate species, are capable of deception that is fashioned to take full account of how their dupes are likely to react to the action of the deceiver. Langer (1972:163) maintains that 'no animal can deliberately feign, deceive, distort evidence, or invent any ruse to trick an antagonist'. She makes her claim by limiting her attention to 'intentional deception' but even with this limitation the proposition is negated by studies of non-human primates. Robert Mitchell (1986:21–29) has proposed a typology in which he distinguishes four levels of deception, increasing in complexity. At the lowest level we find plants and butterflies that deceive by appearance; they cannot do otherwise, and they do so all the time. At the next level some birds attempt to deceive by actions such as feigning injury; the right stimulus has to occur but the response then follows involuntarily. At level three we have animals learning to deceive, as when a dog fakes an injured leg because past experience has taught it that this behaviour evokes sympathetic responses from its human masters. Finally, on level four, we have planned deception, designed to deal with novel circumstances; this level is achieved by at least some chimpanzees and baboons as well as by innumerable humans (cf. Byrne and Whiten 1992; Trivers 1985:395– 420), though the plans seemingly adopted by non-human primates are comparatively simple (Shultz and Cloghesy 1981:466; cf. Premack 1976:676– 677; Whiten and Byrne 1988b).

It is at the fourth level, and to some extent at level three, that what Christie and Geis (1970) call Machiavellian skill is needed (cf. Machiavelli 1965:5–96). This is the ability to take account, in deciding how to act, of the likely responses of others. It is, among other things, the skill needed to succeed in the contests analysed in the theory of games, 'in which the best course of action for each participant depends on what he expects the other participants to do' (Schelling 1960:9–10), but its sphere of application is not confined to this context.

Social psychologists draw a distinction between two kinds of intelligence, Machiavellian and technical (Byrne and Whiten 1988), a distinction corresponding to Cheney and Seyfarth's (1990: chapter 9) social and non-social intelligence, and Jolly's (1988) social intelligence and object-oriented intelligence. All these writers assert that the two kinds of intelligence can be distinguished, and that possession of one kind is not necessarily accompanied by possession of the other. In Cheney and Seyfarth's (1990:261–262) formulation, the two kinds of ability are domain specific.

Technical intelligence is the kind of intelligence needed to cope with the physical or inanimate world, whereas Machiavellian or social intelligence is the ability needed to cope with other animate beings, notably, in the case of humans, with other people. A person using Machiavellian skill takes account of the likely responses of other people in deciding on a course of action. Used in this sense, the exercise of Machiavellian skill is not linked *necessarily* with guile and deceit; indeed Machiavelli (1965:66) himself points out that sometimes, though only sometimes, it might be in the interests of his Prince to *be* 'merciful, trustworthy, humane, blameless' and even religious, and not merely falsely appear to be so. An individual who, in deciding how to act, takes account of the likely responses of others, may well decide to act in an honest, sincere, and even altruistic fashion. What is entailed with this ability, however, as with Machiavelli's own advice to the Prince, is the ever-present possibility of exercising deception if the individual thinks that it would be in his or her interests, short-term or long-term, to do so. It is this possibility of deception that I shall be mainly concerned with, but I must emphasize that in achieving trustful interpersonal cooperation the exercise of Machiavellian skill is equally advantageous. Indeed, according to one view (Cheney and Seyfarth 1990:258; Humphrey 1983:51–52), this skill evolved in early hominid populations because it facilitated cooperation, even though at the same time it enhanced the ability to deceive (Carrithers 1990). Trivers (1971) stresses the complexity of the advantages and costs of altruism and cheating in human populations. He argues that although selection pressures favour those who are 'subtle cheaters', they also favour the ability to detect and discriminate against those who cheat. In his textbook *Social evolution* Trivers (1985) says little about selection for social intelligence used cooperatively but has a great deal to say about selection for the ability to deceive, including the ability to deceive oneself. The Mach scale devised by Christie and Geis (1970), discussed in chapter 8, clearly focusses on the uncooperative rather than the cooperative use of Machiavellian skill.

What distinguishes animate beings from inanimate objects is their ability to act and to react. The social environment is reactive, and humans, like many other animals, take this into account in deciding what to do. In this sense the social world presents a greater challenge to those who try to cope with it than does the physical world of inanimate objects. As noted earlier, this leads to the sciences with softer data being those with the hardest problems of interpretation. My point is that individuals, humans and apes alike, have an advantage if they possess the capacity to infer what is likely to be the response of others should they themselves act in a certain way. If individuals are able to choose from a range of possible actions, and not merely between inaction and a pre-programmed response, they are further advantaged. If they can make their choices in the light of beliefs about what is going on in the minds of their fellows they are advantaged even further. Cheney and Seyfarth (1990:254) suggest that

many of the most fundamental differences between the minds of monkeys and the minds of apes will ultimately be traced to the apes' superior skills in attributing states of mind to each other.

Human infants acquire this skill gradually as part of their growing sense of self-awareness, their sense of differentiation from those around them.

Machiavellian skill is restricted to some primate genera; how it arose in the higher primates is still a matter about which the experts disagree (Byrne and Whiten 1992:624–625; Whiten and Byrne 1988a) and is not of direct concern to us here. We merely note that Nic Humphrey (1983:23) suggests that

the evolution of a social system capable of supporting advanced technology should only happen under conditions where improvements in technique can substantially increase the return on labour.

These conditions were met three or four million years ago when hominids moved into the African savanna, where they 'discovered an environment where technical knowledge began to pay new and continuing dividends'. This thesis seems to depend on the possibility of using increased

Machiavellian intelligence to achieve technical and material ends. Cheney and Seyfarth (1990:262) make the point that although the two contrasted kinds of intelligence may be domain specific, 'rules learned in one domain can be abstracted and extended to other domains'. They support Humphrey's view when they comment that 'a crucial distinction between humans and other primates may be that humans are better able to generalize, or extend, skills used in social interaction to nonsocial domains'.

Dennett (1987:275–276) argues along similar lines. He says that although many non-human primates live as members of cohesive groups, the simplicity of their social organization obviates the need for attributing mental states to other individuals, an ability he terms higher-order intentionality. Humans, spider monkeys and chimpanzees, however, live in more fluid groupings in which this ability is essential. He therefore argues that the ability evolved because of selective pressures favouring individuals who possessed it. Cheney and Seyfarth (1990:252) query this argument. While speculating that, because of the simplicity of their social organization, vervet monkeys 'could not make use of most of the features of human language', they suggest that maybe 'the ability to attribute states of mind to others is what *permits* social groups to become more fluid and less stable'. Maybe both views are partially correct; increasing ecological pressure may favour the survival of groups with complex and fluid types of social organization which can be sustained only by individuals able to attribute mental states to others. Hence the two features, higher-order intentionality and fluid social organization, may have evolved together.

Some primatological evidence seems to indicate that social complexity, and the intelligence that sustains it, can develop ahead of technical intelligence (Jolly 1988; Chevalier-Skolnikoff 1986:211; cf. Jolly 1985:379). The greater importance of social, rather than technical, intelligence is captured by Humphrey (1983:16) when he says:

it was the arrival of Man Friday on the scene which really made things difficult for Crusoe. If Monday and Tuesday, Wednesday, and Thursday had turned up as well then Crusoe would have had every need to keep his wits about him.

Much the same view is taken by Cheney and Seyfarth (1990:252) who note that vervet monkeys have at most a limited ability to take account of what others are likely to do and feel, whereas chimpanzees are better equipped in this respect, and humans better still. They note that this ability may be less useful to vervets, who live in troops, than it is to chimpanzees whose social groupings are more fluid. Yet even so, they provide evidence for one vervet deliberately deceiving another.

Together with Machiavellian skill and its associated theories of mind, the ability to deceive is facilitated by the ability to indulge in fantasy. We cannot tell to what extent non-human primates indulge in fantasy but the human ability to do so is made manifest at an early age. Infants become capable of engaging in fantasy, and thus of distinguishing between what is real and what is imagined, before they become capable of attributing to others states of mind different from their own. As Cheney and Seyfarth (1990:244) put it,

a toddler who is as yet unable to lie successfully about the cookie crumbs on her face can nonetheless invite a teddy bear to a tea party.

Equipped with the ability both to fantasize and to envisage what others will think, lying becomes a feasible option. Piaget (1932:135; cf. Vasek 1986:285) maintains that 'the tendency to tell lies is a natural tendency ... an essential part of a child's egocentric thought'. Victor Tausk (1933:46 n.5), writing in 1919, claimed that lying by infants during their first year of life is not unusual. James Sully (1895:258), a pioneer psychologist, reported a case of a child lying at the tender age of seventeen and a half months. More recently Judy Dunn (1988:160, 163) writes of the growing 'enjoyment of deliberate falsehood or misnaming' by young children in their second year, and sees this as 'further evidence for the children's understanding of the rules of their world and of how to upset others'. Some writers have held that children under four years of age 'seem to have difficulty in recognizing that other individuals' beliefs or thoughts might be different from their own'. By the age of six, most can do so (Cheney and Seyfarth 1990:207–209). The ability to attribute beliefs and attitudes to others enhances one's ability both to elicit cooperation from them and to deceive them, even though both objectives can sometimes be attained without this ability. But once children are able to impute mental states to themselves and to others, thus possessing the ability called by Premack and Woodruff (1978) a 'theory of mind' (cf. Whiten 1991), they have, as it were, creative intelligence, and are appropriately labelled as *Homo sapiens*. Research designed to establish the age at which children acquire this kind of 'theory' indicates that in a sample of fifty-six English-speaking North American children, 90 per cent of the children aged under three and a half 'took active steps to disinform' an adult experimenter (Chandler et al. 1989:1272). This finding is taken as evidence that even before their third birthday, children recognize that other people may hold beliefs different from their own. Sodian and her colleagues (1991:479) challenge this claim; they maintain, on the basis of experimental evidence, that 'an understanding of false beliefs emerges at around 4 years of age'. I would like to see cross-cultural evidence.

As humans, we can choose either to act in a way that will elicit trustful cooperation from others or we can decide that our interests will be best served by provoking hostile responses from them. In either case we have a second choice to make. We can choose to act sincerely, so that our audience is able to draw correct inferences about our intentions. Alternatively, whether we seek cooperation or confrontation, we can be insincere and deliberately mislead our audience about what our real intentions are. Whichever way we choose, our success will depend at least in part on our ability to foresee how others will respond to our actions. Thus to summarize the argument so far we can say that the possession of Machiavellian intelligence is a necessary, but by no means a sufficient, condition for the exercise of the highest form of deception, while simpler kinds of deception can be achieved without this skill.

The possibilities for deception are greatly increased by the use of oral language. Otte (1974:400) notes that 'humans seem to employ an inordinate amount of deceit in communication' and explains this as being due 'in part to the fact that the vehicle for misinformation, symbolic language, is so well developed' compared to the communication systems available to other animals. Hobbes (1840:25) perceptively associates the human ability to 'multiply one untruth by another' with 'the *invention* of *names*'. Weaver (1985) suggests that the capability for complex speech probably evolved later than did Machiavellian skill but we should heed the warning given by Katharine Milton (1988:303) that 'There is little that can be said with any degree of assurance on the evolution of language'. There is considerable controversy about when language evolved; estimates vary widely, depending partly on differing views about what constitutes true language, and range from millions of years ago to only 125,000 (Elia 1988:258–259; Goodenough 1990:605; Lieberman 1991:77). For our present purposes, all we need to say is that language evolved long before the agricultural revolution and that once this step had been taken, with words being used symbolically, lying could really take off. According to Peter Reynolds (1981:232) language may have been acquired by humans for social rather than material reasons. Indeed, Karl Popper (1974:1112–1113) *almost* (but perhaps not quite!) suggests that human language evolved *because* it made lying possible. Similarly Oscar Wilde (1989:227) proclaims that the first liar 'was the true founder of social intercourse'. Rappaport (1979:180, 224, 226) comments:

the very freedom of sign from signified that permits discourse to transcend the here and now, if it does not actually make lying possible, facilitates it enormously and may encourage it as well.

Lies, he says, are 'the bastard offspring of symbols' and he maintains that 'lying expands the possibilities for deceit enormously'.

In evolutionary terms, it was advantageous for our remote ancestors to develop Machiavellian intelligence which, among other things, enabled its possessors to deceive their fellows more effectively than had been possible hitherto; why, then, should the exercise of this ability by human beings, by and large, be regarded as reprehensible? Moreover, this adverse judgment on deceit and lying is no recent phenomenon. Lying, the most developed medium for the conduct of fourth level deception, was condemned by the writers of antiquity, even though some of them made important exceptions. We therefore cannot treat the disapproval of lying as a response to some quite recent global phenomenon like over-population or environmental degradation.

To explain both the sustained disapproval of lying and its persistence despite this disapproval we must look back long before Plato. A capacity or propensity that is advantageous at one stage of human evolution need not necessarily remain advantageous indefinitely. For example, the preference for sweet things rather than sour, which nowadays plays havoc with children's teeth, was advantageous for our remote ancestors, in that it led them to spurn unripe fruit; they were not faced every day with well-stocked supermarket shelves. Direct evidence on the social organization of early hominids is sparse indeed (Tanner 1981:169–190) but even if our very remote ancestors were relatively solitary, studies of non-human primates suggest that group living came to characterize early human social organization. Unlike the genetically uniform eusocial animals such as ants and wasps, our group-living ancestors were social animals, with individual as well as collective reproductive interests. Cooperation entailed trust and hence disapproval of deceit, but Machiavellian skill, essential for cooperation, could continue to be used deceptively to further individual interests. Hence deceit persisted despite disapproval. The exercise of Machiavellian skill in good faith is clearly essential to the maintenance of a complex social order at the present time, and we have no grounds for thinking that it has not been essential throughout hominid and human history; but if its use deceptively has, at least in part, a genetic basis, the reproductive chances of liars and other deceivers would be favoured. Nowadays, as the control and intrusiveness of the communications media approximate ever more closely to Orwell's *1984*, the societal dangers of the untrammelled exercise of Machiavellian skill become more conspicuous. Tension between its sincere and deceptive uses is unavoidable. Locke (1894:147) was not entirely mistaken in saying that 'men find pleasure to be deceived', yet most of the time people dislike being lied to. They feel that the liar is trying to manipulate them, and any trust they may have had in him or her is undermined. Hence they have a hostile attitude to lying, even if they also tell lies.

Whatever may be the reasons for Machiavellian skill being advantageous, the disapproval of lying and other modes of deception constitutes an attempt by the community to set constraints on the deceptive exercise of that skill. All humans, we can argue, benefit by being able to live in complex social systems rather than having to forage and hunt on the savanna. The agricultural revolution, marking the break with foraging and hunting, began some ten thousand years ago. Since that date, increasing numbers of humans have enjoyed the advantages of participating in forms of social organization that are more complex, flexible and diversified and yet which, unlike the societies of the eusocial insects, are not entirely rigid. In this sense all members of a society are advantaged by the exercise of Machiavellian skill, without which these complex societies would collapse, even though the advantages of using this same skill for deception are likely to be unevenly distributed. Without Machiavellian skill, human society as we know it today would not exist. I am not, of course, trying to say that complex societies are in all respects preferable to the societies of hunters and collectors, nor do I deny that many members of complex societies might have lived happier lives if, instead of being slaves or serfs, or even wage slaves, they had faced the freedoms and hardships of foraging and hunting; complex societies are typically societies of inequality. Nevertheless, even from the standpoint of a polluted and overcrowded world, we cannot shut our eyes to the gains achieved during the last ten thousand years through societal complexity.

Yet even if the possession of Machiavellian skill is potentially advantageous for all humans, forager and factory worker, slave and lord, the same potential equality of benefit does not necessarily flow from the constraints on lying which, we postulate, are also in the general interest. Who, then, benefits, and who is disadvantaged, by a limitation on the deceptive use of Machiavellian skill? For purposes of discussion, we can envisage a continuum running between societies characterized by the polar conditions of total truthfulness at one end and random truthfulness and deceit at the other. In the next section we look at this continuum and try to identify a point on it to aim at.

OPTIMAL ARRANGEMENTS

In the absence of published research findings, we can only speculate about the advantages and disadvantages of too much or too little lying in social life. Philosophers and sociologists seem to agree that if everyone told lies all the time, social life would collapse; indeed it would never have begun. There is no empirical evidence for this; indeed, almost by definition there could not possibly be such evidence. Nevertheless the proposition seems eminently plausible. We could perhaps argue that if all utterances are known to be lies, and if all lies are simply deceptive untruths, it is fairly simple to decode them and to arrive at the truth by believing the opposite of whatever has been said or written. But looking for the opposite of what has been said may face us, as Montaigne noted long ago, with a choice of many options. More importantly, if we knew that our audience would take anything we say as a lie, we could simply deceive them by telling them the truth, confident that they would assume wrongly that the truth lay elsewhere, as illustrated in chapter 8.

Discussions about what would happen if there were absolutely no lies must also necessarily be mainly speculative. The sociobiologist Richard Alexander (1987:73) asserts that because of the genetic differences between all humans, with the exception of identical twins, 'nearly all communicative signals ... should be expected to involve significant deceit' (cf. Trivers 1985:395, 420). On the other hand Carrithers (1990:195) argues, with reference to early human society, that:

To the extent that the individual had become dependent on one feature of its environment, namely its conspecifics configured as a group, deception could be only a minor theme, a departure from a basic consensus.

A third speculation is provided by Bok (1978:18) when she speaks of a state of affairs when all statements were 'randomly truthful or deceptive'; then, she says, 'action and choice would be undermined from the outset'. This too is merely a hypothetical condition; it might be simulated in a laboratory but is unlikely to exist in nature. Fewer writers have discussed the extreme condition where everyone tells the whole truth all the time; there is no empirical evidence from the real world as to what would happen in this condition either. I am inclined to agree with Eck (1970:69) when he says: 'Not to speak the truth is sometimes a duty', and: 'A society in which all truths were bluntly exposed would be more like a hell than a paradise.' Indeed, in his allegory of the cave, Plato (1966:123–125) remarks that the man who tried to expose the deceit being practised on his fellow prisoners would be killed by them (cf. Arendt 1968:229). Eck's pronouncements are backed up by Scheibe (1980:18) in his comment on the advice sometimes given to young married couples that they should be utterly honest with one another, practise complete candour and have no secrets. This advice is, he says, regarded by marriage counsellors as advice toward a quick separation. Goffman (1956:42) takes the same view. Although we tend to think of trust and deceit as incompatible, complete trust does not entail telling the whole truth all the time. Likewise, in the special context of nude beaches and casual sex, where, as described by Douglas (1976:67), participants habitually use false names, perfectly enjoyable and satisfying social relations can take place without any general sense of trust about such cognitive matters [i.e. non-beach identities].

Douglas (1976:145) carries this observation a stage further in discussing the statements made by women working in Californian massage parlours about their sexual activities. These women, he says, distinguish between

potential customers who have to be let in on the truth of sex in the parlor; and actual or potential boyfriends who must be fronted out about most of the sex, for fear they will not stand for the whole sex-for-money game.

Douglas emphasizes his point by reference to the treatment of one of his associates in the research:

It was precisely because Rasmussen was so friendly and invited such trust that she had 'put the make on him' and she and all the others had fronted him out.

Here then we have a situation in which the more trustful the relation the greater the likelihood of deceit. But we should note that the deceit is one-sided; the massage girls deceive their boyfriends but the boyfriends, if the girls' trust in them is justified, presumably do not deceive the girls, or at least do not do so systematically. Furthermore it is only the sexual behaviour of the girls that is reported truthfully to clients and deceitfully to boyfriends; this configuration presumably does not apply to other activities, values and beliefs. Indeed, in so far as boyfriends and beach acquaintances understand the rules of the game, they are not deceived but merely knowingly misinformed. Deceit that is expected is only half-hearted deceit.

The sex industry is not the only context in which deceit and trust exist side-by-side. Secrecy, and its near neighbour deceit, is a technique for protecting highly respectable institutions as well as massage parlours. In chapter 3 we saw that even when there is complete trust between lawyers and their spouses, the latter expect to be deceived if deceit is necessary to protect professional relations. The same expectation applies to the spouses of military planners and professional counsellors; indeed it applies to all situations with clear distinctions between professional and domestic spheres of activity, with each sphere having its specific secrets. In general the use of deceit as a mode of bureaucratic or professional confidentiality is directed at all and sundry, not only at trusted spouses. What marks off the massage parlour from other contexts is that here deceit is a consequence of trust, not a limitation of it.

Trust is also a consideration in the use of deceit in social research. Bok (1978:182–202) tends to condemn using deception in social research, but interestingly gives limited approval to its employment in medical contexts through the use of pseudo-patients, healthy investigators who endeavour to be mistaken for genuinely ill patients. O'Connor and Barnes (1983) take an opposite view, rejecting any blanket condemnation of deceit, whether in the laboratory or in covert inquiries in the field; each context has to be examined separately. As most medical settings are predicated on a high level of trust by patients in those who care for them, the adoption of deceptive techniques for investigations in hospitals requires stronger justification; in this view, the adoption of pseudo-patient roles is particularly hard to justify.

Albert's (1972:75) comment, based on two years of empirical research in Africa, gives further support for deception in some situations:

A well-brought-up Murundi would suffer agonies of shame in the presence of the naked truth and would hasten to provide the esthetic coverings called for by the cultural value system.

When Lemuel Gulliver visited the country of the Houyhnhnms, where lies were completely unknown, he found neither a hell, as Eck suggests would occur, nor a paradise, certainly not for the unfortunate Yahoos (Swift 1941:203–280). The obsessively honest Houyhnhnms lack the vitality of the inhabitants of Lilliput and Brobdingnag and seem to confirm Francis Bacon's (1861a:377–378) rhetorical question:

Doth any man doubt, that if there were taken out of men's minds vain opinions, flattering hopes, false valuations, imaginations as one would, and the like, but it would leave the minds of a number of men poor shrunken things, full of melancholy and indisposition, and unpleasing to themselves?

Bok (1978:18) points to an acceptable intermediate state of affairs when she asserts that 'some level of truthfulness has always been seen as essential to human society, no matter how deficient the observance of other moral principles'.

The notion that human beings are constitutionally incapable of surviving a regime of absolute truth was advanced by Edmund Burke (1987:67), in his attack on the ruthlessly rational systematization of social institutions which he believed was taking place in revolutionary France. In order to 'cover the defects of our naked, shivering nature' it was necessary for there to be 'pleasing illusions' which 'incorporated into politics the sentiments which beautify and soften private society,' illusions which in France were 'to be dissolved by this new conquering empire of light and reason'. Despite his patrician stance Burke did not confine these illusions to any segment of society, unlike the theologian Reinhold Niebuhr (1932:221) who, at one point in his career, adopted an unashamedly elitist position when he claimed that the proletariat required 'necessary illusions' on which to base their faith and to maintain their revolutionary purpose. This may be seen as a modern version of Plato's 'noble lie', with lies being generated not only by the ruling elite but also by the revolutionary intelligentsia hoping to overthrow them.

'Noble' lies, mainly those concocted in the United States by the federal government during the last few decades, have been dissected in detail by Chomsky (1989). More recent events in the Gulf showed that governments on both sides of the conflict actively engaged in manipulating the flow of information to both friend and foe. There was the dearth of pictures of dead and wounded bodies, as mentioned in chapter 8, and there was more explicit recognition of the effort made by the military to 'control' or 'constrain' (two commonly used euphemisms for 'censor') the reports appearing in the media. This recognition led, at least in Australia, to media announcers continually stressing that their reports had been 'constrained', the caveat applying to both sides in the conflict. Similar caveats occurred in British television reports of the Falklands fighting, but even without them the juxtaposition of wildly conflicting claims from the two sides would have led to scepticism about where truth lay. Perhaps with the Gulf War we reached the point at which increased lying became counter-productive. For some, this point was reached earlier, during the Reagan presidency in the United States. In 1986 Bernard Kalb, assistant secretary of state for public affairs, resigned 'out of concern for the impact of the disinformation programme [against Moammar Gadaffi] on the credibility of the United States' (Ottaway 1986).

The phenomenon of a self-defeating excess of lying may perhaps have been absent from early hominid society, as Carrithers claims, but in historic times the disadvantages of excess and the advantages of moderation in lying were soon noted by commentators on tactics in the political arena. According to Diogenes Laertius (1959:461), Aristotle noted that known liars are not believed when they tell the truth. Francesco Guicciardini (1965:28), writing in the sixteenth century, said that he

would praise the man who in his daily life lives freely and openly and uses dissimulation only rarely and for some very important reason. ... in matters of the greatest importance you will profit most by dissimulation, the more so since having the reputation of sincerity, your duplicity will the more easily be believed

(cf. Barzini 1964:164). In the eighteenth century the dangers of excessive lying were noted by Arbuthnot (1712:16; cf. Pollard 1897:117) when he explained the

late ill success of the *Whig-Party* to their glutting the Market, and retailing too much of a bad Commodity at once: When there is too great a Quantity of Worms, it is hard to catch Gudgeons.

His contemporary Richard Steele (1898:174) made the same observation in the pages of the *Spectator*; in chapter 2 we saw that much the same advice, given, alas, in less elegant language, is repeated in our own time.

What is clear is that the last fifty years have seen an increase in the incidence of publicly recognized lies. Technological improvements in the mass media have made lying to the multitude much easier for powerful liars and, with the advent of television, much more effective. Hannah Arendt (1968:252) says that organized lying by governments aimed at the masses is a 'relatively recent phenomenon', by which I think she has in mind the twentieth century. But while the scale of organized lying has increased in this century, its onset occurred long before 1900. Arendt may be right in that only in this century have the 'masses' been targeted by governments, but organized deception by governments and other power-ful groups, aimed at selected dupes, has a much longer history. As noted in chapter 3, similar processes occur even in pre-literate societies. Yet if its roots are ancient, its incidence seems to be increasing. Jackall (1980:59) links this increase to the growth of bureaucracies. Associating himself with Max Weber's gloomy prognosis about the growth of repressive bureauc-racy, he says:

The very system of organized efficiency which underpins the material abundance of our civilization threatens to degrade us completely.

These assorted observations and comments do not take us very far towards discovering how much lying would be good for us. We should avoid the extremes of no lies and arbitrarily distributed frequent lies; we should also shun so much lying that it becomes counter-productive. But it is difficult to make any more precise inferences from the evidence.

If attempts to determine the optimal point on the continuum stretching from no lies to ubiquitous and arbitrary lying have so far had only limited success, even less progress has been made on another continuum, stretch-ing from complete detection of all lies to no detection whatsoever. Ekman (1985:281–282) provides a short discussion of the merits and demerits of lie catching, in which he refers to national interests, altruistic intentions and a legitimate wish for privacy as reasons for sometimes not detecting, or at least for not exposing, lies. He says:

I believe it worth noting that *sometimes* lie catching violates a relationship, betrays trust, steals information that was not, for good reason, given.

In chapter 6 we mentioned Scheibe's comment on the therapeutic benefit of some harmless lies and in chapter 7 we noted Snyder's argument in favour of self-deception 'at the planetary level'. Clearly, with some lies, there are advantages to both dupe and liar in avoiding detection. Both ends of the continuum, no detection at all and complete detection, are to be avoided. However, the merits and demerits of detection cannot be discussed in isolation from another phenomenon, exposure. Most writers on lying seem to have neglected this important issue. Detection affects the state of mind of the dupe but it is only with exposure that the fact of detection begins to affect others directly, including the liar. Dupes must live alone with the consequences of unexposed detection, whereas exposure brings different consequences for them as well as affecting other people. The effects of detection, and of failure to detect, vary with the domain in which the lie occurs, as do the advantages and disadvantages of exposure. In warfare, it must surely always be an advantage to commanders on one side to detect the lies told by the other, but the extent to which these lies are then exposed must be a strategic or tactical decision. It is often advantageous to deceive the enemy by not revealing that its lies have been detected. However, in the world of politics, at least in a peacetime democracy, we would be inclined to say that the more lies that are detected and exposed, the better for the community as a whole. Liberty, said John Philpot Curran, is conditional on eternal vigilance. But it was another Irishman, Edmund Burke who, as we have seen, stressed the advantages of 'pleasing illusions' in political life and who took for granted their presence in 'private society'. I take a more optimistic view of 'our naked, shivering nature' than did Burke, and would argue that in public life we should as far as possible avoid the 'pleasing illusions' provided by undetected lies. Furthermore, in this domain, detection should be followed by exposure unless, in a particular case, exposure would harm the dupe more than the liar.

In other domains the advantages and disadvantages of detection and exposure are harder to characterize. The harmless lies told for therapeutic purposes presumably are less effective if they are detected, though even in the sickbed some strong-minded patients would prefer to know the truth about themselves, and would not necessarily lose confidence in a physician if they knew that he or she had tried to deceive them. In chapter 8 we noted DePaulo and Jordan's preference for misplaced trust rather than unpleasant facts. In general, unpleasant facts are easier to bear if they are shared with others, but dupes who cannot do this face anguish in isolation. Hence a powerless and isolated dupe may be happier, though not wiser, if he or she fails to detect the lie told by a trusted liar. The testimony provided by the women interviewed by Werth and Flaherty, cited in chapter 7, illustrates the reluctance of comparatively powerless dupes to face up to unpleasant facts and the anguish they experience when they do. Thus, though we might prefer to contemplate a world in which all citizens were adequately empowered to detect and expose the lies told to deceive them, we have to recognize that in the real world the ability to detect and expose, like all other aspects of lying, is closely related to the distribution of power.

The model of society implied by writers like Sissela Bok who advocate avoiding lying wherever possible seems to be characterized by cooperation and the harmonization of interests. On the other hand we have the pragmatic view expressed in the Rundi proverb: 'The man who tells no lies cannot feed his children' (Albert 1972:90). I propose an intermediate model, drawing on Simmel's comment on the diversity of 'sociological structures', as he called them. Some social institutions, but not all, can operate adequately only if lies are kept to a minimum but are not entirely eliminated. With relations that call for maximum trust we should remember the comment made by T. S. Eliot in his *Four quartets* (1969:172) that human beings can tolerate only a limited exposure to reality. Eliot's caveat may perhaps apply to honesty in the marriage relationship though I am sure that rock climbers would opt for complete trust and truthfulness. Eliot's sentiments were expressed earlier by H. L. Mencken (1924:275) who maintained that 'the truth is something too harsh and devastating for the majority of men to bear'. More recently the American anthropologist Elizabeth Colson (1989:2) has noted that 'people respond to what they believe others are thinking; it may be fortunate that they do not *know* what the other thinks'. Similarly, Kaufmann (1970:9) notes that 'the taste for the truth is an acquired taste that few acquire'. This view is shared by Scheibe (1980:21) who draws upon evidence that patients who 'retained a hope beyond reason' recovered from illness or surgery more quickly than those who were correctly informed of the real risks. This evidence supports his proposition that 'the case for misrepresentation is stronger than the case for the utter truth on the grounds of the requirements for effective psychological functioning'. Colson and Scheibe do not call for deliberate deceit, but only for the exercise of discretion in communication of the truth.

In other social contexts where maximization of trust is not aimed at, lying and deceit may be tolerated and even called for. In these contexts lying should be used in moderation, so that it does not become counterproductive.

Inhabiting a social world entirely devoid of lies would be like living by algorithms, never having to face the challenge of ambiguity and uncertainty. In this connection an interesting observation has been made by Robert Murphy, in his comments on Thomas Gregor's study of the Mehinacu people of the Upper Xingu river area of Brazil. According to Murphy (1971:228), the Mehinacu tell one another many lies because they have 'too much information'. The fifty-seven members of the community live in close proximity; 'almost all activity is visible'. They hear a great deal about one another's activities, but much of what they hear is gossip, and may not necessarily be true, for, says Murphy, 'the Mehinacu are as good at lying as they are at adultery and gossip'. Thus we have a situation in which 'Nobody really knows, then, what is true and what is false: they are given ample doubts and few convictions'.

Omniscience poses a threat to social life, a threat that the Mehinacu meet by widespread lying. Murphy's comments are consonant with Simmel's perception of social life; elsewhere Murphy (1964:1257) refers approvingly to Simmel's (1950:312) statement that:

We simply cannot imagine any interaction or social relation or society which are [sic] *not* based on this teleologically determined non-knowledge of one another.

Murphy's comments are based on Gregor's 1969 Cornell doctoral disser-tation and, in my reading, are not fully confirmed by his later published monograph (Gregor 1977). Nevertheless I think that Murphy's comments are sound, even if they do not apply fully to the Mehinacu, in so far as they draw attention to the need for ambiguity and uncertainty in interpersonal relations. His remarks tally with the warning against complete candour between spouses mentioned earlier in this chapter.

The drabness of a world without lies can easily be inferred by imagining what Shakespeare's plays would be like with all lying removed; the salience of lies in his work has been examined at length by Ewbank (1983). As Bulwer Lytton (1848:433) said, 'no man hath better expounded the mysteries of roguery!' In the survey of contrasting values held by people in western Europe, mentioned in chapter 1, the widely held preference for honesty was found to be contrasted strongly with an emphasis on imagin-ation. Harding and Phillips (1986:22) interpret this as a contrast between 'a dominant traditional ethical value, and values emphasising individual initiative and the autonomous role of the individual'.

I suppose a preference for disciplined imagination might be seen as simply a plea for fewer but more effective lies. So far as benign lies are concerned, this is indeed what my plea amounts to; I am following in the steps of Mark Twain's well-known call for better lying (1961). I am also supported by Samuel Butler (1964:149) when he says that 'the best liar is he who makes the smallest amount of lying go the longest way ...'

The same sort of advice is given, in blunter language, by a character in one of Eric Ambler's novels: 'Never tell a lie when you can bullshit your way through' (Ambler 1969:22). Frankfurt (1986:90), in an extended dis-cussion of the notion of bullshit, says that he regards the essence of this complex concept as an 'indifference to how things really are' and a 'lack of connection to a concern with truth'. In general, bullshit, like humbug, is 'deceptive misrepresentation, short of lying', and hence attracts somewhat less moral censure and less feeling of guilt.

The position of warfare at one end of the spectrum of approval and disapproval of lying is strikingly revealed in a statement by Machiavelli in which he reverses the advice given by Butler, Ambler and innumerable moralists. In his writings Machiavelli continually emphasizes the honour and glory achieved by military success. Yet even so he writes that 'wise commanders never attempt to win by force what they can win by fraud'. This preference for lies rather than casualties is, of course, a preference held by liars; their enemy dupes are not given an opportunity to state theirs.

If the arguments outlined above amount to a plea for more effective, and if possible fewer, benign and protective lies, they do not carry the same implication for malicious lies, except perhaps in the context of war. Rather, a greater recognition that lies are not universally reprehensible, and that even our best friends tell lies, should lead us to a greater awareness of the ubiquity of lying, and hence to a diminution in the occurrence of misplaced trust. Success in malicious lying should thus become harder rather than easier. The level at which lying becomes counter-productive should become lower, not higher. Thus we should have a dialectical process in which excessive malicious lying leads to its own negation. Perhaps more importantly, the removal of the stigma attached to lying should make it easier for individuals to admit to themselves that they too, like everyone else, tell lies from time to time. If the easiest person of all to deceive is oneself, then to avoid this hazard we need all the Machiavellian skill we can muster.

Machiavellian skill is definitely an asset that contributes to general well-being. But that other asset, the enhanced capacity for deception that comes as part of the package, must be used only with moderation and restraint. This caveat is particularly relevant in those domains of social life where some use of deception is regarded as legitimate. The dangers of counter-productive lying are greatest for politicians, police officers, bureaucrats and those in similar occupations where lying in the course of duty is sometimes called for.

We cannot assume that an optimal distribution of honesty and deceit will be reached, even in the long run, by any automatic tendency towards social equilibrium. In the abstract of his classic paper on 'The evolution of reciprocal altruism', written while he was still a graduate student, Trivers (1971:35) claims:

Each individual human is seen as possessing altruistic and cheating tendencies, the expression of which is sensitive to developmental variables that were selected to set the tendencies at a balance appropriate to the local social and ecological environment.

I think it is significant that when, fourteen years later, Trivers published his textbook *Social evolution*, this happy reliance on selection pressures to bring about an appropriate balance had disappeared. We cannot rely on our genes to lead us to Utopia, or even just to optimal arrangements. We cannot be content with merely *possessing* Machiavellian intelligence; we also have to *use* it cooperatively and not only selfishly.

CONCLUSION

The evidence surveyed in this book, gathered from many sources in jackdaw-like fashion with a strong bias towards works in English, would fail dismally any tests for comprehensiveness or statistical adequacy. Quantified information is notably thin on the ground, though I take heart from a comment by Hobbs, in his prizewinning account of the culture of London's East End. To critics who complained of the absence of statistical analysis, Hobbs (1988:15) replied that 'numerically speaking, I have restricted myself to carefully numbering each page'. For despite its lack of quantification, his book, *Doing the business*, is highly persuasive. I have selected data in the first place because they have been available to me in the libraries to which I have had access, and secondly because they appeared to support, qualify or contradict the points I want to make. Given the present state of inquiries into the sociology of telling lies, I think it is worth while attempting to make a few general remarks, despite the partiality of the evidence on which they are based.

J. L. Austin (1975:1) begins his classic William James lecture series *How to do things with words* by saying:

What I shall have to say here is neither difficult nor contentious: the only merit I should like to claim for it is that of being true, at least in parts.

This must also be my limited claim. I have argued elsewhere (Barnes 1990:7) that 'a great deal of empirical inquiry in social science is directed towards discovering which popular assumptions about the workings of society are true and which are false'. Some are false, and hence the sociological effort is worth while, but fortunately for the members of society many are true. We should therefore not be too disappointed if no earthshaking insights emerge from our inquiry. Indeed, Durandin (1972:6), after studying lying for more than twenty years in the hope of coming up with some general conclusions, said he had the feeling of pushing at an open door. My own engagement with this topic has been much shorter than his. The evidence I have presented demonstrates that for the last two thousand years and more the same assorted comments and evaluations have been repeated over and over again by philosophers, theologians, moralists and others without achieving any significant steps towards agreement. The writings of social scientists are more explicitly directed towards the achievement of consensus, but as yet their inquiries are far short of comprehensive and serve to highlight the extent of our ignorance.

Perhaps the first point to make is that the evidence collected here gives strong support to Austin's basic contention that the force of an utterance is determined at least in part by the context in which it is made and heard. Similarly a written statement generates a meaning that may vary according to the context in which it is read. Austin dealt with all kinds of utterances and his claim applies as much to lies as to sincere statements. For example, the remark 'I don't know' may be accepted as true when made to a lover when in fact it is a lie; the same remark made by a prisoner in the dock may be perceived by the court as a lie when in fact it is true. Appearing on the page of a novel readers may guess whether it is true or false, but in neither case do they think that the author is trying to deceive them. When telephone answering machines first came into use, their programmed announcements such as 'This is Joe Bloggs speaking' were often preceded by a disclaiming statement that 'This is a recorded message' to make sure that callers would not be misled into thinking that Joe was really present at the other end of the line. Now that these machines are in wide use, disclaiming statements have largely disappeared, along with the likelihood that a caller would be deceived.

The importance of context, determined along the dimensions of domain, culture and structure, was demonstrated in chapters 2 to 6. Among other things I drew attention to the way in which the dupes targeted by liars are often friends rather than enemies. This inward, not outward, thrust of lies is carried a stage further in the lies considered in chapter 7, where I tried to draw a distinction between self-deception and self-delusion. The process of transformation brought about when liars start to believe their lies to be true was exemplified not only by the testimony of anguished women about their personal relations but also by statements made by American policy makers and their publicists during the Vietnam War. The consequences of self-delusion are in both cases serious, even though very different. The transformation entails a progression, extending over a few months or years, from a fairly straightforward intention to deceive on the part of the liar to a situation where it is no longer clear who, if anyone, is deceiving whom. The initial conflict of interest between liar and dupe is overlaid by a connivance or a tacit collaborative agreement to pretend, if perhaps never fully to believe, that what was formerly a lie is no longer so.

On a longer timescale we saw in chapter 8 how an individual's ability to lie and to detect lies, and his or her perception of what constitutes a lie, develop through childhood into adult life. The comparatively limited, but still significant, ability to deceive possessed by other primate species led us to assume that this process of development in humans has been going on for several tens of thousands of years. On the other hand we noted that during the present century important changes have taken place, in the increased institutionalization of lying and in the greater ease and efficiency with which lies can be generated and disseminated by elite liars. Departments of disinformation and television networks have, at least initially, improved the prospects for lying but at the same time have increased the probability that lying, by becoming excessive, becomes also counter-productive. Politics and what we called in chapter 3 'ambiguous domains' are particularly likely to experience the effects of excessive lying. Would-be free riders proliferate while the supply of naive potential dupes declines. But it would be foolish to rely on excessive lying alone to sustain an adequate level of scepticism in the general public. We need the help of a plurality of sources of information to match one fact and one opinion against another, even if plurality brings with it an increased diversity of lies. Diversity undermines the power of lies.

It is in these ambiguous domains that our regrettably vague recommendation, a call for better but fewer lies, has most relevance. There is, however, nothing vague about our recommendation that everyone should recognize the ubiquity of lying, its inevitability and its beneficial as well as its detrimental attributes, and the need for awareness of the likelihood of becoming a dupe. We should remember Hobbes' (1839:36) warning and promise:

For speech has something in it like to a spider's web ... for by contexture of words tender and delicate wits are ensnared and stopped; but strong wits break easily through them.

Further research should increase our understanding of the phenomenon of lying, and might lead to more narrowly focussed recommendations for public policy and personal conduct. We referred in chapter 1 to DePaulo and Rosenthal's plea for more research into how and when people lie in real life, rather than in psychological laboratories. Field research on this topic may be difficult but should not be impossible. Despite Ochs' (1986) plea for work in this area, one part of the research has so far been conspicuously neglected; this is the investigation of the process whereby children learn when and how to lie and when not to do so, a topic we mentioned in chapter 8. Studying children in the field presents formidable obstacles for adult investigators, but even these should not be insuperable. I am encouraged to see recent signs of revived interest by social scientists of many specializations in the ethnographic study of children (Benthall 1992).

Further inquiry should also be directed at investigating the social consequences of variation in the extent of lying and other modes of deceit in the community. Some twenty years ago two economists, Darby and Karni (1973), looked into what they described as 'the optimal amount of fraud' under certain market conditions. I think their neo-classical analytical framework would be only of limited value in tackling the wider question of determining an optimum level of deceit outside the market-place, but at least they identified an important but neglected topic for research. Maybe we would be foolish to expect ever to reach consensus about optimum levels, even if we could overcome the difficulties in determining valid ways of measuring them. It is more likely that the same diversity of views that has persisted over the centuries would merely shift unhelpfully from a qualitative to a quantitative mode. But even so, more information about the effects of minimal lying and of profligate lying might enable us to narrow the area of contention. Social science is inherently restricted to modest goals.

As an epigraph for this book I have used the first verse of Robert Browning's poem 'Childe Roland to the dark tower came', with its reference to malicious lying. The poem takes its title from a cryptic remark made by Edgar, who 'assumes madness for purposes of disguise and deception' (Kellogg 1866:24), in Shakespeare's *King Lear*. When asked about the poem, which ends somewhat abruptly, Browning said that he did not know what it meant (Pettigrew 1981:1117). In 1974 the *New Statesman* ran a weekend competition in which competitors were asked to provide two additional verses to round off the poem. It seems therefore appropriate to end my attempt to come to grips with the phenomenon of lying, a topic that is touched on in several of Browning's poems, by reprinting one of the entries to the competition. This entry can serve to drive home one of the points I have tried to make: we all tell lies.

> But hardly had the echoes died away
>   When from the crags the watchers all were gone,
>   While from the tower a form appeared alone,
> Black-outlined in the dying glow of day.
> A glance behind me showed now that the way
>   Was barred by buttresses and walls of stone.
>
> No sign or 'scutcheon did his armour show,
>   But, lifting high his sword, as I'd half-known
>   He would, he came. Like old and splintered bone
>
> His helmet shattered underneath my blow
> I saw a face beneath the blade – and lo!
>   The features staring at me were my own.

> (Conway 1974).

References

Abrahams, Raphael Garvin 1987. The name of the game? *Cambridge Anthropology* 11(2):15–20 [133]

Abrahams, Roger D. 1974. Black talking on the streets. In Bauman, Richard, and Sherzer, Joel, eds. *Explorations in the ethnography of speaking*. Cambridge: Cambridge University Press, pp. 240–262 [2]

Ackerman, Raquel 1990. Deception among the southcentral Quechua (unpublished) [103, 142]

Adams, Robert M. 1977. *Bad mouth; fugitive papers on the dark side*. Berkeley: University of California Press [33]

Adams, Timothy Dow 1990. *Telling lies in modern American autobiography*. Chapel Hill: University of North Carolina Press [96, 128]

Adenauer, Konrad 1966. *Memoirs 1945–53*. London: Weidenfeld and Nicolson [93]

Aitken, George Atherton 1892. *The life and works of John Arbuthnot*. Oxford: Clarendon Press [30]

Albert, Ethel M. 1972. Culture patterning of speech behavior in Burundi. In Gumperz, John Joseph, and Hymes, Dell, eds. *Directions in sociolinguistics: the ethnography of communication*. New York: Holt, Rinehart and Winston, pp. 72–105, [37, 51, 81, 83, 106, 116, 138f., 158, 162]

Aldrich, C. Knight 1989. Psychiatric aspects of lying. *American Journal of Psychiatry* 146: 405 [22]

Alexander, Richard D. 1987. *The biology of moral systems*. New York: Aldine de Gruyter [2, 81, 104, 145, 156]

Allen, Walter 1954. *The English novel: a short critical history*. London: Phoenix house [127]

Allon, Dafna 1985. Reflections on the art of lying. *Commentary* 81(6): 47–54 [122]

Ambler, Eric 1969. *Dirty story: a further account of the life and adventures of Arthur Abdel Simpson*. London: Fontana [163]

Amis, Martin 1975. *Dead babies*. London: Jonathan Cape [131]

Ammar, Hamed M. 1954. *Growing up in an Egyptian village: Silwa, Province of Aswan*. London: Routledge & Kegan Paul [163]

Anderson, Alan Ross 1970. St Paul's Epistle to Titus. In Martin, Robert L., ed. *The paradox of the liar*. New Haven: Yale University Press, pp. 1–11 [5]

Anonymous 1763. *Lying Intelligencer* (23 January) 1:3 [2f.]

References

Appell, George Nathan 1978. *Ethical dilemmas in anthropological inquiry: a case book.* Waltham, Mass.: Crossroads Press [61]

Arbuthnot, John 1712. (unsigned) *Proposals for printing the Art of Political Lying* (2 vols.) London: John Morphew [30, 134, 159]

Arendt, Hannah 1968. *Between past and present: eight exercises in political thought.* New York: Viking [3, 28, 30, 50, 93]

1972. *Crises of the republic.* New York: Harcourt Brace Jovanovich [3, 27, 28, 29, 44, 93, 95]

Aronfreed, Justin 1969. The concept of internalization. In Goslin, David A., ed. *Handbook of socialization theory and research.* Chicago: Rand McNally, pp. 263–323 [103]

Asch, Stanley Elliott 1956. Studies of independence and conformity I: A minority of one against a unanimous majority. *Psychological monographs* 70(9) [62]

Aubert, Vilhelm 1965. *The hidden society.* Totowa, N.J.: Bedminster Press [82]

Augustine, Saint 1952. *Treatises on various subjects.* (Deferrari, Roy Joseph, ed.) Washington, D.C.: Catholic University of America Press [12, 14, 113, 137]

Austin, John Langshaw 1975. *How to do things with words* (2nd edn). Oxford: Clarendon Press [165]

Axelrod, Robert M. 1984. *The evolution of cooperation.* New York: Basic Books [5]

Babbage, Charles 1830. *Reflections on the decline of science in England and on some of its causes.* London: Fellows & Booth [56]

Backscheider, Paula R. 1989. *Daniel Defoe: his life.* Baltimore: Johns Hopkins University Press [128]

Bacon, Francis 1861a. *The works of Francis Bacon.* Vol. 6: *Literary and professional works, vol. 1.* London: Longman [158]

1861b. *The works of Francis Bacon.* Vol. 7: *Literary and professional works, vol. 2.* London: Longman [69]

Bailey, Frederick George 1988. *Humbuggery and manipulation: the art of leadership.* Ithaca, N.Y.: Cornell University Press [30, 34f.]

1991. *The prevalence of deceit.* Ithaca, N.Y.: Cornell University Press [16, 66, 81, 83, 91, 109, 133]

Baker, Ernest Albert 1924. *The history of the English novel. The age of romance: from the beginnings to the Renaissance.* London: Witherby [128]

Baker, John Hamilton 1990. *An introduction to English legal history* (3rd edn). London: Butterworths [38]

Baker, John Hamilton, and Milsom, S. F. C. 1986. *Sources of English legal history: private law to 1750.* London: Butterworths [39]

Banville, John 1976. *Doctor Copernicus: a novel.* London: Secker and Warburg [131]

Barnes, John Arundel 1967. Genealogies. In Epstein, Arnold Leonard, ed. *The craft of social anthropology* (Social science paperbacks 22). London: Tavistock, pp. 101–127 [51]

1980. *Who should know what? Social science, privacy and ethics.* Cambridge: Cambridge University Press [47, 58, 59, 61]

1981. Professionalism in British sociology. In Abrams, Philip, Deem, Rosemary, Finch, Janet and Rock, Paul. eds. *Practice and progress: British sociology 1950–1980.* London: Allen & Unwin, pp. 13–24 [60, 132]

1990. *Models and interpretations: selected essays.* Cambridge: Cambridge University Press [10, 51, 57, 60, 165]

Barron, Oswald 1959. Genealogy. In *Encyclopaedia Britannica* 10:103–104 [51]

170

References

Bartoszewski, W. T. 1989. The myth of the spy. *Journal of the Anthropological Society of Oxford* 20:27–35 [24]

Barwise, Jon, and Etchemendy, John 1987. *The liar: an essay on truth and circularity*. New York: Oxford University Press [5]

Barwise, Jon, and Perry, John 1983. *Situations and attitudes*. Cambridge, Mass.: MIT Press [4]

Barzini, Luigi 1964. *The Italians*. New York: Atheneum. [159]

Basso, Ellen B. 1987. *In favor of deceit: a study of tricksters in an Amazonian society*. Tucson: University of Arizona Press [65]

Bateson, Gregory 1951. Conventions of communication: where validity depends upon belief. In Ruesch, Jurgen, and Bateson, Gregory. *Communication: the social matrix of psychiatry*. New York: Norton, pp. 212–227 [16]

    1968. Redundancy and coding. In Sebeok, Thomas A., ed. *Animal communication: techniques of study and results of research*. Bloomington: Indiana University Press, pp. 614–626 [119]

Bateson, Patrick 1988. The biological evolution of cooperation and trust. In Gambetta 1988, pp. 14–30 [119f.]

Battersby, Christine 1981. An enquiry concerning the Humean woman. *Philosophy* 56:303–312 [7]

Beale, Bob 1988. Lying: the unpleasant truth. *Good Weekend* (Sydney) 15 July:20–25 [24]

Beattie, Lester Middleswarth 1935. *John Arbuthnot: mathematician and satirist* (Harvard studies in English 16). Cambridge, Mass.: Harvard University Press [30]

Becker, Ernest 1973. *The denial of death*. New York: Free Press [88]

Benthall, Jonathan 1992. Child-focused research. *Anthropology Today* 8(2):23–25 [167]

Bentham, Jeremy 1843. Swear not at all: ... In *The works of Jeremy Bentham*. Vol. 5. Edinburgh: William Tait, pp. 187–229 [38]

Beringer, Johann Bartholomew Adam 1963. *The lying stones of Dr Johann Bartholomew Adam Beringer being his* Lithographia Wirceburgensis. Berkeley: University of California Press [55]

Berry, Joy 1988. *A children's book about lying*. (?)Danbury, Conn.: Grolier Enterprises. [17, 106]

Bilmes, Jack 1975. Misinformation and ambiguity in verbal interaction: a northern Thai example. *Linguistics* 165:63–75 [139]

Bird, Roger 1983. *Osborn's concise law dictionary*. (7th edn). London: Sweet & Maxwell [91]

Black, Max 1955. Metaphor. *Proceedings of the Aristotelian Society* n.s. 57:273–294 [115]

    1983. *The prevalence of humbug and other essays*. Ithaca, N.Y.: Cornell University Press [4, 111, 113, 125]

Blake, William 1982. *The complete poetry and prose of William Blake*. Berkeley: University of California Press [140]

Blasi, Augusto 1980. Bridging moral cognition and moral action: a critical review of the literature. *Psychological Bulletin* 88:1–45 [9]

Blum, Richard H. 1972. *Deceivers and deceived*. Springfield, Ill.: Charles C. Thomas [80]

Bohannan, Laura 1952. A genealogical charter. *Africa* 22:301–315 [50]

Bok, Sissela 1978. *Lying: moral choice in public and private life*. New York: Pantheon Books [*passim*]

    1980. On lying. *Berkshire Review* 15:7–14 [47, 139]

References

1984. *Secrets: on the ethics of concealment and revelation.* Oxford: Oxford University Press [140]

Boorstin, Daniel Joseph 1962. *The image, or what happened to the American dream.* New York: Atheneum [46]

Borofsky, Robert 1987. *Making history: Pukapukan and anthropological constructions of knowledge.* Cambridge: Cambridge University Press [50]

Boruch, Robert Francis, and Cecil, Joe Shelby 1983. (eds.). *Solutions to ethical and legal problems in social research.* New York: Academic Press [61]

Boswell, James 1934. *Boswell's life of Johnson.* Vol. 4. Oxford: Clarendon Press [15]

Bourrienne, Louis-Antoine Fauvelet de 1893. *Memoirs of Napoleon Bonaparte.* (new edn). Vol. 2. London: Richard Bentley [27]

Boyle, Robert 1744. *The works of the Honorable Robert Boyle.* Vol. 1. London: A. Millar [55]

Bradlee, Benjamin C. 1991. Lies, damned lies, and presidential statements. *Guardian Weekly* 145(22):21 [1]

Branch, Taylor 1982. Closets of power. *Harper's* 265(1589):34–50 [92]

Bridgstock, Martin 1982. A sociological approach to fraud in science. *Australian and New Zealand Journal of Sociology* 18:364–383 [56]

Broad, William, and Wade, Nicholas 1982. *Betrayers of the truth: fraud and deceit in the halls of science.* New York: Simon & Schuster [56]

Broder, David S. 1988. Deception as a way of life. *Guardian Weekly* 138(18):18 [33]

Brodsky, Joseph 1979. Less than one. *New York Review of Books* 26(14):32, 41–48 [8]

Brown, Anthony Cave 1975. *Bodyguard of lies.* New York: Harper & Row [27]

Browne, Sir Thomas, 1964. *Pseudodoxia epidemica.* London: Faber [7]

Browning, Robert 1981. *The poems.* Vol. 1. New Haven: Yale University Press [vii, 3]

Bunyan, John 1967. *The pilgrim's progress* (2nd edn). Oxford: Clarendon Press [126]

Burke, Edmund 1987. *Reflections on the revolution in France.* Indianapolis: Hackett [158]

Burling, Robbins 1993. Primate calls, human language, and nonverbal communication. *Current Anthropology* 34:25–53 [119]

Burridge, Kenelm Oswald Lancelot 1960. *Mambu: a Melanesian millennium.* London: Methuen [69]

Burt, Thomas 1924. *Thomas Burt M.P., D.C.L., pitman and Privy Councillor: an autobiography.* London: Fisher Unwin [127]

Burton, Roger V. 1976. Honesty and dishonesty. In Lickona, Thomas, ed. *Moral development and behavior: theory, research, and social issues.* New York: Holt, Rinehart & Winston, pp. 173–197 [107]

Burton, Roger V., and Reis, Janet 1981. Internalization. In Munroe, Ruth H., Munroe, Robert L.., and Whiting, Beatrice B., eds. *Handbook of cross-cultural human development.* New York: Garland STPM Press, pp. 675–687 [110]

Bush, Christopher 1949. *The case of the purloined picture.* London: Macdonald [130]

Bussey, Kay 1992. Lying and truthfulness: children's definitions, standards, and evaluative reactions. *Child Development* 63:129–137 [138]

Butler, Samuel 1964. *Ernest Pontifex or The way of all flesh.* Boston: Houghton Mifflin [163]

Byatt, Antonia Susan 1990. *Possession: a romance.* London: Chatto & Windus [131]

Byrne, Richard W., and Whiten, Andrew 1988. (eds.). *Machiavellian intelligence: social expertise and the evolution of intellect in monkeys, apes, and humans.* Oxford: Clarendon Press [149]

1992. Cognitive evolution in primates: evidence from tactical deception. *Man* n.s. 27:609–627 [149, 150]

Campbell, John Kennedy 1964. *Honour, family and patronage: a study of institutions and moral values in a Greek mountain community*. Oxford: Clarendon Press [75, 81]

Canberra Times 1992. Married women in PS: govt told a lie. 1 January:10 [34]

Cannon, Lou 1988. President believed not to approve. *Guardian Weekly* 138(17):19 [33]

Carey, Peter 1985. *Illywhacker*. St Lucia: University of Queensland Press [5]

Carrithers, Michael 1990. Why humans have cultures. *Man* n.s. 25:189–206 [149, 156]

Carroll, Lewis 1910. *The hunting of the snark: an agony in eight fits*. London: Macmillan [67]

Castaneda, Alfred, McCandless, Boyd R., and Palermo, David Stuart 1956. The children's form of the manifest anxiety scale. *Child Development* 27:317–326 [106]

Castaneda, Carlos 1968. *The teachings of Don Juan: a Yaqui way of knowledge*. Berkeley: University of California Press [133]

   1971. *A separate reality: further conversations with Don Juan*. New York: Simon & Schuster [133]

   1972. *Journey to Ixtlan: the lessons of Don Juan*. New York: Simon & Schuster [133]

   1974. *Tales of power*. New York: Simon & Schuster [133]

   1977. *The second ring of power*. New York: Simon & Schuster [133]

   1981. *The eagle's gift*. New York: Simon & Schuster [133]

Chagnon, Napoleon A. 1974. *Studying the Yanomamö* (Studies in anthropological method). New York: Holt, Rinehart & Winston [59]

Chandler, Michael, Fritz, Anna S., & Hala, Suzanne 1989. Small-scale deceit: deception as a marker of two-, three-, and four-year-olds' early theories of mind. *Child Development* 60:1263–1277 [152]

Chapman, Leslie 1979. *Your disobedient servant*. (2nd edn). Harmondsworth: Penguin [52]

Chaucer, Geoffrey 1975. The Wife of Bath's prologue. In *Canterbury tales*. London: Dent, pp. 158–180 [7]

Cheney, Dorothy L., and Seyfarth, Robert M 1990. *How monkeys see the world: inside the mind of another species*. Chicago: University of Chicago Press [149ff.]

Chevalier-Skolnikoff, Suzanne 1986. An exploration of the ontogeny of deception in human beings and nonhuman primates. In Mitchell and Thompson 1986, pp. 205–220. [151]

Chisholm, Roderick Milton, and Feehan, Thomas David 1977. The intent to deceive. Journal of Philosophy 74:143–159 [11, 17, 87]

Chomsky, Noam 1989. *Necessary illusions: thought control in democratic societies*. London: Pluto Press [159]

Christie, Richard 1970. Why Machiavelli? In Christie and Geis 1970, pp.1–9 [110]

Christie, Richard, and Geis, Florence Lindauer 1970. (eds.). *Studies in Machiavellianism*. New York: Academic Press [149, 150]

Cirino, Robert 1971. *Don't blame the people: how the news media use bias, distortion and censorship to manipulate public opinion*. Los Angles: Diversity Press [10]

Clifford, James 1983. Power and dialogue in ethnography: Marcel Griaule's initiation. In Stocking, George W., Jr., ed. *Observers observed: essays on ethnographic fieldwork*. Madison: University of Wisconsin Press, pp. 121–156 [60]

References

Colby, Anne, and Kohlberg, Lawrence 1987a. *The measurement of moral judgment.* Vol. 1: *Theoretical foundations and research validation.* Cambridge: Cambridge University Press [9]

1987b. *The measurement of moral judgment.* Vol. 2: *Standard issue scoring manual.* Cambridge: Cambridge University Press [9]

Coleman, Linda, and Kay, Paul 1981. Prototype semantics: the English word 'lie'. *Language* 57:26–44 [10]

Collier, Jane Fishburne 1973. *Law and social change in Zinacantan.* Stanford: Stanford University Press [42, 70]

Collins, Harry 1988. Guilty secrets. *Times Higher Education Supplement* 806:26 [120]

Colson, Elizabeth 1989. Overview. *Annual Review of Anthropology* 18:1–16 [162]

Comer, Michael J., Ardis, Patrick M., and Rice, David H. 1988. *Bad lies in business.* London: McGraw-Hill [80]

Committee on Professional Ethics and Academic Freedom 1980. Report. PS 13:345–348 [12]

Compayré, Gabriel 1902. *Development of the child in later infancy.* New York: Appleton [76, 105]

Connections 1989. From our namesake. *Connections* 12(1):4–5 [16]

Conway, T. M. 1974. Weekend competition entry. *New Statesman* 87:935 [168]

Cooley, Charles Horton 1922. *Human nature and the social order.* New York: Charles Scribner's Sons [81]

Cornish, William Rodolph 1978. Criminal justice and punishment. In Cornish, W. R., Hart, J., Manchester, A. H., and Stevenson, J., eds. *Crime and law in nineteenth century Britain.* Dublin: Irish University Press, pp. 5–109 [39]

Cornish, William Rodolph, and Clark, G. de N. 1989. *Law and society in England 1750–1950.* London: Sweet & Maxwell [39]

Corson, David 1984. Lying and killing: language and moral reasoning of twelve-and fifteen-year-olds by social group. *Adolescence* 19:473–482 [138]

Craswell, Richard 1991. Regulating deceptive advertising: the role of cost–benefit analysis. *Southern California Law Review* 64:549–604 [46]

Criminal Law Revision Committee 1972. *Eleventh report: evidence (general).* London: HMSO, Cmnd 4991 [38, 39f.]

Cruickshank, Charles Greig 1977. *The fourth arm: psychological warfare 1938–1945.* London: Davis-Poynter [24]

1981. *Deception in World War II.* Oxford: Oxford University Press [24, 27]

Culler, Jonathan D. 1975. *Structuralist poetics: structuralism, linguistics and the study of literature.* London: Routledge & Kegan Paul [123]

Curtis, Charles F. 1951. The ethics of advocacy. *Stanford Law Review* 4:3–23 [41]

Dale, David 1992. *The new, improved official liars' handbook.* Pymble: Collins Angus and Robertson [4]

Daniel, Glyn Edward 1986. Piltdown and Professor Hewitt. *Antiquity* 60:59–60 [56]

Daniel, Helen 1988. *Liars: Australian new novelists.* Ringwood, Vic.: Penguin [5, 124]

Darby, Michael R., and Karni, Edi 1973. Free competition and the optimum amount of fraud. *Journal of Law and Economics* 16:67–88 [168]

Davidoff, Eugene 1942. The treatment of pathological liars. *Nervous Child* 1:358–388 (cited Ford et al. 1988; p.555) [22]

References

Davies, Paul Charles William 1979. Reality exists outside of us? In Duncan and Weston-Smith 1979, pp. 143–158 [11]

de Mille, Richard 1980. Editor. *The Don Juan papers: further Castaneda controversies*. Santa Barbara: Ross-Erikson [133f.]

de Villiers, Jill G., and de Villiers, Peter A. 1978. *Language acquisition*. Cambridge, Mass.: Harvard University Press [105, 108]

Dean, John Peebles, and Whyte, William Foote 1958. How do you know if the informant is telling the truth? *Human organization* 17(2):34–38 [37f.]

Deferrari, Roy Joseph 1952. Introduction to 'Against lying' In Augustine 1952, pp.113–120 [137]

Defoe, Daniel 1725. *A new voyage round the world, by a course never sailed before ...* London: Bettesworth and Mears [129]

   1927. *Robinson Crusoe*. Vol. 1. Oxford: Blackwell [127]

   1928. *A journal of the plague year*. Oxford: Blackwell [129]

Demos, Raphael 1960. Lying to oneself. *Journal of Philosophy* 57:588–595 [87, 94]

Denness, Bruce 1988. Divine artefact. *Nature* 336:614 [137]

Dennett, Daniel Clement 1987. *The intentional stance*. Cambridge, Mass.: MIT Press [151]

Dentan, Robert Knox 1970. Living and working with the Semai. In Spindler, George D., ed. *Being an anthropologist: fieldwork in eleven cultures*. New York: Holt, Rinehart & Winston, pp. 85–112 [85]

DePaulo, Bella M., and Jordan, Audrey 1982. Age changes in deceiving and detecting deceit. In Feldman, Robert S., ed. *Development of nonverbal behavior in children*. New York: Springer-Verlag, pp. 151–180 [107, 108f., 110, 111, 117, 118]

DePaulo, Bella M., and Rosenthal, Robert 1979. Telling lies. *Journal of Personality and Social Psychology* 37:1713–1772 [9, 117]

DePaulo, Bella M., Stone, J. I., and Lassiter, G. D. 1985. Deceiving and detecting deceit. In Schlenker, Barry Royce, ed. *The self and social life*. New York: McGraw-Hill, pp. 323–370 [7, 110, 118]

DePaulo, Bella M., Zuckerman, Miron, and Rosenthal, Robert 1980. Humans as lie detectors. *Journal of Communication* 30(2):129–139 [110]

Devons, Ely 1950. *Planning in practice: essays in aircraft planning in war-time*. Cambridge: Cambridge University Press [57]

Dickinson, Emily 1955. *The poems of Emily Dickinson*. Vol. II. Cambridge, Mass.: Harvard University Press, pp. 379–820 [86]

Disraeli, Benjamin 1927. *Tancred or the new crusade* (Bradenham edition 10). London: Peter Davies [17]

D'Israeli, Isaac 1791, 1793. *Curiosities of literature* (2 vols). London: Murray [109, 126]

   1881. *Curiosities of literature*. New ed. Vol. 2, London; Frederick Warner [30]

Douglas, Jack D. 1976. *Investigative social research*. Beverly Hills: Sage [6f., 17, 114, 156f.]

Drinker, Henry Sandwith 1952. Some remarks on Mr Curtis' 'The ethics of advocacy'. *Stanford Law Review* 4:349–357 [41]

du Boulay, Juliet 1974. *Portrait of a Greek mountain village*. Oxford: Clarendon Press [73, 74, 75]

   1976. Lies, mockery and family integrity. In Peristiany, Jean George, ed. *Mediterranean family structures*. Cambridge: Cambridge University Press, pp. 389–406 [72, 73]

175

References

Duncan, Ronald, and Weston-Smith, Miranda 1979. (eds.). *Lying truths: a critical scrutiny of current beliefs and conventions*. Oxford: Pergamon Press [11]

Dunn, Judy 1980. Playing in speech. In Michaels, L., and Ricks, Christopher, eds. *The state of the language*. Berkeley: University of California Press, pp. 202–212 [105, 106]

  1988. *The beginnings of social understanding*. Oxford: Blackwell [105, 152]

Dunn, Judy, and Wooding, Carol 1977. Play in the home and its implications for learning. In Tizard, Barbara, and Harvey, David, eds. *Biology of play*. London: Spastics International Medical Publications, pp. 45–58 [107]

Dupré, Ernest Pierre 1905. *La mythomanie: étude psychologique et médico-legale du mensonge et de la fabulation morbides*. Paris: J. Gainche. (cited in Eck 1970; p. 78) [21]

Durandin, Guy 1972. *Les fondements du mensonge*. Paris: Flammarion [6, 87, 90, 165]

Eagle, Morris 1988. Psychoanalysis and self-deception. In Lockard and Paulhus 1988, pp. 78–95 [6]

Eastwood, Granville 1977. *Harold Laski*. London: Mowbrays [54]

Eck, Marcel 1970. *Lies and truth*. New York: Macmillan. [21, 22, 52, 102, 104, 156]

Eco, Umberto 1976. *A theory of semiotics*. Bloomington: Indiana University Press [4]

Edwards, Carolyn Pope 1981. The comparative study of the development of moral judgment and reasoning. In Munroe, Ruth H., Munroe, Robert L., and Whiting, Beatrice B., eds. *Handbook of cross-cultural human development*. New York: Garland STPM Press, pp. 501–528 [69]

Egan, Ted 1991. *Would I lie to you? The goanna drover and other very true stories*. Ringwood, Vic.: Viking O'Neil [135]

Ekman, Paul 1985. *Telling lies: clues to deceit in the marketplace, politics, and marriage*. New York: Norton [8, 30, 91, 104, 160]

  1989. *Why kids lie*. New York: Charles Scribner's Sons [8]

  1992. *Telling lies* (2nd edn). New York: Norton [23]

Elia, Irene 1988. *The female animal*. New York: Henry Holt [153]

Eliot, Thomas Stearns 1969. *The complete poems and plays*. London: Faber & Faber [162]

English, Jack 1986. *Police training manual*. London: McGraw-Hill [38]

Epstein, Edward Jay 1989. *Deception: the invisible war between the KGB and the CIA*. New York: Simon & Schuster [23, 93]

Evans-Pritchard, Edward Evan 1956. Sanza, a characteristic feature of Zande language and thought. *Bulletin of the School of Oriental and African Studies* 18:161–180 [66]

Ewbank, Inga-Stina 1983. Shakespeare's liars. *Proceedings of the British Academy* 69:137–168 [6, 89, 163]

Exline, Ralph V., Thibaut, John Hickey, Carole B., and Gumpert, Peter, 1970. Visual interaction in relation to Machiavellianism and an unethical act. In Christie and Geis 1970, pp. 53–75 [110]

Farb, Peter 1973. *Word play: what happens when people talk*. London: Jonathan Cape [5, 129]

Farber, Leslie H. 1974. Lying on the couch. *Review of Existential Psychology and Psychiatry* 13:125–135 [88]

Feldman, Robert Stephen, and Custrini, Robert J. 1988. Learning to lie and self-deceive. In Lockard and Paulhus 1988, pp. 40–53 [107]

Ferenczi, Sandor 1955. *Final contributions to problems and methods of psycho-analysis*. London: Hogarth Press [3, 6, 105]

Festinger, Leon 1957. *A theory of cognitive dissonance*. Evanston, Ill.: Row Peterson [92]

References

Festinger, Leon, Riecken, Henry William, and Schachter, Stanley 1956. *When prophecy fails*. Minneapolis: University of Minnesota Press [61]

Fingarette, Herbert 1969. *Self-deception* (Studies in philosophical psychology). London: Routledge & Kegan Paul [88]

Foot, Paul 1989. *Who framed Colin Wallace?* London: Macmillan [29]

Ford, Charles V., and Hollender, Marc H. 1988. Drs. Ford and Hollender reply. *American Journal of Psychiatry* 145:1611 [139]

Ford, Charles V., King, Bryan H., and Hollender, Marc H. 1988. Lies and liars: psychiatric aspects of prevarication. *American Journal of Psychiatry* 145:554–562 [6, 7, 8, 22]

Forrester, John 1980. *Language and the origins of psychoanalysis*. New York: Columbia University Press [6]

   1989. Lying on the couch. In Lawson, Hilary, and Appignanesi, Lisa, eds. *Dismantling truth*. London: Weidenfeld & Nicolson, pp. 145–165 [6, 137, 142]

   1990. *The seductions of psychoanalysis. Freud, Lacan and Derrida*. Cambridge: Cambridge University Press [6]

Forsdyke, John 1956. *Greece before Homer: ancient chronology and mythology*. London: Max Parrish [125]

Fortes, Meyer 1957. Malinowski and the study of kinship. In Firth, Raymond William, ed. *Man and culture*. London: Routledge & Kegan Paul, pp. 157–188 [5]

Foster, George McClelland 1979. *Tzintzuntzan: Mexican peasants in a changing world* (rev. edn). New York: Elsevier [68]

Frankel, Marvin E. 1975. The search for truth: an umpireal view. *University of Pennsylvania Law Review* 123:1031–1059 [41]

Frankfurt, Harry 1986. On bullshit. *Raritan* 6(2):81–100 [163]

Freedman, Monroe H. 1975. *Lawyers' ethics in an adversary system*. Indianapolis: Bobbs-Merrill [41]

Freilich, Morris 1970. Toward a formalization of field work. In Freilich, M., ed. *Marginal natives: anthropologists at work*. New York: Harper & Row, pp. 485–594 [60]

Freud, Sigmund 1958. Two lies told by children. In *Standard edition*. Vol. 12. London: Hogarth Press, pp. 303–311 [6]

   1960. *Jokes and their relation to the unconscious*. London: Routledge & Kegan Paul [113]

Friedl, Ernestine 1962. *Vasilika: a village in modern Greece*. New York: Holt, Rinehart & Winston [2]

Gale, Anthony 1988. (ed.). *The polygraph test: lies, truth and science*. London: Sage [120]

Gambetta, Diego 1988. (ed.). *Trust: making and breaking cooperative relations*. New York: Blackwell

Garfinkel, Andrew 1977. Truths, half-truths and deception in advertising. *Papers in Linguistics* 10:135–149 [45]

Geertz, Clifford 1968. Thinking as a moral act: ethical dimensions of anthropological fieldwork in the new states. *Antioch Review* 33(1):139–158 [58]

Gifford, Prosser 1980. Comments on Moomaw. *Berkshire Review* 15:40–42 [56]

Gilsenan, Michael 1976. Lying, honor and contradiction. In Kapferer, Bruce, ed. *Transaction and meaning: directions in the anthropology of exchange and symbolic behavior*. (ASA essays in social anthropology 1). Philadelphia: Institute for the Study of Human Issues, pp. 191–219 [2, 18, 70ff., 82f., 145]

References

Glasgow University Media Group 1976. *Bad News*. London: Routledge & Kegan Paul [2]
    1980. *More bad news*. London: Routledge & Kegan Paul [2]
Goffman, Erving 1956. *The presentation of self in everyday life* (Monograph 2). Edinburgh: University of Edinburgh, Social Sciences Research Centre [156]
    1975. *Frame analysis: an essay on the organization of experience*. Harmondsworth: Penguin [17]
Goldberg, Arnold 1973. On telling the truth. In Feinstein, Sherman C., and Giovacchini, Peter L., eds. *Adolescent psychiatry*. Vol. II: *Developmental and clinical studies*. New York: Basic Books, pp. 98–112 [6, 21]
Goldman, Alan H. 1980. *The moral foundations of professional ethics*. Totowa, N.J.: Rowman & Littlefield [47]
Goleman, Daniel 1985. *Vital lies: simple truths: the psychology of self-deception*. New York: Simon & Schuster [88, 96]
Gombrich, Richard Francis 1971. *Precept and practice: traditional Buddhism in the rural highlands of Ceylon*. Oxford: Clarendon Press [137]
Goodenough, Ward Hunt 1990. Evolution of the human capacity for beliefs. *American Anthropologist* 92:597–612 [153]
Gordon, Richard 1957. *Doctor in love*. London: Michael Joseph [130]
Gosse, Edmund 1949. *Father and son: a study of two temperaments*. Harmondsworth: Penguin [130]
Gourevitch, Victor 1980. Rousseau on lying: a provisional reading of the fourth Rêverie. *Berkshire Review* 15:93–107 [84f., 129]
Granovetter, Mark 1985. Economic action and social structure: the problem of embeddedness. *American Journal of Sociology* 91:481–510 [63]
Green, Mark J., and MacColl, Gail 1983. *There he goes again: Ronald Reagan's reign of error*. New York: Pantheon Books [32]
Greenwald, Anthony G. 1988. Self-knowledge and self-deception. In Lockard and Paulhus 1988, pp. 113–131 [88]
Gregor, Thomas 1969. Roles in a small society: a study of the Mehinacu Indians. Ph.D. dissertation, Cornell University [163]
    1977. *Mehinaku: the drama of everyday life in a Brazilian Indian village*. Chicago: University of Chicago Press [163]
Griaule, Marcel 1957. *Méthode de l'ethnographie*. Paris: Presses Universitaires de France [59]
Grice, Herbert Paul 1989. *Studies in the way of words*. Cambridge, Mass.: Harvard University Press [9, 111]
Grotius, Hugo 1925. *On the law of war and peace*. Book 3. Oxford: Clarendon Press, pp. 599–946 [9f., 87]
Guamán Poma de Ayala, Felipe 1980. *El primer nueva corónica y buen gobierno*. Vol. 1. Mexico D.F.: Siglo Veintiuno [142]
Guicciardini, Francesco 1965. *Selected writings*. London: Oxford University Press [159]
Guthrie, William Keith Chambers 1953. Foreword. In Cornford, Francis Macdonald, *Microcosmographia academica, being a guide for young academic politicians* (5th edn). Cambridge: Bowes and Bowes [26]
Gutmann, Bruno 1926. *Das Recht der Dschagga* (Arbeiten zur Entwicklungspsychologie 7). Munich: C. H. Beck'sche Verlagsbuchhandlung [65f.]

References

Habermas, Jürgen 1970. On systematically distorted communication. *Inquiry* 13:205–218 [4, 68]

1979. *Communication and the evolution of society.* London: Heinemann [12]

Hall, Granville Stanley 1890. Children's lies. *American Journal of Psychology* 32:59–70 [104, 107, 108]

1891. Children's lies. *Pedagogical Seminary* 1:211–218 [7, 62]

Hall, Oakley Maxwell 1973. *Warlock.* London: White Lion [132]

Harding, Stephen, and Phillips, David 1986. *Contrasting values in western Europe: unity, diversity and change* (Studies in the contemporary values of modern society). London: Macmillan [1, 66, 163]

Hardy, Frank Joseph 1971. *The hard way: the story behind 'Power without glory'.* Hawthorn: Gold Star Publications (Aust.) [130]

Harris, Marvin 1979. *Cultural materialism: the struggle for a science of culture.* New York: Random House [133f.]

Hartshorne, Hugh, and May, Mark Arthur 1928. *Studies in deceit.* Book 1. *General methods and results.* (Studies in the nature of character 1.) New York: Macmillan [68, 110]

Hartung, John 1988. Deceiving down: conjectures on the management of subordinate status. In Lockard and Paulhus 1988, pp. 170–185 [86, 88]

Haviland, John Beard 1977. *Gossip, reputation, and knowledge in Zinacantan.* Chicago: University of Chicago Press [13]

Hawthorne, Nathaniel 1900. *The house of the seven gables: a romance.* Boston: Houghton Mifflin [131]

Hayano, David Mamoru 1980. Communicative competency among poker players. *Journal of Communication* 30(2):113–120 [4]

1982. *Poker faces: the life and work of professional card players.* Berkeley: University of California Press [4]

Heath, Shirley Brice 1983. *Ways with words: language, life, and work in communities and classrooms.* Cambridge: Cambridge University Press [75]

Henderson, Lawrence Joseph 1970 [1935]. Physician and patient as a social system. In his *On the social system: selected writings.* Chicago: University of Chicago Press, pp. 202–213 [84]

Hendry, Joy 1989. To wrap or not to wrap: politeness and penetration in ethnographic inquiry. *Man* n.s. 24:620–635 [66]

Herzfeld, Michael 1990. Pride and perjury: time and the oath in the mountain villages of Crete. *Man* n.s. 25:305–322 [40]

Hewitt, John P., and Stokes, Randall 1975. Disclaimers. *American Sociological Review* 40:1–11 [130]

Hillerman, Tony 1986. *Skinwalkers.* New York: Harper Paperbacks. [67]

Hingley, Ronald 1978. *The Russian mind.* London: Bodley Head [18, 67]

Hobbes, Thomas 1839. *Elements of philosophy. First section.* (English works, vol. 1.) London: Bohn [3, 167]

1840. *The English works of Thomas Hobbes of Malmesbury.* Vol. 4. London: Bohn [3, 153]

Hobbs, Fred 1989. *Doing the business: entrepreneurship, the working class, and detectives in the East End of London.* Oxford: Oxford University Press [165]

Hoffman, David 1986. Reagan denies Libya plan involved 'disinformation'. *Guardian Weekly* 135(15):17 [28]

References

Hollis, Martin 1989. Honour among thieves. *Proceedings of the British Academy* 75:163–180 [5]

Homer 1974. *The Odyssey.* New York: Norton [136]

Horace, 1929. *Satires, epistles and Ars poetica.* London; Heinemann [124]

Howe, James, and Sherzer, Joel 1986. Friend Hairyfish and friend Rattlesnake or keeping anthropologists in their place. *Man* n.s. 21:680–696 [65]

Hume, David 1987. Of the study of history. In *Essays moral, political and literary.* Indianapolis: Liberty classics, pp. 563–568 [7]

Humphrey, Nicholas 1983. *Consciousness regained: chapters in the development of the mind.* Oxford: Oxford University Press [149, 150, 151]

Humphreys, Laud 1975. *Tearoom trade: impersonal sex in public places.* (enlarged edn). Chicago: Aldine [61]

Ibsen, Henrik 1960. *Ibsen.* Vol. 6. London: Oxford University Press [88]

Irving, Clive, Hall, Ron, and Wallington, Jeremy 1963. *Scandal '63. A study of the Profumo affair.* London: Heinemann [32]

Jackall, Robert 1980. Structural invitations to deceit: some reflections on bureaucracy and morality. *Berkshire Review* 15:49–61 [47f., 160]

Jakobson, Roman 1981. Linguistics and poetics. In *Poetry of grammar and grammar of poetry* (Selected writings 3). The Hague: Mouton pp. 18–51 [113]

Johnson, Samuel 1905. *Lives of the English poets.* Vol. 1. Oxford: Clarendon Press [122]
1963. *The idler* and *The adventurer* (Yale edition 2). New Haven: Yale University Press [8, 15, 54]

Jolly, Alison 1985. *The evolution of primate behavior* (2nd edn). New York: Macmillan [151]
1988. Lemur social behaviour and primate intelligence. In Bryne and Whiten 1988, pp. 27–49 [149, 151]

Jones, Frank Lancaster 1989. Changing attitudes and values in post-war Australia. In Hancock, Keith Jackson, ed. *Australian society.* Cambridge: Cambridge University Press, pp. 94–118 [66]

Jones, Graham 1984. *Forked tongues: the book of lies, half truths and excuses.* London: Century [3]

Kant, Immanuel 1930. *Lectures on ethics.* London: Methuen [137]
1949. On a supposed right to lie from altruistic motives. In Beck, Lewis White, ed. *Critique of practical reason and other writings.* Chicago: University of Chicago Press, pp. 346–350. [14, 137]
1964. *The doctrine of virtue.* New York: Harper & Row [137]

Kateb, George 1980. Comments on Gourevitch. *Berkshire Review* 15:122–129 [137]

Kaufmann, Walter Arnold 1950. *Nietzsche: philosopher, psychologist, antichrist.* Princeton: Princeton University Press [15]
1970. I and you: a prologue. In Buber, Martin. *I and Thou.* New York: Charles Scribner's Sons, pp. 7–48 [162]

Kavka, Jerome 1985. Wordsworth on teaching a child to lie: some thoughts on creative fictionalism. *Annual of Psychoanalysis* 12/13:395–414 [8]

Kawharu, Ian Hugh 1989. *Waitangi: Maori and Pakeha perspectives of the treaty of Waitangi.* Auckland: Oxford University Press [29]

Keenan, Elinor Ochs 1976. The Universality of conversational postulates. *Language in Society* 5:67–80 [67f.]

References

Keesing, Roger Maxwell, and Tonkinson, Robert 1982 (eds.). Reinventing traditional culture: the politics of *Kastom* in Melanesia. *Mankind* 13:297–399 [51]

Kellogg, Abner Otis 1866. *Shakspeare's delineations of insanity, imbecility and suicide*. New York: Hurd & Houghton [168]

Kelman, Herbert Chanoch 1967. Human use of human subjects: the problem of deception in social psychological experiments. *Psychological Bulletin* 67:1–11 [61]

1968. *A time to speak: on human values and social research*. San Francisco: Jossey Bass [61]

Kermode, Frank 1991. Theory and truth. *London Review of Books* 13(22):9–10 [13]

Kerr, Philip 1990. (ed.). *The Penguin book of lies*. London: Viking [3, 109]

Kintz, B. L. 1977. College student attitudes about telling lies. *Bulletin of the Psychonomic Society* 10:490–492 [30, 63]

Kipling, Rudyard 1965. *Puck of Pook's Hill*. London: Macmillan [68]

Klockars, Carl B. 1974. *The professional fence*. New York: Free Press [45]

1984a. Introduction. In Klockars 1984c, pp. 413–422 [42f., 49]

1984b. Blue lies and police placebos. In Klockars 1984c, pp. 529–544 [43f.]

1984c. (ed.). Lies, secrets, and social control. *American Behavioral Scientist* 27:411–544

Kloos, Peter 1983–84. Nothing but the truth, a question of power. *Journal of Northern Luzon* 14:121–137 [60f.]

Knightley, Phillip 1991. Lies, damned lies and military briefings. *New Statesman and Society* 4(137):26–27 [23]

Kohlberg, Lawrence 1964. Development of moral character and moral ideology. In Hoffman, Martin L., and Hoffman, Lois Wladis, eds. *Review of child development research*. Vol. 1. New York: Russell Sage Foundation, pp. 383–431 [9]

Kohlberg, Lawrence, Levine, Charles, and Hewer, Alexandra 1983. *Moral stages: a current formulation and a response to critics* (Contributions to human development 10). Basel: S. Karger [9]

Kohlberg, Lawrence, and Turiel, Elliot 1971. Moral development and moral education. In Lesser, Gerald S., ed. *Psychology and educational practice*. Glenview, Ill.: Scott, Foresman, pp. 410–465 [9]

Kovar, Leo 1974. The pursuit of self-deception. *Review of Existential Psychology and Psychiatry* 13:136–149 [88, 91, 99]

Koyré, Alexandre 1943. Réflexions sur le mensonge. *Renaissance* 1:95–111 [142]

Kuhn, Alfred 1963. *The study of society: a multidisciplinary approach*. Holmwood, Ill.: Richard D. Irwin [5]

Lacan, Jacques 1988. *The seminar of Jacques Lacan*. Book 2. Cambridge: Cambridge University Press [3]

Laertius, Diogenes 1959. *Lives of eminent philosophers*. London: Heinemann [159]

LaFrenière, Peter J. 1988. The ontogeny of tactical deception in humans. In Byrne and Whiten 1988, pp. 238–252 [105]

Langdon, John H. 1991. Misinterpreting Piltdown. *Current Anthropology* 32:627–631 [56]

Langer, Susanne Katherina 1972. *Mind: an essay on human feeling*. Vol. 2. Baltimore: Johns Hopkins University Press [148]

LaPiere, Richard Tracy 1934. Attitudes vs. actions. *Social Forces* 13:230–237 [61]

Larsen, Tony 1979. *Trust yourself: you have the power*. San Luis Obispo, Calif.: Impact Publishers [138]

Larson, John Augustus 1932. *Lying and its detection: a study of deception and deception tests.* Chicago: University of Chicago Press [5]

Leach, Edmund Ronald 1987. Tribal ethnography: past, present, future. *Cambridge Anthropology* 11(2):1–14 [133]

Leonard, Eugenie Andruss 1920. A parent's study of children's lies. *Pedagogical seminary* 27:105–136 [138]

Levinson, Stephen Curtis 1983. *Pragmatics.* Cambridge: Cambridge University Press. [67]

Lévi-Strauss, Claude 1970. *The raw and the cooked.* London: Jonathan Cape [133]

1981. *The naked man.* London: Jonathan Cape. [125]

Levitt, Morton, and Levitt, Michael 1979. *A tissue of lies: Nixon vs. Hiss.* New York: McGraw-Hill. [33]

Lewis, Michael, Stanger, Catherine, and Sullivan, Margaret W. 1989. Deception in 3-year-olds. *Developmental Psychology* 25:439–443 [104, 105]

Lieberman, Philip 1991. *Uniquely human: the evolution of language, thought, and selfless behavior.* Cambridge, Mass.: Harvard University Press. [153]

Lindskold, Svenn, and Walters, Pamela S. 1983. Categories for acceptability of lies. *Journal of Social Psychology* [79, 138]

Lindstrom, Lamont Carl 1990. *Knowledge and power in a South Pacific society.* Washington: Smithsonian Institution Press. [69]

Lipmann, Otto, and Plaut, Paul 1927. (eds.). *Die Lüge in psychologischer, philosophischer, juristischer, pädagogischer, historischer, sociologischer, sprach- und literaturwissenschaftlicher und entwicklungsgeschichtlicher Betrachtung.* Leipzig: Johann Ambrosius Barth [5]

Lockard, Joan S., and Paulhus, Delroy L. 1988 (eds.) *Self-deception: an adaptive mechanism?* Englewood Cliffs: Prentice-Hall [96]

Locke, John 1894. *An essay concerning human understanding.* Vol. 2. Oxford: Clarendon Press [3, 154]

Lott, Tim 1990. Life of the land in the land of the lie. *Weekend Guardian* 14–15 July:12 [1]

Ludwig, Arnold M. 1965. *The importance of lying.* Springfield, Ill.: Charles C. Thomas [10, 134]

Lutman, Stephen 1988. Giving the lie to the study of deceit. *Guardian* (London) 22 April [6]

Lykken, David T. 1984. Detecting deception in 1984. *American Behavioral Scientist* 27:481–499 [120]

Lytton, Edward George Earle Bulwer 1848. *Paul Clifford.* London: Routledge & Sons [163]

1852. *The disowned.* London: Routledge & Sons [87]

McCarthy, Thomas A. 1973. A theory of communications competence. *Philosophy of the Social Sciences* 3:135–156 [4]

Macdonald, Fiona 1990. Man of 1000 faces. *Australian Magazine* 26–27 May:44–45, 47–48 [134]

Macdonald, Margaret 1954. [Contribution to] The language of fiction. *Aristotelian Society* (supplementary vol.) 28:165–184 [123]

Machiavelli, Niccolò 1965. *The chief works and others.* Vol. 1. Durham, N.C.: Duke University Press [149]

McKenzie, Donald Francis 1987. The sociology of a text: oral culture, literacy and print in early New Zealand. In Burke, Peter, and Porter, Roy, eds. *The social history of language*. Cambridge: Cambridge University Press, pp. 161–197 [29]

McKeon, Michael 1987. *The origins of the English novel 1600–1740*. Baltimore: Johns Hopkins University Press [126f.]

McLuhan, Marshall 1962. *The Gutenberg galaxy*. Toronto: University of Toronto Press [68]

Maier, Richard A., and Lovrakas, Paul J. 1976. Lying behavior and evaluation of lies. *Perceptual and Motor Skills* 42:575–581 [79]

Malouf, David 1976. *Johnno*. Ringwood, Vic.: Penguin [9]

Manning, Peter Kirby 1977. *Police work: the organization of policing*. Cambridge, Mass.: MIT Press [42]

Marro, Anthony 1985. When the government tells lies. *Columbia Journalism Review* 23(6):29–41 [27]

Martin, Kingsley 1953. *Harold Laski (1893–1950): a biographical memoir*. London: Gollancz [54]

Marx, Gary T., and Reichman, Nancy 1984. Routinizing the discovery of secrets: computers as informants. *American Behavioral Scientist* 27:423–452 [120]

Masterman, Sir John Cecil 1972. *The double-cross system in the war of 1939 to 1945*. New Haven: Yale University Press [23, 25]

Mates, Benson 1981. *Skeptical essays*. Chicago: University of Chicago Press [5]

Maugham, 1st Viscount Frederic Herbert, 1941. *Lies as allies: or Hitler at war*. (Oxford giant pamphlet). London: Oxford University Press [25]

May, Mark Arthur, and Hartshorne, Hugh 1928. *Studies in deceit*. Book 2. *Statistical methods and results*. New York: Macmillan [62]

Mencken, Henry Louis 1924. *Prejudices*. (fourth series). New York: Knopf [96, 162]

Merton, Robert King (1984). Scientific fraud and the fight to be first. *Times Literary Supplement*:1265 [56]

Michaels, Eric 1985. Constraints on knowledge in an economy of oral information. *Current Anthropology* 26:505–510 [68]

    1987. The last of the nomads, the last of the ethnographies or 'All anthropologists are liars'. *Mankind* 17:34–46 [133]

Michell, Gillian. 1990. Women and lying: a pragmatic and semantic analysis of 'saying it slant'. In Hibri, Azizah Y., and Simons, Margaret A., eds. *Hypatia reborn: essays in feminist philosophy*. Bloomington: Indiana University Press, pp. 175–191 [85, 86]

Milgram, Stanley 1974. *Obedience to authority: an experimental view*. New York: Harper & Row [62]

Miller, Arthur G. 1986. *The obedience experiments: a case study of controversy in social science*. New York: Praeger [62]

Miller, Gerald R., de Turck, Mark A., and Albfleisch, Pamela J., 1983. Self-monitoring, rehearsal, and deceptive communication. *Human Communication Research* 10:97–117 [81]

Miller, Walter B. 1958. Lower class culture as a generating milieu of gang delinquency. *Journal of Social Issues* 14(3):5–19 [76f.]

Milton, John 1934. *De doctrina christiana (continued)*. New York: Columbia University Press [22]

Milton, Katharine 1988. Foraging behaviour and the evolution of primate intelligence. In Byrne and Whiten 1988, pp. 285–305 [153]

Mitchell, Robert W. 1986. A framework for discussing deception. In Mitchell and Thompson 1986, pp. 3–40 [148]

Mitchell, Robert W., and Thompson, Nicholas S. 1986 (eds.). *Deception: perspectives on human and nonhuman deceit*. Albany: State University of New York Press.

Mitchell, W. J. Thomas 1992. Culture wars. *London Review of Books* 14(8):7–10 [115]

Modjeska, Drusilla 1990. *Poppy*. Ringwood, Vic.: McPhee Gribble [124]

Monmonier, Mark 1991. *How to lie with maps*. Chicago: University of Chicago Press [17]

Montaigne, Michel Eyquem de 1926. *The essays of Michel de Montaigne*. Vol. 1. London: Bell [12, 17, 31]

Montanino, Fred 1984. Protecting the Federal witness: burying past life and biography. *American Behavioral Scientist* 27:501–528 [19]

Moomaw, William R. 1980. Deception, distortion, and delusion in science. *Berkshire Review* 15:25–39 [56]

Moore, John Robert 1955. Defoe's project for lie-detection. *American Journal of Psychology* 68:672 [120]

Murphy, Robert Francis 1964. Social distance and the veil. *American Anthropologist* 66:1257–1274 [163]

1971 *The dialectics of social life: alarms and excursions in anthropological theory*. New York: Basic Books [162f.]

Nature 1989. Correspondence: Is there a God? *Nature* 337:498 [137]

Necker de Saussure, Albertine Adrienne 1839. *Progressive education, or considerations on the course of life*. Vol. 1. London: Longman, Orme, Brown [76]

Newberry, Benjamin H. 1973. Truth telling in subjects with information about experiments: who is being deceived? *Journal of personality and Social Psychology* 25:369–374 [62]

Newey, Vincent 1980. Bunyan and the confines of the mind. In Newey, V., ed. *The pilgrim's progress: critical and historical views*. Liverpool: Liverpool University Press, pp. 21–48 [126]

Newson, John, and Newson, Elizabeth 1968. *Four years old in an urban community*. London: Allen & Unwin [77, 106]

Nicholson, Watson 1919. *The historical sources of Defoe's 'Journal of the plague year'*. Boston: Stratford [129]

Niebuhr, Reinhold 1932. *Moral man and immoral society: a study in ethics and politics*. New York: Charles Scribner's Sons [158]

Nietzsche, Friedrich Wilhelm 1911. *The twilight of the idols . . .* (Complete Works. Vol. 16) (Ludovici, Anthony M., trans). Edinburgh: Foulis [16, 87, 92, 141]

1968a. *The will to power* (Kaufmann, Walter Arnold, and Hollingdale, R. J., trans.). New York: Vintage Books [16, 92, 140]

1968b. *Basic writings of Nietzsche* (Kaufmann, Walter, trans.). New York: Random House [140]

1979. *Philosophy and truth* (Breazeale, Daniel, trans.). Atlantic Highlands, N.J.: Humanities Press [141]

North, Oliver L 1987. *Taking the stand; the testimony of Lieutenant Colonel Oliver L. North*. New York: Pocket Books [23]

Novack, Dennis H., Detering, Barbara J., Arnold, Robert, Farrow, Lachlan, Ladinsky, Morissa, and Pezzullo, John C., 1989. Physicians' attitudes toward using deception to resolve difficult ethical problems. *Journal of the American Medical Association* 261:2980–2985 [79, 138]

Ochs, Elinor 1986. Introduction. In Schieffelin, Bambi Bernhard, and Oochs, E., eds. *Language socialization across cultures*. Cambridge: Cambridge University Press, pp. 1–13 [8, 167]

O'Connor, Michael Edward, and Barnes, John Arundel 1983. Bulmer on pseudo-patient studies: a critique. *Sociological Review* n.s. 31:753–758 [158]

O'Grady, Frank 1964. *The sun breaks through*. Sydney: Angus and Robertson [131]

O'Hair, Dan, and Cody, Michael J. 1987. Gender and vocal stress differences during truthful and deceptive information sequences. *Human Relations* 40:1–13 [120]

O'Neill, Graeme 1991. Truth hurts US scientific 'facts'. *Age* (Melbourne) 5 June [56]

Orne, Martin T. 1962. On the social psychology of the psychological experiment: with particular reference to demand characteristics and their implications. *American Psychologist* 17:776–783 [62]

Orne, Martin T., Thackray, Richard I., and Paskewitz, David A., 1972. On the detection of deception: a model for the study of physiological effects of psychological stimuli. In Greenfield, Norman Samuel, and Sternbach, Richard A., eds. *Handbook of psychophysiology*. New York: Holt, Rinehart & Winston, pp. 743–785 [119]

Orwell, George 1984. *1984*. Oxford: Clarendon Press [92, 115]

Ottaway, David B. 1986. State department spokesman resigns. *Guardian Weekly* 135(16):16 [159]

Otte, Daniel 1974. Effects and functions in the evolution of signalling systems. *Annual Review of Ecology and Systematics* 5:385–417 [153]

Paley, William 1825. *The principles of moral and political philosophy*. (Works, vol. 4) London: Rivington [9, 29]

Pascal, Blaise 1967. *The provincial letters*. Harmondsworth: Penguin [109]

Passin, Herbert 1942. Tarahumara prevarication: a problem in field method. *American Anthropologist* 44:235–247 [59, 114]

Patai, Raphael 1987. Druze. In Eliade, Mircea, ed. *The encyclopedia of religion*. Vol. 4. New York: Macmillan, pp. 503–506 [137]

Patton, Walter M. 1920. Shi'ahs. In Hastings, James, ed. *Encyclopædia of religion and ethics*. Vol. 11. Edinburgh: Clark, pp. 453–458 [137]

Paulhus, Delroy L. 1988a. General introduction. In Lockard and Paulhus 1988, pp. 1–7 [87]

    1988b. Psychological theories. In Lockard and Paulhus 1988, pp. 71–77 [90]

    1988c. Self-deception: where do we stand? In Lockard and Paulhus 1988, pp. 251–257 [96]

Pavel, Thomas G. 1986. *Fictional worlds*. Cambridge, Mass.: Harvard University Press [122, 130]

Perez, Bernard 1885. *The first three years of childhood*. London: Swan Sonnenschein [105]

Peristiany, Jean George 1976. Introduction. In Peristiany, J. G., ed. *Mediterranean family structures*. Cambridge studies in social anthropology 13. Cambridge: Cambridge University Press, pp. 1–26 [72]

Perry, John Anthony Godwin 1981. Land, power and the lie. *Man* n.s. 16:235–250 [70]

Peters, Geoffrey M. 1987. The use of lies in negotiation. *Ohio State Law Journal* 48:1–50 [41]

References

Peters, Richard Stanley 1971. Moral development: a plea for pluralism. In Mischel, Theodore, ed., *Cognitive development and epistemology*. New York: Academic Press, pp. 237–267 [9]

Peterson, Candida Clifford, Peterson, James L., and Seeto, Diane 1983. Developmental changes in ideas about lying. *Child development* 54:1529–1535 [11]

Pettigrew, John 1981. Notes. In Browning 1981, pp. 1019–1184 [168]

Phillips, Herbert P. *Thai peasant personality*. Berkeley: University of California Press [139]

Phillips, Melanie 1991. Private lies and public servants. *Guardian* (London) 9 January:21 [32, 48]

Piaget, Jean 1932. *The moral judgment of the child*. London: Routledge & Kegan Paul [152]

Picton-Warlow, T. 1967. *O. E.* Sydney: Angus and Robertson [131]

Plato 1935. *Plato's Republic* (Lindsay, A. D., trans.). London: Dent [83]
    1966. *Plato's Republic* (Richards, I. A., trans.). Cambridge: Cambridge University Press [106, 136, 156]

Pleynet, Marcelin 1968. La poesie doit avoir pour but . . . In Foucault, Michel, Barthes, Roland, Derrida, Jacques, Baudry, Jean Louis, et al. *Théorie d'ensemble*. Paris: Éditions du seuil, pp. 94–126 [123]

Pollard, Albert Frederick 1897. (ed.). *Political pamphlets selected and arranged*. London: Kegan Paul, Trench, Trubner [30, 134, 154]

Popper, Karl Raimund 1974. Replies to my critics. 32. Ayer on empiricism and against verisimilitude. In Schilpp, Paul Arthur, ed. *The philosophy of Karl Popper* (Library of living philosophers 14) Book 2. La Salle, Ill.: Open court, pp. 1100–1114 [153]

Powell, Jody 1984. *The other side of the story*. New York: William Morrow. [34]

Premack, David 1976. Language and intelligence in ape and man. *American Scientist* 64:674–683 [149]

Premack, David, and Woodruff, Guy 1978. Does the chimpanzee have a theory of mind? *Behavioral and Brain Sciences* 4:515–526 [152]

Quintilian 1921. *Institutio oratoria*. Vol. 2. London: Heinemann [31]

Raiffa, Howard. 1982. *The art and science of negotiation*. Cambridge, Mass.: Harvard University Press [10, 40]

Rappaport, Roy Abraham 1979. *Ecology, meaning, and religion*. Richmond, Calif.: North Atlantic Books [3, 16, 105, 153]

Rasberry, Robert W. 1981. *The 'technique' of political lying*. Washington, D.C.: University Press of America [1, 27, 28]

Reamer, Frederic G. 1982. *Ethical dilemmas in social service*. New York: Columbia University Press [37, 47]

Repina, T. A. 1971. Development of imagination. In Zaporozhets, Aleksandr Vladimirovich, and Elkonin, D. B., eds. *The psychology of preschool children*. Cambridge, Mass.: MIT Press, pp. 255–277 [117]

Reynolds, Peter C. 1981. *On the evolution of human behavior: the argument from animals to man*. Berkeley: University of California Press [153]

Rich, Adrienne Cecile 1980. *On lies, secrets, and silence: selected prose 1966–1978*. London: Virago [27, 87]

Rich, John Martin 1986. Morality, reason and emotions. In Modgil, Sohan, and Modgil, Celia, eds. *Lawrence Kohlberg: consensus and controversy*. Philadelphia: Falmer Press, pp. 209–219 [9]

References

Ricks, Christopher 1975. Lies. *Critical Inquiry* 2:121–142 [6, 15]

Roberts, Thomas John 1972. *When is something fiction?* Carbondale, Ill.: Southern Illinois University Press [123, 130]

Rotenberg, Ken J., Simourd, Linda, and Moore, Deborah 1989. Children's use of a verbal–nonverbal consistency principle to infer truth and lying. *Child development* 60:309–322 [118]

Rousseau, Jean-Jacques 1946. *Les rêveries du promeneur solitaire*. Paris: Association pour la diffusion de la pensée française [14]

    1953. *The confessions of Jean-Jacques Rousseau*. Harmondsworth: Penguin [85]

    1973. *The social contract and discourses*. London: Dent [141]

    1979. *Reveries of the solitary walker*. Harmondsworth: Penguin [129f.]

    1991. *Emile* or *On education*. Harmondsworth: Penguin [85]

Royle, Trevor 1987. *War report: the war correspondent's view of battle from the Crimea to the Falklands*. Edinburgh: Mainstream Books [29]

Ruskin, John 1905. *Modern painters*. Vol. 5. London: George Allen [2, 109]

Sackeim, Harold A. 1988. Self-deception: a synthesis. In Lockard and Paulhus 1988, pp. 146–165 [87]

Sacks, Harvey 1980. Button button who's got the button? *Sociological Inquiry* 50:318–327 [110]

Sacks, Oliver 1986. *The man who mistook his wife for a hat*. London: Pan Books [18]

Sahlins, Marshall 1983. Other times, other customs: the anthropology of history. *American Anthropologist* 85:517–544 [29]

Salamone, Frank A. 1977. The methodological significance of the lying informant. *Anthropological Quarterly* 50:117–124 [59]

Scheibe, Karl E. 1979. *Mirrors masks lies and secrets: the limits of human predictability*. New York: Praeger [2]

    1980. In defense of lying: on the moral neutrality of misrepresentation. *Berkshire Review* 15:15–24 [8, 84, 132, 137, 156, 162]

Schelling, Thomas Crombie 1960. *The strategy of conflict*. Cambridge, Mass.: Harvard University Press [5, 149]

Scheppele, Kim Lane 1988. *Legal secrets: equality and efficiency in the common law*. Chicago: University of Chicago Press [40]

Sciama, Lidia 1981. The problem of privacy in Mediterranean anthropology. In Ardener, Shirley, ed. *Women and space: ground rules and social maps*. London: Croom Helm, pp. 89–111 [75]

Scriven, Michael 1954. [Contribution to] The language of fiction. *Aristotelian Society* (supplementary vol.) 28:185–196 [123]

Searle, John Rogers 1975. The logical status of fictional discourse. *New Literary History* 6:319–332 [4, 122]

Seaton, Thomas 1720. *The conduct of servants in great families* ... London: Tim Goodwin [52]

Selling, Lowell Sinn 1947. *Synopsis of neuropsychiatry*. (2nd edn). London: Henry Kimpton [22]

Sexton, Michael 1986. The theory and psychology of military deception. In Mitchell and Thompson 1986, pp. 349–356 [27]

Sharrock, Roger 1954. *John Bunyan*. London: Hutchinson [126]

References

Shaw, George Bernard 1970. *Shaw: an autobiography 1856–1898*. London: Max Reinhardt [96]

Sheehan, Neil 1988. *A bright shining lie: John Paul Vann and America in Vietnam*. New York: Random House [23]

Shultz, Thomas R., and Cloghesy, Karen 1981. Development of recursive awareness of intention. *Developmental Psychology* 17:465–471 [149]

Sidgwick, Henry 1907. *Methods of ethics* (7th edn). London: Macmillan [52]

Siegler, Frederick A. 1966. Lying. *American Philosophical Quarterly* 3:128–136 [113]

Silverman, David 1975. *Reading Castaneda: a prologue to the social sciences*. London: Routledge & Kegan Paul [134]

Simmel, Georg 1906. The sociology of secrecy and of secret societies. *American Journal of Sociology* 11:441–498 [142f., 144]

  1950. *The sociology of Georg Simmel*. Glencoe, Ill.: Free Press [22, 45f., 97, 143f., 163]

  1958. *Soziologie: Untersuchungen über die Formen der Vergesellschaftung*. Berlin: Duncker und Humblot [97]

Simpson-Herbert, Mayling 1987. Women, food and hospitality in Iranian society. *Canberra Anthropology* 10(1):24–34 [67]

Siskind, Janet 1973. *To hunt in the morning*. New York: Oxford University Press [69f.]

Smith, Barbara Herrnstein 1978. *On the margins of discourse: the relation of literature to language*. Chicago: University of Chicago Press [122]

Smith, Francis Barrymore 1973. *Radical artisan: William James Linton 1812–97*. Manchester: Manchester University Press [116]

Smith, Joseph 1968. The first lie. *Psychiatry* 31:61–68 [8]

Smith, Logan Pearsall 1907. *The life and letters of Sir Henry Wotton*. Vol. 1. Oxford: Clarendon Press [23]

Smith, Sandi W., Cody, Michael J., LoVette, Shannon and Canary, Daniel J., 1990. Self-monitoring, gender and compliance-gaining goals. In Cody, Michael J. and McLaughlin, Margaret L., eds. *The psychology of tactical communication*. Clevedon: Multilingual Matters, pp. 91–135 [108]

Snarey, John R. 1985. Cross-cultural universality of social–moral development: a critical review of Kohlbergian research. *Psychological Bulletin* 97:202–232 [9]

Snyder, Charles Richard 1989. Reality negotiation: from excuses to hope and beyond. *Journal of Social and Clinical Psychology* 8:130–157 [89]

  1991. *The negotiation of self realities: psychic shootout at the I'm OK corral*. Paper presented at the Washington meeting of the American association for the advancement of science, mimeo. [89]

Snyder, Charles Richard, and Higgins, Raymond L. 1990. Reality negotiation and excuse-making: President Reagan's 4 March 1987 Iran arms scandal speech and other literature. In Cody, Michael J., and McLaughlin, Margaret L., eds. *The psychology of tactical communication*. Clevedon: Multilingual Matters, pp. 207–228 [88, 90]

Snyder, Charles Richard, Irving, Lori M., Sigman, Sandra T., and Holleran, Sharon, 1992. Reality negotiation and valence/linkage self- theories: psychic showdown at the I'm OK corral and beyond. In Montada, Leo, Filipp, Sigrun-Heide, and Lerner, Melvin J., eds. *Life crises and experiences of loss in adulthood*. Hillsdale, N.J.: Lawrence Erlbaum Associates, pp. 275–297 [89]

References

Snyder, Scott 1986. Pseudologia fantastica in the borderline patient. *American Journal of Psychiatry* 143:1287–1289 [22]

Sodian, Beate, Taylor, Catherine, Harris, Paul L., and Perner, Josef, 1991. Early deception and the child's theory of mind: false trails and genuine markers. *Child Development* 62:468–483 [152]

Somerville, Edith Œnone, and Ross, Martin 1944. *Experiences of an Irish R.M.* London: Dent [20]

Speakes, Larry 1989. *Speaking out: the Reagan presidency from inside the White House.* New York: Scribner [33]

Spencer, Frank 1990a. *Piltdown: a scientific forgery.* London: British Museum (Natural History) [56]

1990b. *The Piltdown papers 1908–1955: the correspondence and other documents relating to the Piltdown forgery.* London: Natural History Museum Publications [56]

Spencer, Herbert 1892. *The principles of ethics.* Vol. 1. London: Williams and Norgate [65, 141]

1902. *The principles of sociology.* Vol. 2 (3rd edn). London: Williams and Norgate [144]

Spencer, John Rason, and Flin, Rhona H. 1990. *The evidence of children: the law and the psychology.* London: Blackstone Press [38, 39]

Steele, Richard 1898. No. 352: 14 April 1712. In *The Spectator.* Vol. 5. London: Nimmo, pp. 170–175 [60]

Steiner, Franz Baermann 1954. Chagga truth: a note on Gutmann's account of the Chagga concept of truth in *Das Recht der Dschagga. Africa* 24:364–369 [66]

Steiner, George 1975. *After Babel: aspects of language and translation.* Oxford: Oxford University Press [4, 5, 37, 124f.]

Stouffer, Samuel Andrew, and Toby, Jackson 1951. Role conflict and personality. *American Journal of Sociology* 56:395–406 [67]

Stricker, Lawrence J. 1967. The true deceiver. *Psychological Bulletin* 68:13–20 [62]

Stricker, Lawrence J., Messick, Samuel, and Jackson, Douglas Northrop 1969. Evaluating deception in psychological research. *Psychological Bulletin* 71:343–351 [62]

Sully, James 1895. *Studies of childhood.* London: Longmans Green [152]

Sunday Sport 1991. Issue of 25 August [132]

Sutherland, John 1978. Norman Mailer's *Marilyn*: a reassessment. *Bennington Review.* February:36–41 [133]

Sweetser, Eve E. 1987. The definition of 'lie': an examination of the folk models underlying a semantic prototype. In Holland, Dorothy C., and Quinn, Naomi, eds. *Cultural models in language and thought.* Cambridge: Cambridge University Press, pp. 43–66 [11]

Swift, Jonathan 1940. *The Examiner and other pieces written in 1710–11.* Oxford: Blackwell [31]

1941. *Gulliver's travels.* Oxford: Blackwell [127f., 158]

Szasz, Thomas 1979. The lying truths of psychiatry. In Duncan and Weston-Smith 1979, pp. 121–142 [11]

Taietz, Philip 1962. Conflicting group norms and the 'third' person in the interview. *American Journal of Sociology* 68:97–104 [60]

Tallis, Raymond 1988. *Not Saussure: a critique of post-Saussurean literary theory.* Basingstoke: Macmillan [36f.]

References

Tanner, Nancy Makepeace 1981. *On becoming human.* Cambridge: Cambridge University Press [154]

Tarski, Alfred 1956. The concept of truth in formalized languages. In his *Logic, semantics, metamathematics: papers from 1923 to 1938.* Oxford: Clarendon Press, pp. 152–278 [113]

Taubman, William 1980. Lying as a way of life: the Soviet Union (A conversation with Viktoria and Mikhail Schweitzer). *Berkshire Review* 15:62–82 [49]

Tausk, Victor 1933. On the origin of the 'influencing machine' in schizophrenia. In Fliess, Robert, ed. *The psycho-analytic reader.* New York: International Universities Press, pp. 31–64 [152]

Taylor, Shelley E. 1990. *Positive illusions: creative self-deception and the healthy mind.* New York: Basic Books [89]

Thomas Aquinas, Saint 1972. *Summa theologiae.* Vol. 41. London: Eyre and Spottiswoode [14]

Thorold, Algar Labouchere 1913. *The life of Henry Labouchere.* London: Constable [135]

Thorpe, William Homan 1972. The comparison of vocal communication in animals and man. In Hinde, Robert Aubrey, ed. *Non-verbal communication.* Cambridge: Cambridge University Press, pp. 27–48 [3]

Toland, John 1982. *Infamy: Pearl Harbor and its aftermath.* London: Methuen [26]

Toynbee, Arnold Joseph 1935. *A study of history.* Vol. 3 (2nd edn). London: Oxford University Press [136]

Trivers, Robert L. 1971. The evolution of reciprocal altruism. *Quarterly Review of Biology* 46:35–57 [149f., 164]

1985. *Social evolution.* Menlo park: Benjamin/Cummings [68, 87, 95, 149, 150, 156]

1988. Foreword. In Lockard and Paulhus 1988, pp. vii–ix [87]

Tudor-Hart, B. E 1926. Are there cases in which lies are necessary? *Pedagogical Seminary* 33:586–641 [8]

Twain, Mark 1897, 1899. *Following the equator.* (2 vols.) New York: Harper and brothers [37, 113]

1960. *The autobiography of Mark Twain* (Neider, Charles, ed.). London: Chatto & Windus [10]

1961. On the decay of the art of lying. In *The complete humorous sketches and tales of Mark Twain.* Garden City, N.Y.: Doubleday, pp. 503–508 [163]

Uberoi, Jitendra Pal Singh 1978. *Science and culture.* Delhi: Oxford University Press [137]

Uphaus, Robert W. 1988. Preface. In Uphaus, R. W., ed. *The idea of the novel in the eighteenth century* (Studies in literature, 1500–1800, no. 3). East Lansing, Mich.: Colleagues Press, pp. vii–x [126]

Valentine, Charles Wilfred 1938. A study of the beginnings and significance of play in infancy. Part 2. *British Journal of Educational Psychology* 8:285–306 [105]

Van den Berghe, Pierre Louis 1967. Research in South Africa: the story of my experiences with tyranny. In Sjoberg, Gideon, ed. *Ethics, politics, and social research.* Cambridge, Mass.: Schenkman, pp. 183–197 [61]

Vasek, Marie E. 1986. Lying as a skill: the development of deception in children. In Mitchell and Thompson 1986, pp. 271–292 [152]

Veatch, Robert M. 1978. Truth-telling I: Attitudes. In Reich, Warren T., ed. *Encyclopedia of bioethics.* New York: Free Press, pp. 1676–1682 [139]

Vernant, Jean-Pierre 1980. *Myth and society in ancient Greece.* Sussex: Harvester Press [49]

Vinacke, William Edgar 1954. Deceiving experimental subjects. *American Psychologist* 9:155 [62]

Vincent, Jocelyne M., and Castelfranchi, Christiano 1981. On the art of deception: how to lie while saying the truth. In Perret, Herman, Sbisa, Marina and Verschueren, Jeff, eds. *Possibilities and limitations of pragmatics* (Studies in language companion series 7). Amsterdam: John Benjamins, pp. 749–777 [113]

Vincenzi, Penny 1977. *The compleat liar.* London: Cassell [103]

Virgo, Sean 1981. *White lies and other fictions.* London; Hamish Hamilton [14]

Voegelin, Eric 1957. *Order and history.* Vol. 3: *Plato and Aristotle.* Baton Rouge: Louisiana State University Press [136]

Walton, Izaak 1951. *The lives of John Donne* ... London: Falcon Educational Books [23]

Washington Post 1987. Poindexter's testimony. *Guardian Weekly* 137(4):15–16 [111f.]

Wat, Aleksander 1988. *My century: the odyssey of a Polish intellectual.* Berkeley: University of California Press [115]

Watt, Ian 1957. *The rise of the novel: studies in Defoe, Richardson and Fielding.* London: Chatto and Windus [130]

Waugh, Patricia 1984. *Metafiction: the theory and practice of self-conscious fiction.* London: Methuen [123, 132]

Wax, Murray L 1986. Reflections on fieldwork reciprocity and ethical theories. *Anthropology and Humanism Quarterly* 11(1):2–8 [136]

Weaver, Kenneth F 1985. The search for our ancestors. *National Geographic* 168:561–629 [153]

Weinstein, Deena 1979. Fraud in science. *Social Science Quarterly* 59:639–652 [55, 56]

Weintraub, Stanley 1970. G. B. S.: sketches for 'A self-portrait'. In Shaw 1970, pp. vii–xvi [96]

Werth, Lucy Fontaine, and Flaherty, Jenny 1986. A phenomenological approach to human deception. In Mitchell and Thompson 1986, pp. 293–311 [90ff., 98ff., 145]

Wesley, John 1986. *The works of John Wesley.* Vol. 3. Nashville: Abingdon Press [14]

Whaley, Barton 1984. *Covert German rearmament, 1919–1939: deception and misperception.* Frederick, Md.: University Publications of America [26, 29]

White, Patrick 1989. A sense of integrity. In (White, P.) *Patrick White speaks.* Sydney: Primavera Press, pp. 189–195. [49]

Whiten, Andrew 1991. (ed.). *Natural theories of mind: evolution, development and simulation of everyday mindreading.* Oxford: Blackwell [152]

Whiten, Andrew, and Byrne, Richard W. 1988a. The Machiavellian intelligence hypothesis: editorial. In Byrne and Whiten 1988, pp. 1–9 [150]

    1988b. Tactical deception in primates. *Behavioral and Brain Sciences* 11:233–273 [149]

Wigmore, John Henry 1976. *Evidence in trials at common law.* Vol. 6. Boston: Little, Brown [38, 40]

Wilde, Oscar 1989. The decay of lying (1889) In (Wilde, O.) *Oscar Wilde.* Oxford: Oxford University Press, pp. 215–239 [1, 49, 153]

Williams, Bernard 1988. Formal structures and social reality. In Gambetta 1988, pp. 3–13 [5]

Williams, Glanville Llewelyn 1963. *The proof of guilt: a study of the English criminal trial.* (3rd edn). London: Stevenson & Sons [39]

Williams, Harold 1941. Introduction. In Swift 1941, pp. ix–xxviii [128]

References

Wise, David 1973. *The politics of lying: government deception, secrecy, and power*. New York: Random House [23]

Wittgenstein, Ludwig 1953. *Philosophical investigations*. (Anscombe, G. E. M., trans.). Oxford: Blackwell [4]

Wolf, Jane M. 1988. Psychiatric aspects of lying. *American Journal of Psychiatry* 145:1611 [6]

Wolfe, Alan 1989. *Whose keeper? Social science and moral obligation*. Berkeley: University of California Press [5]

Wolozin, Harold 1974. Lying and economic dogma. *Review of Existential Psychology and Psychiatry* 13:196–203 [63]

Woodbury, Hanni 1984. The strategic use of questions in court. *Semiotica* 48:197–228 [42]

Yerkes, Robert Mearns, and Berry, Charles S 1909. The association reaction method of mental diagnosis (*Tatbestandsdiagnostik*). *American Journal of Psychology* 20:22–37 [59]

Young, Wayland, 2nd Baron Kennet 1963. *The Profumo affair: aspects of conservatism* (Penguin special S152). Harmondsworth: Penguin [32]

Index

Asterisks indicate authors whose work appears in the list of references. Other citations are not indexed here; their locations are shown in the list of references, at the end of each item.

193

Index

196